The Swedish Presence in Afghanistan

This book delivers on two analytical levels. First, it is a broad study of Sweden as an international actor, an actor that at least for a brief period tried to play a different international role than that to which it was accustomed. Second, the book problematizes the role of international military missions as drivers for change in the security and defence field. Several perspectives and levels of analysis are covered, from the macro level of strategic discourse to the micro level of the experiences of individual commanders. The book focuses upon Sweden and its participation in the international military mission in Afghanistan during 2002–12. It contributes to the growing literature evaluating the mission in Afghanistan and explores the implications of the security and defence practices that have dominated Western Europe for the last decade.

Arita Holmberg is Associate Professor in Political Science at the Department of Security, Strategy and Leadership at the Swedish Defence University, Sweden.

Jan Hallenberg is Professor in Political Science at the Department of Security, Strategy and Leadership at the Swedish Defence University, Sweden.

Military Strategy and Operational Art
Edited by Professor Howard M. Hensel,
Air War College, USA

The Routledge Series on Military Strategy and Operational Art analyzes and assesses the synergistic interrelationship between joint and combined military operations, national military strategy, grand strategy, and national political objectives in peacetime, as well as during periods of armed conflict. In doing so, the series highlights how various patterns of civil–military relations, as well as styles of political and military leadership influence the outcome of armed conflicts. In addition, the series highlights both the advantages and challenges associated with the joint and combined use of military forces involved in humanitarian relief, nation building, and peacekeeping operations, as well as across the spectrum of conflict extending from limited conflicts fought for limited political objectives to total war fought for unlimited objectives. Finally, the series highlights the complexity and challenges associated with insurgency and counter-insurgency operations, as well as conventional operations and operations involving the possible use of weapons of mass destruction.

Also in this series:

The Transformation of
Italian Armed Forces in
Comparative Perspective
Adapt, Improvise, Overcome?
Fabrizio Coticchia and Francesco N. Moro
ISBN 978 1 4724 2751 9

The Failure to Prevent
World War I
The Unexpected
Armageddon
Hall Gardner
ISBN 978 1 4724 3056 4

The Powell Doctrine and US
Foreign Policy
Luke Middup
ISBN 978 1 4724 2565 2

Air Power in UN
Operations
Wings for Peace
Edited by A. Walter Dorn
ISBN 978 1 4724 3546 0

Inside Cambodian Insurgency
A Sociological Perspective on Civil
Wars and Conflict
Daniel Bultmann
ISBN 978 1 4724 4305 2

The Swedish Presence in Afghanistan
Security and Defence Transformation

**Edited by
Arita Holmberg and Jan Hallenberg**

LONDON AND NEW YORK

First published 2017
by Routledge
2 Park Square, Milton Park, Abingdon, Oxon OX14 4RN

and by Routledge
711 Third Avenue, New York, NY 10017

Routledge is an imprint of the Taylor & Francis Group, an informa business

© 2017 selection and editorial material, Arita Holmberg and Jan Hallenberg; individual chapters, the contributors.

The right of the editors to be identified as the authors of the editorial material, and of the authors for their individual chapters, has been asserted in accordance with sections 77 and 78 of the Copyright, Designs and Patents Act 1988.

All rights reserved. No part of this book may be reprinted or reproduced or utilised in any form or by any electronic, mechanical, or other means, now known or hereafter invented, including photocopying and recording, or in any information storage or retrieval system, without permission in writing from the publishers.

Trademark notice: Product or corporate names may be trademarks or registered trademarks, and are used only for identification and explanation without intent to infringe.

British Library Cataloguing in Publication Data
A catalogue record for this book is available from the British Library

Library of Congress Cataloguing in Publication Data
Names: Holmberg, Arita, editor. | Hallenberg, Jan, editor.
Title: The Swedish presence in Afghanistan : security and defence transformation / edited by Arita Holmberg and Jan Hallenberg.
Description: Abingdon, Oxon; New York, NY : Routledge, 2017. |
Includes index. Identifiers: LCCN 2016004282 |
ISBN 9781472474094 (hardback) | ISBN 9781315552415 (e-book)
Subjects: LCSH: Afghan War, 2001–Participation, Swedish. |
Sweden–Military policy. Classification: LCC DS371.412.S94 2017 |
DDC 958.104/7409485–dc23
LC record available at https://lccn.loc.gov/2016004282

ISBN: 978-1-4724-7409-4 (hbk)
ISBN: 978-1-315-55241-5 (ebk)

Typeset in Times New Roman
by Out of House Publishing

Contents

List of figures	vii
List of tables	viii
Notes on contributors	ix

1 **Introduction** 1
ARITA HOLMBERG AND JAN HALLENBERG

2 **Conceptual framework** 19
ARITA HOLMBERG AND JAN HALLENBERG

3 **Swedish strategy and the Afghan experience: from neutrality to ambiguity** 31
JAN ANGSTROM AND ERIK NOREEN

4 **Swedish use of force and the international legal framework: the legacy of Afghanistan** 55
INGER OSTERDAHL

5 **MOTs, Juliette and omelettes: temporary tactical adaptations as the postmodern, interoperable force awaits the anticipated operation?** 78
MAGNUS JOHNSSON

6 **Military–technological aspects of the Swedish mission to Afghanistan** 100
AKE SIVERTUN

7 **Leadership lessons: new challenges for smaller nations in multinational, highly stressful missions** 116
GERRY LARSSON, AIDA ALVINIUS, MARIA FORS BRANDEBO, PEDER HYLLENGREN, SOFIA NILSSON AND ALICIA OHLSSON

8 **Introducing gender perspectives in operations: Afghanistan as a catalyst** 138
ROBERT EGNELL

9 **A veteran at last: the Afghan experience and Swedish veterans policy** 160
RALPH SUNDBERG

10 **Conclusions** 182
ARITA HOLMBERG AND JAN HALLENBERG

Index 196

List of figures

3.1	The Swedish catch-all narrative	38
3.2	The number of Swedish officers appointed at NATO Training Mission in Afghanistan (NTM-A), Headquarters Joint Command (HQ IJC) and Headquarters ISAF (HQ ISAF), 2005–12	43
3.3	Number of Swedish officers serving in NATO or EU staffs outside the immediate theatre of operations	44
5.1	The relationship between place of origin and place of realization in military change	80
7.1	Theoretical model of leadership	118
7.2	Examples of collaborating actors	129

List of tables

5.1	Analytical scheme	84
7.1	Specific individual aspects of importance to military officers at the strategic level	121
7.2	Specific organizational aspects of importance to military officers at the strategic level	123
7.3	Specific group aspects of importance to military Officers at the strategic level	124
7.4	Collaboration actors and key leadership behaviours for military officers at the strategic level	130

Notes on contributors

Aida Alvinius (Ph.D., Karlstad University, Sweden) is a researcher in Sociology at the Department of Security, Strategy and Leadership, Swedish Defence University.

Jan Angstrom (Ph.D., King's College, London) is Professor in War Studies at the Department of Security, Strategy and Leadership, Swedish Defence University.

Maria Fors Brandebo (Ph.D., Karlstad University, Sweden) is a researcher at the Department of Security, Strategy and Leadership, Swedish Defence University.

Robert Egnell (Ph.D., King's College, London) is Professor of Leadership at the Department of Security, Strategy and Leadership, Swedish Defence University.

Jan Hallenberg (Ph.D., Stockholm University, Sweden) is Professor in Political Science at the Department of Security, Strategy and Leadership, Swedish Defence University.

Arita Holmberg (Ph.D., Stockholm University, Sweden) is Associate Professor in Political Science at the Department of Security, Strategy and Leadership, Swedish Defence University.

Peder Hyllengren (M.A., Karlstad University, Sweden) is a university adjunct at the Department of Security, Strategy and Leadership, Swedish Defence University.

Magnus Johnsson (Ph.D. Candidate, Uppsala University, Sweden) is a researcher in War Studies at the Department of Security, Strategy and Leadership, Swedish Defence University.

Gerry Larsson (Ph.D., Gothenburg University, Sweden) is Professor of Leadership Psychology at the Department of Security, Strategy and Leadership, Swedish Defence University. He also holds an adjunct professor position at the Hedmark University College, Norway.

Sofia Nilsson (Ph.D., Karlstad University, Sweden) is a researcher at the Department of Security, Strategy and Leadership at the Swedish Defence University.

Erik Noreen (Ph.D., Uppsala University, Sweden) is Associate Professor at the Department of Peace and Conflict Research at Uppsala University.

Alicia Ohlsson (M.A.) is a researcher in Psychology at the Department of Security, Strategy and Leadership at the Swedish Defence University.

Inger Osterdahl (L.L.D., Uppsala University, Sweden) is Professor in Public International Law at the Faculty of Law, Uppsala University.

Ake Sivertun (Ph.D., Umea University, Sweden) is Professor in Military Technology at the Department of Military Studies at the Swedish Defence University.

Ralph Sundberg (Ph.D., Uppsala University, Sweden) is Lecturer and a post-doctoral researcher at the Department of Peace and Conflict Research, Uppsala University.

1 Introduction

Arita Holmberg and Jan Hallenberg

International engagement: influence and consequences?

The transformation of the security and defence fields has been debated for decades in security and strategic studies, with the focus ranging from structural power shifts to technological innovation to institutional development. This debate has mainly been devoted to material factors and to multilateral top-down processes of managing what could be seen as an increasingly complex and challenging security environment in which the European state as a single entity has undoubtedly lost much of the capability to act and pursue policy independently (Haaland Matláry 2009). The literature has, however, also captured the less material move towards what has been characterized as post-Westphalian states and modes of security governance, which have gained ground mainly in Europe (Kirchner & Sperling (Eds) 2007, Wagnsson *et al.* (Eds) 2009).

The literature has so far mainly concentrated on explaining what has enabled these changes. There has been less interest directed at how transformations materialize and what their consequences are. In particular, the influence of substantial engagement in international military missions during the last two decades is largely overlooked: it has rather been seen as a consequence of the wider changes in the security and defence field. This book aims to look carefully at the role that international engagement can play in the ongoing transformation processes. This is done through a detailed analysis of the role of a particular case: the Swedish presence in Afghanistan from 2002 to 2012. How have the experiences gained during this international endeavour fed into the transformation processes in the security and defence fields?

This book thus focuses on the transformation of the security and defence fields in one particular European state: Sweden. The new Swedish identity that was developed after the end of the Cold War made international action involving the use of force possible. Sweden's national identity in terms of international security affairs during the period from the late 1950s to the end of the millennium had been that of a very loyal member of the United Nations, which sent its forces on multilateral expeditions but was very careful indeed about using force internationally and more or less self-sufficient regarding its security and defence policy orientation. We argue that the Swedish military engagement in Afghanistan from 2002 to 2012 captures several important traits of the evolution of a new self-image. During the expedition to Afghanistan, Swedish politicians began to project a national image that was different in several respects from the old one, not least in terms of the legitimacy of the use of force (Osterdahl 2010). The ambition here is to understand how international military missions relate to, and possibly influence, these processes of transformation in the security and defence field. The conceptual framework is further elaborated upon in Chapter 2.

Several areas are analyzed in the chapters: Swedish strategy and the Afghan experience; issues pertaining to international law; tactical developments; military technological developments; leadership lessons, processes of gender mainstreaming and veteran policies. These areas are chosen for the volume because they constitute the bulk of the security and defence field and include some upcoming trends related to military–society relationships. They also relate to international engagement in various contexts and on different levels. By bringing these different areas together in a comprehensive analysis, a wider understanding of the influence of international engagement is reached.

The book addresses the following main questions: does international engagement influence the security and defence fields at the national level – and, if so, how and with what consequences? To what extent (if any) has the more than ten years of Swedish presence in Afghanistan changed policies, strategies, organization or practices in various areas of the field? If such change has occurred, what are the consequences for the various areas and for the field as a whole?

Our purpose is to shed light on the role of international engagement for the transformations taking place in the security and defence field. We choose to focus on one experience that has been very prominent in many European states: the international military presence in Afghanistan. The more than 10-year-long Swedish involvement in Afghanistan is used to capture the possible influence and consequences of international engagement from different angles and perspectives. Each chapter is guided by the following research questions:

- What influence has the Swedish engagement in Afghanistan had for each chapter's area of study during the past decade?
- What consequences can be identified for the chapter's area of study and the security and defence field as a whole?

The chapters are structured broadly around the research questions in their area of study. Policies, strategies, organization or practices are highlighted to various degrees in the different chapters, depending on their focus and level of analysis. There is no doubt that this research task is complex. The development of the Swedish security and defence fields is multifaceted, with many nuances and sources of change. However, the long Swedish involvement in Afghanistan appears to have been an important factor in several respects and a thorough analysis is needed to assess the role of this engagement.

The results can contribute to theoretical development in relation both to the literature that considers broader changes in the security and defence field and to the research that focuses on the transformation of the Armed Forces of the world, in particular small- and medium-sized European militaries. In addition, several of the chapters illustrate how changing security policies and the transformation of the field both nourish and challenge the evolution of the Swedish self-image. The introduction and the concluding chapter, in particular, address these larger questions pertaining to the Swedish national image in connection to international security affairs.

In the following, the Swedish empirical landscape and previous research in relation to the theme of this book is introduced. We also present the international setting in which the International Security Assistance Force (ISAF) has operated: Afghanistan. The literature concerning other countries that have participated in the military mission in Afghanistan is touched upon to see whether there are any relevant comparisons that can be made between their experiences and those that Sweden has had. Finally, the chapters are introduced.

Empirical background

What can be said about the empirical starting point in the Swedish case? We argue that expressions of Swedish identity can be found by focusing on policies, strategies, organization and practices, and therefore provide the reader with a starting point as to where these appeared in the shift from the 1990s to the 2000s. The aim is both to provide a departure for the analysis in the subsequent empirical chapters and to present analytical aspects with which to assess conclusions about possible changes due to international engagement.

Explanations for Swedish participation in international operations since the end of the Cold War are multiple, ranging from the defence of values to the protection of the Swedish homeland beyond its borders to opportunities for the military to train (Angstrom 2010, Holmberg 2013). Swedish politicians have made enormous efforts to defend and explain the use of force, both to a national (public) and an international (elite) audience. If Ringmar's (2007, pp. 90–1) checklist of requirements for explaining action through identity is applied, there are clear indications that international operations played a significant role in the telling of the story of the new Swedish security policy in a situation where security was seen as gained through cooperation rather than isolation.

The Social Democrats may have had difficulties with telling this story convincingly; their mindset was likely to have been particularly influenced by the dominance of the neutrality policy as a result of years of social democratic hegemony in Swedish politics during the Cold War. However, the decades before and after the new millennium saw a break with the long-time dominance of Social Democratic rule in Sweden. Between the autumn of 2006 and the autumn of 2014, Sweden was governed by a four-party coalition of non-socialist parties. This period can be seen as the height of security policy change; the story of international engagement was accepted by the public, dominating policies and strategies in the security and defence field and plans for organizational change.

In the beginning of 2008, a policy paper entitled *National Strategy for Swedish Participation in International Peace and Security Promoting Activities* was issued (Government Communication 2008). This was the first time that a Swedish Government issued a national strategy pertaining to these matters (compare Osterdahl, 2010, p. 156). There were several elements in this strategy that contrasted with previous Swedish policy and practice. First, the paper made clear that Sweden would henceforth play an increasing role in multilateral international military missions (Government Communication 2008, p. 5). Second, while the typical Swedish participation in international military missions would take place following an explicit mandate from the UN Security Council (UNSC), there were circumstances when the newly-minted 'responsibility to protect' might lead the Swedish Government to consider intervening internationally even in the absence of such a mandate (Government Communication 2008, p. 9). Third, on the point of using military force, the paper states:

> A military peace-support operation can use force in all these situations and in self-defence, but the use of force may also be permitted in other situations in which it would be allowed under international law. This view is shared within the EU. The right of self-defence is accompanied by a right for the state that is contributing troops, if it proves necessary in order to relieve its own personnel, to reinforce the operation and also use military means to evacuate the force.
> (Government Communication 2008, p. 9.
> Translated from Swedish by the authors.)

These sentences indicate that the Swedish Government at the time envisioned a role for Sweden that was more proactive, on a larger scale and with the option of the use of military force to a larger extent than traditionally had been the case. It is difficult not to link these views directly to the Swedish military mission in Afghanistan. During these years (from perhaps 2006 to 2012), several if not most of the countries participating with forces in Afghanistan had a positive view of the chances for a transformation of Afghan society as a result of a successful international mission in Afghanistan. The Swedish Government clearly shared this optimism and the document cited is an indication of this. At the time of writing in late 2015, with the clear majority of the foreign forces having left Afghanistan at the end of 2014, this optimism no longer exists. Instead, the participating countries seem to concentrate on leaving the country in the best possible condition, albeit far from the ideals imagined some 5 years earlier. In assessing the role of international engagement for transformation in the security and defence field, we have an opportunity to consider the state of this change in the Swedish self-image. This discussion is pursued in the concluding chapter.

Policies

Sweden has not been at war with another state for over 200 years. During the twentieth century its ability to stay outside great power conflict was seen as linked to its policy of neutrality, which became an important part of the Swedish identity. The neutrality policy implied that a relatively strong national defence capability was maintained, since Sweden did not join any of the alliances that were established in Europe following the Second World War (as a consequence, it is one of few countries in Europe that until the end of the Cold War lacked major experience of defence integration in the form of membership in alliances). With EU membership in the mid 1990s, the neutrality and non-alignment policy became obsolete. Neutrality was abandoned and non-alignment evolved into military non-alignment, a policy that has gradually become less important: largely as a consequence of Sweden's membership in the EU and the development of the Common European Security and Defence Policy (Eriksson 2006).

Sweden has also gradually enhanced its partnership with NATO (Edstrom *et al.* (Eds) 2011, Wagnsson 2011). With the changed foreign and security policy orientation, the strategies, organization and practices of the Swedish Armed Forces (SAF) gradually changed. Starting with the 1992 Government Bill, the SAF were reformed and resources reduced. In 1995, the Swedish security policy was said to contain both a national and an international dimension. Still, however, defence policy remained part of the national domain. The defence policy decision in 1999 introduced a new main task for the SAF: international operations. This development was due to a changed threat perception and a widened view of security policy. During the following years, the reform of Swedish security and defence policy was to accelerate (Eriksson 2006).

Strategies

It could be argued that the main Swedish security and defence strategy at the time of the Cold War was to pursue an independent policy and organize the defence on a national basis. As indicated, the new situation following the fall of the Berlin Wall and the broadened perception of security changed this strategy. During the 1990s, the focus upon territorial defence was gradually abolished – although a strategy of recapturing the territorial defence was present on paper (Rydén 2003). Sweden started to seek security solutions in cooperation with others, in particular in the EU, but also in partnership with NATO. An active engagement in both these contexts became the main strategy in the years following the 1999 defence decision. This also included participation in international operations. By 2004, the development in the EU's defence policy dimension also gained influence upon Swedish defence strategy and the evolution of military capabilities (Eriksson 2006, p. 145).

The end point of the transformation process from a territorial defence to an expeditionary defence is, according to Petersson (2010), the 2009 defence decision, which states that Swedish military capabilities should be immediately accessible for different tasks: nationally, in the close neighbourhood or far away. He argues that:

> when it comes to defence planning, or the thinking behind the development of capabilities, it is reasonable to conclude that changes have taken place that imply that a threat-based perspective has been replaced by a capability- or intention-based perspective – to a rather high degree.
>
> (Petersson 2010, p. 154. Translated from Swedish by the authors.)

Petersson argues that, in the 20-year period following the end of the Cold War, all the fundamental aspects constituting Swedish security and defence were changed: the goals, the means and the methods (Petersson 2010, p. 148). In the spring of 2015, the Swedish Government submitted a defence bill to Parliament that radically contradicts this view. We return to this in the concluding chapter.

Organization

During the Cold War, both the organization of the defence policy process in Sweden and the Swedish Armed Forces (SAF) as an authority were quite static, and the SAF independently developed doctrines and military thinking (Zetterberg 1999, p. 57). Due to the changed policies and strategies, the organization of the Swedish security and defence policy has become a more dynamic process that is of concern to more actors. Internationalization and Europeanization hit rather directly into the heart of the organization of the SAF, and as the use of military means and the Armed Forces becomes more political, so does their organization.

In many ways, the Swedish Armed Forces have – during the years following the end of the Cold War – evolved in ways that largely correspond to Moskos's (2000) postmodern Armed Forces (Petersson 2010, Holmberg 2015). Since the end of the Cold War, Sweden has gone through much the same transformation with respect to its Armed Forces as many other European small- and medium-sized countries. The focus has been on downsizing and reorientation away from a national defence towards an interoperable defence to be used in international operations. The economic constraints on the defence sector are also likely to be similar to those in most other countries.

The number of military forces has, according to estimations made by Petersson (2010, p. 155), decreased by approximately 72–93 per cent (there are differences between the defence branches) from 1988 to 2009. As a consequence of the neutrality policy and the substantial long-term investments in modern technology, Swedish air force capabilities are, however, still relatively large in comparison to similar states.

Practices

Internationalization and Europeanization have constituted prominent aspects of the transformation of the security and defence fields in Sweden since the end of the Cold War. In the context of this book, we consider *practices* in relation to participation in international operations. Naturally, different parts of the field have different forms of practices. Like several of the other Nordic countries, Swedish identity has a self-perception of being a do-gooder in international affairs – which implies that, politically, military force is not used without hesitation. Concerning participation in international missions, the Swedish position has traditionally been dual: both sceptical and activist (Andrén 1996, p. 214 concerning the United Nations (UN)). On the one hand, Swedish politicians have been sceptical towards using the military instrument for security policy purposes (Petersson 2002); on the other hand, they have supported the UN and decided upon participation in many UN and NATO operations of various kinds. The Swedish Governments have made a priority of participating in EU operations, contributing to more or less every single EU mission undertaken. Swedish rationalizations for the use of force are a complex affair, and many a reason for international participation has been brought forward over the years. It is, however, reasonable to conclude that mainly political considerations have driven Swedish engagement (Petersson 2002, Angstrom 2010, Holmberg 2013).

The international tasks have, however, to be weighed against the defence of the homeland. This is a balancing act that may in practice become difficult for both politicians and the military to pursue (Edstrom & Gyllensporre 2014). Angstrom has argued that the Swedish strategic culture, which is divided into one national and one international part, has constituted an obstacle for transformation due to experiences connected to international operations, particularly at the organizational level (Angstrom 2010). One of the most interesting aspects to analyze is whether or not this division of strategic culture in Sweden has been overcome due to the influence of the international engagement in Afghanistan.

Capturing the influence of international military missions: the Swedish Afghanistan mission as an example

If we look strictly at the Swedish experience, Afghanistan could be seen as merely one case in a long line of international military expeditions in which Swedish forces have taken part.

The Swedish presence in Afghanistan has been both military and civilian, and connected to the work of the international community mainly through NATO, the UN, the World Bank and the EU. Sweden participated militarily in the ISAF in Afghanistan between 2002 and 2014 (the contribution was then severely reduced). With the changing goals and mandates of the mission, the Swedish contribution gradually developed and increased to about 500 troops at most. In 2006, Sweden accepted responsibility for a Provincial Reconstruction Team (PRT), situated in the northern part of the country. In 2012, this institution was transformed to a Transition Support Team (TST), following a transition to civilian leadership (the military command, however, still being ISAF). During 2013, the Swedish contribution became part of Nordic–Baltic cooperation.

Swedish development support to Afghanistan was, for several years, the country's largest undertaking in terms of international aid, totalling about 750 million SEK (80 million EUR) in 2009. At the same time, the military contribution was about 1.5 billion SEK (175 million EUR) (Swedish Government 2010). In 2010, the numbers of military troops contributed by Sweden placed it at number 14 out of the total coalition contributions to ISAF, number 13 in terms of population per soldier deployed and number 19 in terms of million GDP dollars per soldier deployed (Hynek & Marton 2012, p. 17).

Afghanistan is one case among many in which the experiences that the Swedish forces encountered on their mission were bound to influence the future developments of the Swedish Armed Forces, as well as to have an impact on the Swedish security and defence sector more generally. Seen from another perspective, the military experiences in Afghanistan could have a very different impact upon the aforementioned developments than just about any other mission in the 50-year-plus history of international engagement. This is because the Afghanistan experience coincided with the height of the transformation of the security and defence fields in Sweden. The fact that a multiyear international military mission took place alongside these important changes meant that the domestic environment that was to absorb pressures for change was very different from that in previous periods. The Swedish military mission to Afghanistan is thus both representative (as one case among many of Swedish military expeditions abroad since the mid 1950s and unrepresentative (as it took place during wide-ranging changes in Europe).

One of the first comprehensive analyses of the Swedish mission to Afghanistan has been conducted by Agrell (2013). His main points include that the changes in the goals of the mission – particularly during 2009 – were not fully comprehended or debated by the Swedish political and military establishment. The focus is thus on the interaction between policies, strategies and practice. Agrell is critical of what he holds to be a general lack of transparency on the part of Swedish politicians in relation to the Swedish mission to Afghanistan (Agrell 2013, p. 324). As regards the consequences of the Swedish participation, he claims that:

With the Afghanistan mission much was changed in the reference points of Swedish security policy and military, to the extent that the changes may be hard to detect and consider. The realities of coalition warfare are only one of the lessons of the Afghanistan war. Other lessons are the Swedish inability to create functioning civil–military coordination (not only in rhetoric), the sluggishness of the military adaptation process in the face of changed circumstances in the operations area, in terms of materiel, organization and mental [preparedness]. Last but not least, the Afghanistan mission made visible the existence of a remarkably great democratic deficit in the security policy area.

(Agrell 2013, p. 331. Translated from Swedish by the authors.)

In another assessment of Swedish lessons from Afghanistan, Roosberg and Weibull (covering the period 2002–14) focus in particular on the physical, conceptual and moral dimensions of the Swedish warfighting capacity. Concerning physical factors, they find that the ground forces have adjusted their capabilities and systems; for instance, the need for protection has increased – something that has affected the choice of equipment, including the acquisition of new equipment. New (or previously degraded) capabilities have come into focus, in particular Unmanned Aerial Vehicles (UAVs), medical evacuation and Forward Air Control. Certain deficiencies, such as a lack of personnel in specific functions, have been highlighted. These factors have affected priorities in the organization of the SAF (Roosberg & Weibull, 2014, pp. 56–7). Overall, the influence of physical factors is related to strategy, organization and practice.

When it comes to conceptual factors, Roosberg and Weibull argue that the developments of doctrines and concepts in Sweden have been heavily influenced by the engagement in Afghanistan. They offer several examples, including the attempt at contextualizing the use of military force in a military–strategic context and knowledge of new methods and tactics, including those related to UNSC Resolution 1325. The comprehensive approach has also highlighted difficulties in coordinating a Swedish mission with both civilian and military elements (Roosberg & Weibull 2014, p. 69). Finally, the establishment of veteran policies is found to be a change in relation to moral factors that has its roots in the experiences in the Afghanistan mission (Roosberg & Weibull 2014, p. 78).

Sweden has been just one of more than 40 countries to send military forces to Afghanistan after 2001. What other cases of countries are there with which the Swedish experiences could be compared? Our book explicitly refrains from comparing Swedish experiences with those of the United States. The reason is simple: the global role of the United States and the role of the military in that country, as well as the structure and volume of US military forces themselves, are all so vastly different from the conditions prevailing in Sweden that we find any real comparison meaningless. Canada is another country that was very active militarily in Afghanistan during the period under study here. There are similarities between Sweden and Canada in the sense that both countries have been very active as providers of troops for UN missions after the Second World War. There are thus grounds for an overall comparison.

One result of the study of Canadian decisions regarding its actions in Afghanistan is understanding how very important these seem to have been for Canada's overall security and defence policy. A factor strongly influencing the original decision to intervene in Afghanistan was clearly solidarity with its neighbour and fellow NATO member the United States after the terrorist attacks on the latter on 11 September 2001. When the international military mission in Afghanistan expanded after 2003, Canada's political leadership decided that Ottawa needed to be a very active member in the new, larger mission. In addition to solidarity with the US, a further reason for this was grounded in the fact that the political leadership in Canada decided to stay out of the Iraq War, and thus perceived a need to prove to the political leadership in Washington that Canada was still a valuable ally (Marten 2010, Bercuson & Granatstein with Pearson Mackie 2011, Kirkey & Ostroy 2010). In line with these findings are Larsen's conclusions regarding the interaction between the US; the UK; France, Germany and Poland in relation to the Afghanistan mission. He finds that national political and strategic considerations, rather than operational needs or financial matters alone, guided the formation of national standpoints in relation to the development of the operation (Larsen 2013, pp. 57–8).

A second finding regarding Canada is that the military establishment used the Afghanistan mission as a vehicle for proving that the Canadian Armed Forces were indeed still a true fighting force (rather than merely UN peace-keepers), as well as a tool for increasing direct military influence over military operations in Afghanistan and – for a limited time – to serve as policy advisors to Afghan President Hamid Karzai. Regarding the latter at least, civilian bureaucracies eventually regained control over Canadian action in Afghanistan; lessons regarding the former are less clear-cut (Marten 2010, Bercuson & Granatstein with Pearson Mackie 2011, Saideman 2014).

Three of Sweden's neighbours also sent military forces to Afghanistan and can therefore also serve as comparisons to the Swedish experiences. As NATO members, Denmark and Norway are different from Sweden in one very crucial respect, whereas Finland shares Sweden's status as militarily non-aligned. However, formal NATO membership need not be necessary to evaluate experiences and lessons; as stated by Haaland Matláry, 'Sweden is perhaps more important in NATO today than states that are formal members but do not contribute to coalition warfare' (Haaland Matláry 2014, p. 252).

In a research report focusing on Norway, Denmark and the Netherlands, it was difficult to isolate effects specifically related to the mission in Afghanistan. These small states frame their interactions with the international military strategic environment very much in relation to their national narratives concerning security and defence policy. The international engagement seems rather to reinforce existing national developments (Eriksson *et al.* 2013, pp. 66–8, Rasmussen 2014). In the case of Denmark, Rasmussen notes that adaptation was 'second-order'; that is, the Danish military adapted to changes in the British military's approach and the Danish civilian effort adapted to the UN's development in Afghanistan (Rasmussen 2014, p. 155).

One assessment of the Danish participation in both the Afghanistan mission and the war in Iraq concludes that particularly Copenhagen's role in the latter war meant that Denmark's leaders had access to the White House to an extent that is unusual for such a small NATO member (Henriksen & Ringsmose 2012). In the case of Norway, Heier argues that the balancing between national and international operations had become more and more difficult to handle during the period of the Afghanistan mission (Heier 2014, pp. 232–5). New tasks gave the military more of an expertise function, the new role brought a new sense of individual responsibility and a new identity as warfighters was born (and shared among the segment of the military organization that has this experience) (Heier 2014, pp. 227–30). This observation has similarities with the Canadian experience.

Finally, a note on the German experience is required. Hilpert views this operational experience as the last step in transforming German strategic culture regarding the use of force, making it acceptable for the country to participate in combat operations (Hilpert 2014, p. 186). In the beginning of the 2000s, the discourse was similar to the one present a decade earlier, focusing on peacekeeping in the Balkans. However, with the introduction of the Counterinsurgency (COIN) doctrine, the understanding of warfare and the soldier's role started to change slowly. Operational equipment needs were dealt with, but procurement patterns adapted slowly. Hilpert argues that change was undertaken only after external influence, which some agents acted upon (Hilpert 2014, pp. 187–8). Since the Afghanistan operation and its development constitutes the external factor, this can also be seen as a bottom-up process.

The Afghanistan context and ISAF

The land figuring in important transformations of many European militaries in the decade after 2002 is one of the world's poorest and least developed (see, for example, Barfield 2010). Afghanistan has undergone decades of war since the invasion by the Soviet Union in the last days of 1979 (Rubin 2002, Maley 2006, Rashid 2008). It is not the task of this book to undertake new, independent research on developments in Afghanistan. Still, we the editors feel that an overview of our broad understanding of the main strands of developments in Afghanistan, and of foreign influences on the country during the same period, are necessary to put our research on the Swedish mission in Afghanistan into its proper context.

If modern Afghanistan is characterized by poverty and a low level of development, there is also ample historical data to support the notion that throughout the country's recent history (the last two and a half centuries at least) the Government in Kabul has been fairly impotent in exercising power throughout a large country with often forbidding terrain (Barfield 2010, pp. 66–163). Politics and power in the country are also strongly influenced by the ethnic complexities characterizing it.[1] There are layers of complications with political and strategic implications on top of this already fairly complex population mix. First, Afghanistan is a Muslim country with a large Sunni majority. However, the Hazara, who mainly reside in the middle of the country, are Shia. This has resulted in oppression and persecution of the Hazara by various representatives of the majority population in Afghanistan: a situation ongoing at the time of writing. A second highly relevant fact for understanding the conflicts in modern Afghanistan is that the Pashtun, the largest single group in the population of the country, reside not only in Afghanistan but also across the border in Pakistan.[2] Third, a characteristic of the Pashtun in both Afghanistan and Pakistan is that the members of that ethnic group do not accept the legitimacy of the border between those two countries, which was established in 1893 in the form of the Durand line (see Barfield 2010, pp. 48, 54, 89, 153–6). If a government in Kabul tries to seal the border with Pakistan, it is thus bound to encounter severe difficulties (see Lieven 2011, particularly Chapter 10). Fourth, the politics and security of Afghanistan are intimately linked to developments with its large eastern neighbour, Pakistan. The Pakistani authorities, both political and military, intimately link developments in Afghanistan to Islamabad's relations with its traditional rival and sometime enemy: India. Indeed, it seems to be an axiom of modern Pakistani politics that the regime in Kabul should have as good relations as possible with Islamabad and that the establishment of good relations between New Delhi and Kabul must be prevented. All Pakistani governments in recent decades have pursued this strategy (compare Rashid 2008, Roy-Chaudhury 2011).

Into this multifaceted ethnic, political, religious and strategic mosaic, a new type of player was created in the first half of the 1990s: the Taliban. The creation of this group can be said to be a result of many years of civil and insurrectionary wars in Afghanistan. Pakistani journalist Ahmed Rashid, in his standard work *Taliban*, regards the group's origins as largely a reaction against the cruelties, corruption, chaos and the violence that had characterized Afghanistan for so many years by 1994. The Taliban – a group of young Pashtun men with Islamic education – promised a return to an older type of society, largely ruled by Islam. This society would be non-corrupt and would apply a rule of law that – however vindictive and old–fashioned it may appear to European eyes – at least initially contrasted favourably with the corruption and the lack of any rule of law in Afghanistan in the early 1990s. The Taliban gradually gained power and, in 1996, Kabul fell into their hands. At this time, only one important domestic enemy remained – the so-called Northern Alliance, led by the 'Lion of Panshir': the Tajik leader Ahmad Shah Masud.

A final aspect should be mentioned in our attempt to achieve a brief clarification of the vital ingredients of a very complex conflict situation. This is that, ever since their inception in 1994, the Taliban in Afghanistan has been supported (with varying intensity, but seemingly without end) by the ISI: the Inter-Services Intelligence Agency of Pakistan (See Rashid 2008, particularly pp. 84–96 and 110–24, Roy-Chaudhury 2011).

During the second half of the 1990s, Afghanistan was gradually pulled into what was to become an internationalized conflict: the struggle between the United States and the self-proclaimed guardian of Islamic virtue, Al Qaeda, led by the Saudi exile Osama bin Laden. When the Sudanese authorities, responding to pressure from Washington, decided to expel Osama bin Laden from the country in 1996, bin Laden and his allies were given sanctuary by Mullah Omar, the leader of the Taliban in Afghanistan. During five years of existence and build-up in Afghanistan, Al Qaeda created what are reported by some to have been more than 120 training camps in Afghanistan (see 'Strategic Geography', Dodge & Redman (Eds) 2011). On 11 September 2001, Al Qaeda was ready to strike at the United States.

It was in direct response to the Al Qaeda attacks against the United States in September 2001 that first US and then other international forces entered Afghanistan, starting with some US special operations forces in October 2001. A large international conference on the future of Afghanistan was held in December 2001. Starting in 2002, military forces from many members of the UN – including Sweden – started to arrive in Afghanistan. Their mission was to stabilize and rebuild a country ravaged by many years of war. What started as a US- and to some extent a UN-led mission gradually evolved into a NATO mission in 2003. The creation of ISAF – the International Security Assistance Force – was to serve as the nucleus of the international mission in Afghanistan for many years.

ISAF has gone through many different phases. The complexity and development of the mission itself is thus an additional dimension of the case that makes it stand out somewhat in comparison to other international missions conducted by the international community since the end of the Cold War (the Iraq War being the most similar example, although in that case the international community was less united). The initial phase of the ISAF operation in Afghanistan was characterized by the challenges of trying to meet the mission's state-building aims, which largely required capabilities that NATO did not have at its disposal. An awareness of the need for coordination with other actors in the international community emerged; in 2006, the comprehensive approach was adopted and intense coordination efforts followed (Yost 2014, pp. 138–9).

By 2006–10, the operation encountered growing resistance, which led to a focus upon counterinsurgency. From 2011–14, a period of withdrawal, downsizing and training took place, with the aim of transferring responsibility for Afghanistan's security to its national forces in 2014. Subsequently, a training, advice and assistance mission called 'Resolute Support' has been approved by the parties (Russel 2014, p. 67 on the American experience, Yost 2014, pp. 145–9). Russel argues that this development is in itself something that requires immense adaptation at the military level:

> Over the decade, the American military footprint increased from approximately 1,000 Special Forces troops in 2001 to nearly 100,000 mostly conventional troops and several thousand civilians from various agencies by mid-2011. This increased level of effort and broadened strategic focus in itself represented a monumental adaptation that dramatically affected the conduct of units in the field.
>
> (Russel 2014, p. 55)

The complex character and evolution of the Afghanistan mission needs to be taken into consideration when the impact of this international endeavour is assessed. Indeed, the more distance that different observers (both political and academic) get in relation to the conduct of this mission, the more it seems to be a case of 'negative' learning: something that should not stand as a model for the future, or have any substantial impact upon how things are done in the future (for example, Yost 2014, p. 154).

Experiences are, however, diverse. To take just one illustration of this, the experiences of the Swedish force contingent in Afghanistan, which has been based in the relatively stable north of the country, are vastly different from those of the British contingent, which has been fighting (at least during periods) a fairly regular war with the Taliban and their allies during its postings in southeastern Afghanistan. European militaries, while all facing some pressures for change resulting from their experiences in Afghanistan, have thus been subject to very differing experiences there (Angstrom & Honig 2012). This means that the experiences of the Swedish forces in Afghanistan have been very different from, for instance, those of the Canadian forces. The Swedish military contingents in Afghanistan have lost five soldiers during their more than 10-year long mission. In the case of Canada, the corresponding figure is 157 (Bercuson & Granatstein, with Pearson Mackie 2011, p. 1) While the experiences of both countries' militaries in Afghanistan can certainly be presumed to have led to changes in the defence and security field in both countries, the two missions have been so different that it is very likely indeed that the lessons learned are highly distinctive.

Outline

Following this introduction, the conceptual framework of the book is developed in Chapter 2. Starting at the political–strategic level, Jan Angstrom and Erik Noreen aim in Chapter 3 to study the imprints that the Afghanistan intervention has made on Swedish strategy, drawing attention to the strains between the national and the international in Swedish strategic culture. In Chapter 4, Inger Osterdahl reflects on the developments in international law and how the Swedish Government related to these in its reasoning regarding the Swedish use of force. Turning to the events in the field, in Chapter 5, Magnus Johnsson analyzes organizational innovations at the tactical level that have taken place in Afghanistan during the 10 years of the Swedish mission that this book covers. In Chapter 6, Ake Sivertun, in an empirical essay of slightly different character than our other chapters, addresses military–technological aspects of the mission, experiences related to these and their possible imprints at different levels. Gerry Larsson and his colleagues draw 'leadership lessons' in Chapter 7, highlighting individual experiences with implications for organizational development. Chapter 8 by Robert Egnell looks at how gender mainstreaming and issues relating to UN resolution 1325 became a focal point of the mission and fed into organizational change in the SAF. In Chapter 9, Ralph Sundberg studies the veteran policy that the Swedish Government developed and conducted during the years of the Afghanistan mission, reflecting on changes in views of the profession. Finally, in Chapter 10 the editors draw conclusions from the empirical chapters and compare and contrast these findings with what we know from previous research about the role of international operations in transformation processes. This chapter also further addresses the changing identity of Sweden, highlighting both prospects and constraints for its future sustainability.

Notes

1 A good account of the ethnic groups in Afghanistan can be found in Dodge & Redman (Eds) (2011). Compare Barfield 2010, pp. 24–31.
2 Indeed, one estimate is that there are currently more than 7 million Pashtun in Afghanistan and 14 million in neighbouring Pakistan (Encyclopaedia Britannica 2013).

References

Agrell, W. (2013) *Ett krig har och nu: Sveriges vag till vapnad konflikt i Afghanistan* [*A war here and now: Sweden's road to armed conflict in Afghanistan*]. Stockholm: Atlantis.

Andrén, N. (1996) *Maktbalans och alliansfrihet: Svensk utrikespolitik under 1900–talet* [*Balance of power and non-alignment: Swedish foreign policy during the twentieth century*]. Stockholm: Norsteds juridik.

Angstrom, J. (2010) 'Forsvarsmaktens internationella insatser: I den svenska sakerheten eller identitetens tjanst?' [International missions: In the service of Swedish security or identity?] in Engelbrekt, K. & J. Angstrom (Eds) *Svensk sakerhetspolitik i Europa och varlden* [*Swedish security policy in Europe and the world*]. Stockholm: Norstedts Juridik, pp. 169–202.

Angstrom, J. & J.W. Honig (2012) 'Regaining strategy: Small powers, strategic culture, and escalation in Afghanistan' *The Journal of Strategic Studies* Vol. 35, No. 5, pp. 663–87.

Barfield, T. (2010) *Afghanistan: A cultural and political history*. Princeton, NJ/London: Princeton University Press.

Bercuson, D. & J.L. Granatstein with N. Pearson Mackie (2011) *Lessons learned? What Canada should learn from Afghanistan*. Calgary: Canadian Defence & Foreign Affairs Institute.

Dodge, T. & N. Redman (Eds) (2011) *Afghanistan: To 2015 and beyond*. London: International Institute for Strategic Studies/Routledge.

Edstrom, H., J. Haaland Matláry & M. Petersson (Eds) (2011) *NATO: The power of partnerships*. Basingstoke: Palgrave.

Edstrom, H. & D. Gyllensporre (2014) *Svensk forsvarsdoktrin efter kalla kriget: Forlorade decennier eller vunna insikter?* [*Swedish defence doctrine after the Cold War: Lost decades or lessons learned?*]. Stockholm: Santérus Academic Press.

Encyclopaedia Britannica (2013) Pashtun *Encyclopaedia Britannica Ultimate Reference Suite 2013*. Chicago: Encyclopaedia Britannica.

Eriksson, A. (2006) 'Europeanization and governance in defence policy: The example of Sweden' *Stockholm Studies in Politics*, 117, Stockholm: Department of Political Science, Stockholm University.

Eriksson, P., E. Hagstrom Frisell & T. Ahman (2013) 'Afghanistan – lardomar och paverkan pa nationell militar utveckling' [Afghanistan – lessons and consequences on national military development] FOI report, FOI-R-3592-SE, February 2013.

Government Communication (2008) *Nationell strategi for svenskt deltagande i internationell freds- och sakerhetsframjande verksamhet* [*National strategy for Swedish participation in international peace and security support activities*], Regeringens skrivelse 2007/08:51, 13 March 2008.

Haaland Matláry, J. (2009) *European Union security dynamics: In the new national interest*. Basingstoke: Palgrave.

Haaland Matláry, J. (2014) 'Partners versus members? NATO as an arena for coalitions' in Mayer, S. (Ed) (2014) *NATO's post-Cold War politics: The changing provisions of security*. Basingstoke: Palgrave Macmillan, pp. 251–66.

Hilpert, C. (2014) *Strategic cultural change and the challenge for security policy: Germany and the Bunderswehr's deployment to Afghanistan*. Basingstoke: Palgrave Macmillan.

Heier, T. (2014) 'Hvordan påvirker internasjonale operasjoner Forsvaret?' [How do international operations affect the the defence?] in Heier, T., A. Kjølberg & C. F. Rønnfeldt (Eds) (2014) *Norge I internasjonale operasjoner: Militærmakt mellom idealer og realpolitikk* [*Norway In International Operations: Military Power between Ideals and Realpolitik*]. Oslo: Universitetsforlaget, pp. 225–36.

Henriksen, A. & J. Ringsmose (2012) 'What did Denmark gain? Iraq, Afghanistan and the relationship with Washington' in N. Hvidt & H. Mouritzen (Eds) *Danish Foreign Policy Yearbook 2012*. Copenhagen: Danish Institute for International Studies, pp. 157–81.

Holmberg, A. (2013) 'Swedish security strategy in the twenty-first century: What role for human security?' in M. Kaldor, M. Martin & N. Serra (Eds) *National, European and human security: From co-existence to convergence*. Abingdon, London and New York: Routledge, pp. 110–29.

Holmberg, A. (2015) 'A demilitarization process under challenge? The example of Sweden' *Defence Studies*, Vol. 15, No. 3, pp. 235–53.

Hynek, N. & P. Marton (2012) 'Introduction: What makes coalitions s/tick?' in Hynek, N. & P. Marton (Eds) *Statebuilding in Afghanistan: Multinational contributions to reconstruction*. Abingdon, London and New York: Routledge, pp. 1–26.

Kirchner, E.J. & J. Sperling (Eds) (2007) *Global security governance: Competing perceptions of security in the twenty-first century* 1st Edition. London: Routledge.

Kirkey, C. & N. Ostroy (2010) 'Why is Canada in Afghanistan? Explaining Canada's military commitment' *Special Issue: Canada's Commitment to Afghanistan, American Journal of Canadian Studies*, Vol. 40, No. 2, pp. 200–13.

Larsen, H.B.L. (2013) 'NATO in Afghanistan: Democratization warfare, national narratives and budgetary austerity'. Cambridge, MA: Belfer Center for Science and International Affairs, Harvard University.

Lieven, A. (2011) *Pakistan: A hard country* London/New York: Allen Lane.

Maley, W. (2006) *Rescuing Afghanistan*. London: Hurst & Co.

Marten, K. (2010) 'From Kabul to Kandahar: The Canadian forces and change,' *Special Issue: Canada's Commitment to Afghanistan, American Journal of Canadian Studies*, Vol. 40, No. 2, pp. 214–36.

Moskos, C.C. (2000) 'Toward a postmodern military: The United States as a paradigm', in Moskos, C., C.J. Allen Williams & D.R. Segal (Eds) *The postmodern military: Armed Forces after the Cold War.* New York: Oxford University Press, pp. 14–31.

Osterdahl, I. (2010) 'The use of force: Sweden, the *Jus ad Bellum* and the European Security and Defence Policy,' *Nordic Journal of International Law* Vol. 79, pp. 141–88.

Petersson, M. (2002) 'Break glass only in case of war...' *IFS Info* Vol. 5, No. 2, pp. 4–21.

Petersson, M. (2010) 'Forsvarstransformeringen efter det kalla krigets slut: klassificering, forklaring, karakteristik' ['Defence transformation after the end of the Cold War: Classification, explanation and characteristics'] in Engelbrekt, K. & J. Angstrom (Eds) *Svensk sakerhetspolitik i Europa och varlden* [*Swedish security policy in Europe and the World*]. Stockholm: Norstedts Juridik, pp.147–67.

Rashid, A. (2001) *Taliban*. New Haven, CN/London: Yale Nota Bene, Yale University Press.

Rashid, A. (2008) *Descent into chaos: The United States and the failure of nation building in Pakistan, Afghanistan and Central Asia.* New York: Viking.

Rasmussen, M.L V. (2014) 'The military metier: Second order adaptation and the Danish experience in task force Helmand' in Farrell, T., F. Osinga & J.A. Russell (Eds) *Military adaptation in Afghanistan*. Stanford: Stanford University Press.

Ringmar, E. (2007) *Identity, interest and action A cultural explanation of Sweden's intervention in the Thirty Years War.* Cambridge: Cambridge University Press.

Roosberg, H. & A. Weibull (2014) 'Forsvarsmakten efter ISAF: Lardomar och paverkan pa militarstrategisk niva' [The Swedish Armed Forces after ISAF: Lessons learned and consequences at the military strategic level] FOI report, FOI-R-3914-SE, August 2014.

Roy-Chaudhury, R. (2011) 'Pakistan' in (Eds) Dodge, T. & N. Redman *Afghanistan: 2015 and beyond.* London: International Institute for Strategic Studies/Routledge, pp. 167–85.

Rubin, B. (2002) *The fragmentation of Afghanistan: State formation and collapse in the international system* 2nd edition. New Haven, CT: Yale University Press.

Russel, J.A. (2014) 'Into the great Wadi: The United States and the war in Afghanistan' in Farrell, T., F. Osinga & J.A. Russell (Eds) *Military adaptation in Afghanistan*. Stanford: Stanford University Press, pp. 51–82.

Rydén, B. (2003) *Principen om den anpassningsbara forsvarsformagan: Ett implementeringsperspektiv pa svensk forsvarspolitik under forsvarsbeslutsperioden 1997–2001* [The principle of the adaptable defence capability: An implementation perspective on Swedish defence policy 1997–2001] Ph.D. dissertation. Orebro: Orebro University.

Saideman, S.M. (2014) 'Canadian force in Afghanistan: Minority government and generational change while under fire' in Farrell, T., F. Osinga & J.A. Russell (Eds) *Military adaptation in Afghanistan.* Stanford: Stanford University Press, pp. 219–41.

Swedish Armed Forces (2014) *Completed missions* Available online at www.forsvarsmakten.se/en/about/our-mission-in-sweden-and-abroad/completed-operations/ (accessed 10 August 2014).

Swedish Government (2010) *Strategi for Sveriges stod till det internationella engagemanget i Afghanistan* [Strategy for Swedish support for the international engagement in Afghanistan] Available online at www.regeringen.se/contentassets/6284170ece4f493cad8960d2369bbcf6/strategi-for-sveriges-stod-till-det-internationella-engagemanget-i-afghanistan (accessed 25 August 2015).

Wagnsson, C. (2011) 'A security community in the making? Sweden and NATO post Libya'. *European Security*, Vol. 20, No. 4, pp. 585–603.

Wagnsson, C., J. Sperling & J. Hallenberg (Eds) (2009) *European security governance: The European Union in a westphalian world.* London/New York: Routledge.

Zetterberg, K. (1999) 'Det strategiska samspelet' [The strategic interplay] in Wedin, L. & G. Aselius (Eds) (1999) *Mellan byrakrati och krigskonst. Svenska strategier for det kalla kriget* [*Between bureaucracy and the art of war: Swedish strategies for the Cold War*] Forsvarshogskolans ACTA B19. Stockholm: Forsvarshogskolan

Yost, D. (2014) *NATO's balancing act.* Washington, DC: United States Institute of Peace Press.

2 Conceptual framework

Arita Holmberg and Jan Hallenberg

Understanding transformation in the security and defence fields

During the last decades, substantial developments in the security and defence fields have led to an ongoing, major transformation of the European Armed Forces, the results of which have yet to be analyzed and comprehended fully. Global and local developments continue to influence how states, bureaucracies, non-state actors and public opinion conceive of security and defence, the role of Armed Forces, the use of military means and of war. This affects patterns of meaning-making and organizing at various levels in the security and defence fields. In processes of transformation, however, actors are not only being influenced, but also, through social interaction of various kinds, influence the processes themselves.

Different theoretical perspectives and levels of analysis have been applied to make sense of the changes in the security and defence fields. At the systemic level they can, from a realist perspective, be seen as the result of changes in the existing, measurable, strategic power relationships at the global level; the classic examples from the second half of the twentieth century are the demise of the Soviet Union (see, for example, Hallenberg 2002) and the rise of China as a strategic actor (Foot & Walter 2011, Friedberg 2011, Subramanian 2011, Tselichtchev 2012). Changes can also be seen as the result of major trends such as globalization and transformations in the economic sector, driving transnationalization and influencing (for instance) defence industries through various forms of institutionalization (Morth 2003).

If the focus is on civil–military relations and the developments of politics and society in regard to the security and defence fields, we get yet another picture. Researchers in history, sociology and political science speak of demilitarization and denationalization processes in Europe, changing the role of the military in society (Moskos 2000, Sheehan 2008, Haaland Matláry 2009). We can also choose to look at the micro level and focus, for instance, on how individuals assess and process the new context in which they are to function; from state officials to soldiers on the ground (Weibull 2012, Alvinius 2013, Fors Brandebo *et al.* 2013). The level of analysis varies: from the global to the local and the individual.

Both material and immaterial transformations affect the capability of the European states to pursue security and defence policies in the way they used to during the twentieth century. As the resources devoted to military acquisitions are limited and the technological development continues, it becomes more and more difficult for states to keep up in terms of material capabilities. With changing threats, new solutions cross boundaries and require cooperation in parts of the field that used to be strictly national. Changing norms and ideas regarding the military and society may also contribute to transformation (see, for example, Finnemore 2003).

In relation to our particular focus of the transformation of the security and defence fields, much of the attention has been directed at material factors (such as technological changes) rather than immaterial factors (such as identity and culture). In recent years, the debate about the EU as a normative actor can be seen as an example of an alternative perspective to the focus on material factors. From a social constructivist perspective, the focus in analyzing transformation is upon the societal changes that transform identities and contribute to the evolution of new forms of security communities, which alter how states view security and how it should be achieved (Katzenstein (Ed) 1996, Adler & Barnett 1998, Rieker 2006). One of the first academic works on norms, identity and culture to have considerable impact was the edited volume by Katzenstein (1996). Since then, however, the amount of literature devoted to norms and identity has exploded in the research field of international relations (IR). Within the subfield of strategic studies it is not as widespread, although the number of works dealing with the concept of strategic culture is growing.

When we approach the concept of identity in this book, we choose to depart from the understanding made explicit by Lebow:

> most definitions start from the premise that it embodies some sense of who we are that connects us to and differentiates us from others. [note omitted] Identity can be constructed around membership in a community and a set of roles it expects us to fulfil.
>
> (Lebow 2009, p. 562)

Katzenstein and his colleagues understood identity in a similar fashion, as a 'shorthand label for varying constructions of nation- and statehood [...] [that] depict varying national ideologies of collective distinctiveness and purpose' (Katzenstein 1996, p. 6). Identities may differ in the domestic and the international context (Katzenstein 1996, p. 6). Jepperson *et al.* argue that external cultural sources can influence a state's identity in at least three ways: 'they may affect states' prospects for survival as entities [...] change the modal character of statehood in the system over time [...] cause variation in the character of statehood within a given international system' (Jepperson *et al.* 1996, pp. 35–6).

The decades around the millennium shift can be seen as a formative moment (Ringmar 2007, p. 85) when many European states struggled with establishing new self-images that would ensure them a place in the new European security policy context. In this process of identity change, states needed to tell narratives about themselves and their actions that also fit with the international collective. We argue that rationalizing and participating in international operations were crucial components in the making of new self-images, and that this book gives us an opportunity to reflect on the meaning of international engagement for the evolution of self-images related to international security affairs following the end of the Cold War and 9/11.

In this book, we consider the role of international engagement in the ongoing transformation process. The partly new pattern of participation in international operations can in itself be seen as an expression of the transformation of the field (Finnemore 2003, Coleman 2007). However, it also has the potential to reinforce the transformation process in different ways, both at the international and at the national level. We direct our research at how the experiences gained during operations feed back into (and possibly transform) the security and defence fields at the national level.

At the most abstract level of analysis, we consider how participation in an international mission like the International Security Assistance Force (ISAF) fits with the identity, or self-image, of a state. The four dimensions upon which we focus our analysis – policy, strategy, organization and practice – are all seen as gateways to the discovery of expressions of identity. We delimit our study to this focus, although we recognize that identity may take many expressions. In the rest of this chapter our view of the dimensions of policy, strategy, organization and practice are developed. Since our approach is inductive, we refrain from developing a map over the relationship between the dimensions. The relationship between them and the broader transformation processes in the security and defence fields are further analyzed in the concluding chapter.

Policy

Policy in the transatlantic security and defence fields can be said to have been characterized by a number of features since the end of the Cold War: internationalization/Europeanization, joint action in the form of international operations and an increasing blurring of the borders between the previously more distinct policy areas of foreign, security, and defence policy. International operations can be seen as the perfect example of this blurring, when military means are used as foreign policy tools and are not confined to an instrument of national security policy. In this context, questions of legitimacy are increasingly relevant. The differing roles of Armed Forces and the new society relations that some of these require may create challenges with respect to views of appropriateness. One area is the relationship between security and development, which has been contested, for instance in Afghanistan (Forster

2006, pp. 81–2, Holmberg 2011, Larsen 2013). Policy-making in the security and defence fields are potentially influenced by this new setting.

A process of both deepened and broadened European integration in security and defence has developed in both the EU and NATO (Howorth 2007; Wagnsson 2011a, 2011b; Norheim-Martinsen 2013; Boin et al. 2013; Pohl 2014; Yost 2014). Discourses in relation to this internationalization and Europeanization tend, at the national level, to evolve in close relation to the domestic context and identity of a specific country. Processes of transformation that are connected to identity take time, because new discourses and processes of meaning-making in relation to security and defence need to develop and become accepted by the relevant audiences. In both Sweden and Norway, there has been political opposition present during these processes (Graeger 2011, Petersson 2011). This indicates that there are clear limits to changes in domestic politics in relation to a new external environment, in particular if they are deeply rooted in the state's self-image. Studies of the Nordic countries show that factors that could be labelled internal – having to do with domestic politics, historical experiences and perceptions of identity – have, alongside external influences, been important for how the new security and defence fields have been approached politically (Rieker 2006, Eriksson 2006, Moller & Bjereld 2010, Graeger 2011). The decreasing functionality of old policies in relation to the new environment has been highlighted as an explanation for why neutrality was finally abandoned in Sweden (Moller & Bjereld 2011, p. 377).

The Europeanization literature focuses to a large extent upon top-down processes involving formal pressure, various forms of institutionalization and learning. To some extent, the security and defence fields are also characterized by policy change derived from international top-down processes. With threats being perceived as more diffuse and with high economic strains upon state budgets, the costs of security and defence are increasingly being questioned (Hartley 2010). A strand of debate that discusses this is engaged with the concepts of burden-sharing and the pooling of resources as a solution to some of the problems. Burden-sharing was debated in relation to NATO and its European capabilities already during the Cold War; in the twenty-first century it has reappeared in relation to capability development, acquisition and participation in international missions such as ISAF (Oma 2012).

What about policy change due to bottom-up experiences of military operations? A long-term endeavour like the one in Afghanistan may not be characterized by the sort of interaction and pressure common to the regular, institutionalized processes taking place in Brussels and capitals. This does not mean, however, that the operational dynamic does not have any influence upon the larger processes of transformation in the security and defence fields. Farrell et al. (2014) analyze the effects of participation in international operations and discuss whether or not processes of institutionalization in participating Armed Forces organizations are needed for the spread of adaptation originating in the field. There are examples that indicate that this is not the case; in small states the military organizations may be small enough for experiences from the field to have effect anyway, although it may take longer and the result be more varied. Varied results are also found with respect to diffusion between participating countries (what is referred to as 'second-order adaptation') (Osinga & Russell 2014, pp. 306–8). Policy change originating in operational experience may thus materialize bottom-up, even without institutionalization. If this result is transferred to the Swedish case, participation in ISAF could lead to change in the security and defence fields, even though Sweden is not a member of NATO.

Strategy

Strategy is usually conceived of as an operationalization of policy into practice. Scholars focused on strategy and military transformation have started to analyze the consequences of international operations conducted in the 2000s. King's study of the experiences of Europe's forces in Afghanistan concludes that profound changes have taken place:

> At the operational level, new highly capable rapid reaction corps are appearing in each country to form a crystallising transnational military network. At the tactical level, defence resources are being concentrated on favoured elite brigades in Europe to produce nodes of military capability in each country, connected to other military assets across the services. Interestingly, these nodes of military power are increasingly interacting with similarly empowered brigades in other countries to share expertise, training opportunities and to conduct increasingly difficult operations together. In comparison with the solidity of the NATO layer-cake, a quite different military geography is appearing in Europe; a more fluid, porous transnational network of smaller, more specialised centres of military excellence.
> (King 2011, p. 270)

But what is the exact role of international operations in these changes? Farrell sees the drivers for change as connected to either operational experiences or new technologies. Through either domestic or alliance politics, challenges in operations are channelled into strategic adaptations. New technologies work through strategic culture and the civil–military relations that organize the use of force (a bureaucratic structure that is known to be quite difficult to change) (Farrell 2014, pp. 8–12). His conclusion is that, in relation to the mission in Afghanistan, adaptation took place at the tactical level (due to operational pressures) but did not reach the strategic level except in the case of the US. Most other countries studied were inhibited from adapting at the strategic level due to 'domestic politics, strategic culture and alliance politics' (Osinga & Russell 2014, p. 290). There is, however, one exception where strategic adaptation took place: the need for a fast-track acquisition process was acknowledged by many countries (Osinga & Russell 2014, p. 298). There may also have been other more general lessons learned in relation to the experiences gained as the operation proceeded. One such area is the realization of the importance of knowing and using the social and cultural context in the theatre (Osinga & Russell 2014, p. 294). Another, on a completely different level, is the awareness of the difficulty and complexity of civil–military coordination and state building as a political/strategic goal of a mission.

It is too early to assess whether these adaptations or lessons will have an impact in the long run. Rid and Zapfe, analyzing the German case, suggest that adaptation might be short-lived as the bottom-up pressure of the mission diminishes:

> Adaptation in Afghanistan emerged bottom-up, and was later passively permitted on the political–strategic level. Easing these bottom-up pressures comes with an immediate risk of stalled adaptation. Afghanistan will, for the years to come, heavily influence the Bundeswehr. A substantial part of exercise scenarios up to the division level are designed around counterinsurgency scenarios. While Balkan-centric doctrine exercises have shaped the Bundeswehr of the 2000s, Afghanistan will do so for the 2010s.
>
> (Rid & Zapfe 2014, p. 214)

Osinga and Russell conclude that at the political level, some European countries participating in Afghanistan were affected by a strategic culture according to which military force is to be used mainly for humanitarian purposes, others were seeking international reputation for their military involvement and some participated to show alliance solidarity. At the military level, an eagerness to demonstrate capability and professionalism were important factors in some military organizations (Osinga & Russell 2014, pp. 301–2). The authors argue that these factors interacted with the operational ones, something that explains why strategic adaptation often failed to materialize. It seems, thus, as if top-down factors overruled bottom-up factors in the interaction between the state involved and the international operation. One possible reason for the lack of strategic adaptation is simple: Osinga and Russel argue that most European states had no strategic evaluation of the mission, and that the changes eventually made had little to do with reasoning in relation to ends and means but rather pertained to possibilities available at the time (Osinga & Russell 2014, p. 310).

From this brief literature review, the transformation of strategy appears to be a complex affair. Strategy seems caught between political top-down processes and operational bottom-up processes that render it to be something less prioritized.

Organization

The organizational level is of particular interest in the research community when it comes to the Armed Forces. A frequently cited representative of the sociologically-oriented defence transformation literature presents an ideal typology of three different military organizations: modern, late modern and postmodern (Moskos 2000). The three types differ along 11 dimensions: threat perceptions; force structure; the major tasks of the defence; how the military profession is conceived of; public attitudes toward the defence; media relations; the role of civilian employees; the role of women; the role of wives, the status of homosexuals and how resistance towards military service is handled (Moskos 2000, p. 15). Research on defence transformations in different countries allows for an analysis of the different factors behind the evolution of defence organization. The argument proposed by Moskos, Williams and Segal is that the Armed Forces of the Western states are developing towards the postmodern type. The most prominent characteristics of this are:

> the increasing interpenetrability of civilian and military spheres, both structurally and culturally. The second is the diminution of differences within the armed services based on branch of service, rank, and combat versus support roles. The third is the change in the military purpose from fighting wars to missions that would not be considered military in the traditional sense. The fourth change is that the military forces are used more in the international missions authorized (or at least legitimated) by entities beyond the nation state. The final change is the internationalization of military forces themselves.
>
> (Moskos *et al.* 2000, p. 2)

This argument has received criticism, which holds that the theories underlying the changes (post-industrialism, post-Fordism and globalization) can be seen as part of the discourse on postmodernity but they are processes of change that are also largely part of the modern era and cannot be related solely to the end of the Cold War (Booth *et al.* 2001). However, the critics seem to support the essence of the empirical analysis of the development of the Armed Forces. From this we may conclude that international missions are an important ingredient in the organizational transformation of the Armed Forces.

What is interesting in relation to the sociologically-oriented transformation literature is that, paradoxically, it appears to analyze the military largely in its ordinary (national/Western) social context. What happens when a military organization set in a postmodern social context is placed in a modern or even pre-modern social context – such as Afghanistan – and is supposed to interact with the actors present there and solve problems in that milieu? Results from the literature concerned with the effects of international operations show that military organizations are affected in a number of ways. One is through changes in how the military profession is perceived (Heier 2014, pp. 227–30). This volume is able to add to this picture covering the tactical perspective as well as a micro-level perspective focusing on leadership experiences in demanding missions.

Practice

The constructivist turn developed in the 2010s directs focus not only towards ideas, norms and discourse in finding expressions of identity, but also on 'practice'. Pouliot states: '*it is not only who we are that drives what we do; it is also what we do that determines who we are*' (Pouliot 2010, p. 5, italics in original). Inspired by Bourdieu, this approach directs attention towards a different kind of empirical material, towards identifying the kind of social action that is considered normal. It is this practice, not a pre-defined collective identity, which is crucial for a security community, argues Pouliot (2010, pp. 1–5). This leads us to include 'practice' as a dimension in this study. What states do when it comes to international military operations can be seen as part of their self-image, and the (changing) practice in this field can also feed back into and change this identity.

Although much of the literature in security and strategic studies does not yet employ the practice vocabulary to any large extent, a few patterns of behaviour can be distinguished that appear to have been developing into norms in the transatlantic security and defence fields during the last decades. The use of military means has experienced a revival as military forces are to an increasing extent part of operations with various goals in different institutional and geographical settings (Forster 2006, pp. 196–8, Angstrom & Duyvesteyn 2010). The Armed Forces of many West European states have developed and transformed their capabilities from being focused on territorial defence towards expeditionary forces aimed to be used on a global scale. However, the range of reform differs, with variations in the professional goals, methods and means chosen, and the motivations for reform, in the various European countries (Forster 2006, pp. 44–7, Loo 2009). At the same time, the roles of the Armed Forces are being broadened and the internal security role is being emphasized – both domestically and internationally – for instance in efforts relating to security sector reform (Edmunds 2006, p. 1071, Forster 2006, p. 41). Many European states have also abandoned their systems of conscription and are now instead creating professional military forces. Thus, the role of the Armed Forces as a nation-building institution may be up for debate (Leander 2004), and the military profession as such is faced with increasingly complex challenges.

The practice part of international engagement is likely to have an effect not only upon participating states but also on the international organizations that provide the framework for the operations. Rynning argues that ISAF, with its adoption of the counterinsurgency doctrine, went through innovation in Afghanistan 2008–10. This change was driven by operational and geopolitical factors 'on the ground', and also led to strategic and operational adaptation (a more modest form of change) in NATO as a whole (Rynning 2014). Indeed, the creation of the Connected Forces Initiative (CFI) in 2012 is described as a project aimed to fulfil the gap created by the lack of major NATO missions, and the interaction between forces that these creates. This indicates that the dynamic of interaction created through the 'practice part' of international operations is important for the security and defence fields. Indeed, it could be seen as the 'glue' that has kept NATO together during parts of the post-Cold War period.

As the military mission in Afghanistan was wrapping up in 2014, the academic community began to assess its overall impact. Some early accounts are already available. For instance, Alexander Mattelaer argues:

> In military terms, the Afghan campaign has served as a critical wake-up call for European militaries, many of which had not seen genuine combat action since the Korean War. Due to the large number of European personnel rotating through ISAF positions, the impact of the Afghan campaign on the military mindset in Europe cannot be underestimated.
> (Mattelaer 2011, p. 132).

Mattelaer argues that the transformation within NATO related to Afghanistan has driven the evolution of a civil–military reorientation, a revival of the military as a political instrument and a development of the European militaries' doctrines and strategies (Mattelaer 2011, pp. 131–5, see also King 2011, Angstrom & Honig 2012). However, though it is possible to discern some patterns of change that are similar in most countries in the Western world, most researchers recognize that national experiences, identities and institutions are crucial for developments on this level. Therefore, research with a national perspective is needed to acquire a deeper knowledge of how these developments manifest themselves at this level.

Through this brief overview of some of the scholarly work dealing with various aspects and levels of the changes taking place in the security and defence fields, it should be clear that international engagement and the processes it creates need to be further researched and mapped in order to achieve a better understanding of the consequences of the major operations undertaken during the last decades. Experiences from different countries and milieus should be studied and linked to the larger picture of the role of these endeavours for the transformation processes in the security and defence fields. This book proposes to study these questions based on the fundamental analytic concepts – policy, strategy, organization and practice – as they have been presented in this chapter.

References

Adler, E. & M. Barnett (Eds) (1998) *Security Communities.* Cambridge: Cambridge University Press.

Alvinius, A. (2013) *Bridging boundaries in the borderland of bureaucracies: Individual impact on organizational adaptation to demanding situations in civil and military contexts.* Ph.D. thesis, Karlstad: Karlstad University.

Angstrom, J. & I. Duyvesteyn (Eds) (2010) *Modern war and the utility of force: Challenges, methods and strategy.* Abingdon: Routledge.

Angstrom, J. & J.W. Honig (2012) 'Regaining strategy: Small powers, strategic culture, and escalation in Afghanistan' *The Journal of Strategic Studies* Vol. 35, No. 5, pp. 663–87.

Boin, A., M. Ekengren & M. Rhinard (2013) *The EU as crisis manager: Patterns and prospects.* Cambridge: Cambridge University Press.

Booth, B., M. Kestenbaum & D.R. Segal (2001) 'Are post-Cold War militaries postmodern?' *Armed Forces and Society* Vol. 27, No. 3, pp. 319–42.

Coleman, K.P. (2007) *International organisations and peace enforcement: The politics of international legitimacy.* Cambridge: Cambridge University Press.

Edmunds, T. (2006) "What *are* Armed Forces for? The changing nature of military roles in Europe' *International Affairs* Vol. 82, No.6, pp. 1059–75.

Edstrom, H., J. Haaland Matláry & M. Petersson (Eds) (2011) *NATO: The power of partnerships.* Basingstoke: Palgrave.

Eriksson, A. (2006) Europeanization and governance in defence policy: The example of Sweden *Stockholm Studies in Politics*, 117, Stockholm Department of Political Science, Stockholm University.

Farrell, T. (2014) 'Introduction: Military adaptation in war' in Farrell, T., F. Osinga & J.A. Russell (Eds) *Military adaptation in Afghanistan.* Stanford: Stanford University Press, pp. 1–23.

Farrell, T., F. Osinga & J.A. Russell (Eds) *Military adaptation in Afghanistan.* Stanford: Stanford University Press.

Finnemore, M. (2003) *The purpose of intervention: changing beliefs about the use of force.* Ithaca and London: Cornell University Press.

Foot, R. & A. Walter (2011): *China, The United States and global order.* Cambridge/New York: Cambridge University Press.

Fors Brandebo, M., M. Sjoberg, G. Larsson, J. Eid & O. Kjellevold Olsen (2013) 'Trust in a military context: What contributes to trust in superior and subordinate leaders?' *Journal of Trust Research*, Vol. 3, pp. 125–45.

Forster, A. (2006) *Armed forces and society in Europe* Basingstoke: Palgrave Macmillan.

Friedberg, A. (2011) *A contest for supremacy: China, America, and the struggle for mastery in Asia.* New York/London: Norton.

Graeger, N. (2011) ' "Home and away?" Internationalism and territory in the post-1990 Norwegian defence discourse' *Cooperation and Conflict* Vol. 46, No. 1, pp. 3–20.

Haaland Matláry, J. (2009) *European Union security dynamics: In the new national interest.* Basingstoke: Palgrave.

Haaland Matláry, J. (2014) 'Partners versus members? NATO as an arena for coalitions in Mayer, S. (Ed) (2014) *NATO's post-Cold War politics: The changing provisions of security.* Basingstoke: Palgrave Macmillan, pp. 251–66.

Haaland Matláry, J. & O. Osterud (Eds) (2005) *Mot et avnasjonalisert forsvar? [Towards a de-nationalized defence?].* Oslo: Abstrakt forlag.

Hallenberg, J. (2002) *The demise of the Soviet Union: Analysing the collapse of a state.* Aldershot, Hants: Ashgate.

Hartley, K. (2010) 'The case for defence' *Defence and Peace Economics* Vol. 21, No. 5–6, October–December, pp. 409–26.

Heier, T. (2014) 'Hvordan pavirker internasjonale operasjoner Forsvaret?' [How do international operations affect the the defence?] in Heier, T., A. Kjølberg & C. F. Rønnfeldt (Eds) (2014) *Norge I internasjonale operasjoner: Militærmakt mellom idealer og realpolitikk* [*Norway In International Operations: Military Power between Ideals and Realpolitik*]. Oslo: Universitetsforlaget, pp. 225–36.

Holmberg, A. (2011) 'The changing role of NATO: Exploring the implications for security governance and legitimacy' *European Security* Vol. 20, No. 4, pp. 529–46.

Howorth, J. (2007) *Security and defence policy in the European Union*. Basingstoke: Palgrave Macmillan.

Jepperson, R.L., A Wendt & P.J. Katzenstein (1996) 'Norms, identity, and culture in National Security' in Katzenstein, P. (Ed) (1996) *The culture of national security: Norms and identity in world politics*. New York: Columbia University Press, pp. 33–75.

Katzenstein, P. (1996) 'Introduction: alternative perspectives on national security' in Katzenstein, P. (Ed) (1996) *The culture of national security: Norms and identity in world politics*. New York: Columbia University Press, pp. 1–32.

Katzenstein, P. (Ed) (1996) *The culture of national security: Norms and identity in world politics*. New York: Columbia University Press.

King, A. (2011) *The transformation of Europe's Armed Forces: From the Rhine to Afghanistan*. Cambridge/New York: Cambridge University Press.

Leander, A. (2004) 'Drafting community: Understanding the fate of conscription' *Armed Forces and Society* Vol. 30, No.4, pp. 571–99.

Lebow R.N. (2009) *A cultural theory of international relations*. Cambridge/New York: Cambridge University Press.

Loo, B. (Ed) (2009) *Military transformation and strategy: Revolutions in military affairs and small states*. Abingdon: Routledge.

Mattelaer, A. (2011) 'How Afghanistan has strengthened NATO' *Survival: Global Politics and Strategy*, Vol. 53, No. 6, pp. 127–40.

Moller, U. & U. Bjereld (2010) 'From Nordic neutrals to post-neutral Europeans: Differences in Finnish and Swedish policy transformation' *Cooperation and Conflict* Vol. 45, No. 4, pp. 363–86.

Morth, U. (2003) *Organizing European cooperation: The case of armaments*. Rowman & Littlefield.

Morth, U. (2003) *Organizing European cooperation: The case of armaments*. Rowman & Littlefield.

Moskos, C.C. (2000) 'Toward a postmodern military: The United States as a paradigm' in Moskos, C.C., J.A. Williams & D.R. Segal (Eds) *The postmodern military: Armed forces after the Cold War*. New York: Oxford University Press, pp. 14–31.

Moskos, C., J.A. Williams & D.R. Segal (2000) 'Armed forces after the Cold War' in Moskos, C.C., J.A. Williams & D.R. Segal (Eds) *The postmodern military: Armed forces after the Cold War*. New York: Oxford University Press, pp. 1–13.

Norheim-Martinsen, P.M. (2013) *The European Union and military force: Governance and strategy*. Cambridge: Cambridge University Press.

Oma, I.M (2012) 'Explaining states' burden-sharing behavior within NATO' *Cooperation and Conflict* Vol. 47, No. 4, pp. 562–72.

Osinga, F. & J.A Russell (2014) 'Conclusion: Military adaptation and the war in Afghanistan' in Farrell, T., F. Osinga & J.A. Russell (Eds) *Military adaptation in Afghanistan*. Stanford: Stanford University Press, pp. 288–326.

Petersson, M. (2011) 'Defence transformation and legitimacy in Scandinavia after the Cold War: Theoretical and practical implications' *Armed Forces & Society* Vol. 37, No. 4, pp. 701–24.

Pohl, B. (2014) *EU foreign policy and crisis management operations*. Abingdon: Routledge.

Pouliot, V. (2010) *International security in practice: The politics of NATO–Russia diplomacy*. Cambridge: Cambridge University Press.

Rid, T. & M. Zapfe (2014) 'Mission command without a mission: German military adaptation in Afghanistan' in Farrell, T., F. Osinga & J. A. Russell (Eds) *Military adaptation in Afghanistan*. Stanford: Stanford University Press, pp. 192–218.

Rieker, P. (2006) *Europeanization of national security identity: The EU and the changing security identities of the Nordic states*. Abingdon: Routledge.

Rynning, S. (2014) 'ISAF and NATO: Campaign innovation and organizational adaptation' in Farrell, T., F. Osinga & J.A. Russell (Eds) *Military adaptation in Afghanistan*. Stanford: Stanford University Press, pp. 51–83.

Sheehan, J. (2008) *Where have all the soldiers gone? The transformation of modern Europe*. New York: Mariner Books.

Subramanian, A. (2011) *Eclipse: Living in the shadow of China's economic dominance*. Washington, DC: Peterson Institute for International Economics Press.

Tselichtchev, I. (2012) *China versus the West: The global power shift of the 21st century*. Singapore: John Wiley & Sons Singapore.

Wagnsson, C. (2011a) 'NATO's role in the strategic concept debate: Watchdog, fire-fighter, neighbour or seminar leader?' *Cooperation and Conflict*, Vol. 46, No. 4, pp. 482–501.

Wagnsson, C. (2011b) 'A security community in the making? Sweden and NATO post Libya' *European Security*, Vol. 20, No. 4, pp. 585–603.

Weibull, L. (2012) *Emotion management in Swedish peace support operations* Ph.D. dissertation. Karlstad: Karlstad University Studies.

Yost, D. (2014) *NATO's balancing act*. Washington, DC: United States Institute of Peace Press.

3 Swedish strategy and the Afghan experience
From neutrality to ambiguity

Jan Angstrom and Erik Noreen

Introduction

During the Cold War, Sweden pursued a relatively coherent grand strategy. It had a straightforward narrative that was reasonably well communicated, shared among an overwhelming majority of national elites and the national electorate. In order to achieve the political end of continued national independence, its main focus was to avoid being dragged into a devastating war between the superpowers. For this purpose, Sweden pursued a policy of non-alignment in peace, aiming to be neutral in war. If the neutrality should fail in war, Sweden had also made preparations to get support from the West. It had a strong, national defence industry that supported the Armed Forces with equipment, thus maintaining the image of a self-sustainable country, not dependent upon either superpower for its military capabilities, and reassuring the superpowers that it would not quickly join the other side and change the so-called Nordic balance (for example Andrén 1996, Eriksson 2004, Dalsjo 2006, Bjereld *et al.* 2008, Holmstrom 2011, Kronvall & Petersson 2012).

The military strategy was equally straightforward. Sweden knew its main opponent in case of war and it had adopted a basic strategy of deterrence, aiming to sustain its forces at a level at which it would cost the Soviet Union more to attack Swedish soil than it would gain in case it managed to overrun the Swedish Armed Forces. The Navy and Air Force, in particular, were considered to be the main pillars upon which the credibility of the deterrent rested. It was through the efforts of these two branches that a large-scale Soviet invasion fleet across the Baltic could be, if not stopped, at least punished to a degree that the costs exceeded the gains of the effort. Early on during the Cold War, Sweden harboured hopes to be able to sustain this deterrent even in case of a separate Soviet–Swedish war, but from the late 1960s, Swedish decision-makers calculated that Sweden would only be the northern flank in a war between the East and the West. As such, it was able to downgrade its military capabilities and cut its defence spending considerably.

Since the Cold War, however, Swedish security policy and strategy has gone through several processes of change. It is easy to pinpoint a number of developments in Swedish strategy that denote change over the last two decades; it is considerably more difficult to pinpoint how these developments are linked and what they tell us about current strategy on the eve of withdrawal from Afghanistan. How should we understand the development of Swedish strategy since the Cold War? What role has the intervention in Afghanistan played in shaping Swedish strategy? What are the strategic consequences of the more than decade-long intervention?

Our main argument is that the series of overlapping changes in Swedish strategy since the end of the Cold War are not a result of the Afghan intervention in and of itself, but that the military needs and political circumstances of the Afghan intervention accentuated a process of military reform already underway and fuelled its pace. After the Cold War there were structural pressures for military reform, and participation in the war in Afghanistan channelled these pressures and became part of the more immediate motivation behind the changes. As such, the Afghan intervention contributed to a shift from international peacekeeping to warfighting, from conscript large-scale Armed Forces to professional forces and from a strategy founded on neutrality in case of war to one of international collaboration. However, rather than this shift being the result of a carefully crafted overall plan, we suggest that these changes have come about independent of each other and thus created an unintentional pattern of ambiguity. We demonstrate empirically that the political ends, military means and preferred ways of using force have all become ambiguous after the end of the Cold War.

This chapter proceeds as follows. After an account of strategic changes in the post-Cold War era we demonstrate, in three analytical sections, how ambiguity is manifested through strategic choices. By demonstrating how the intervention in Afghanistan influenced Sweden to pursue ambiguous political ends – with military means that partly strengthen this ambiguity and using methods that are ambiguous – we show that, rather than a straightforward linear development, there are multiple, partly overlapping and partly contradicting developments and practices in Swedish strategy. In the conclusion, we elaborate on the consequences of ambiguity for Sweden. While ambiguity can be an advantageous strategy for a small state in uncertain surroundings, it also has distinct disadvantages, such as not clearly signalling intentions and commitments.

Strategic changes after the Cold War

During the last two decades Swedish security policy and military strategy have been in near constant processes of change. These changes have been far-reaching and have influenced policies, strategies, organization and practices in often fundamental ways. If we think of strategy as 'the use, and threat of use, of organized force for political purposes', including the creation and organization of armed force (Gray 1999, p. 1), it is clear that the practice of formulating and pursuing strategy in Sweden has undergone changes during the Afghan intervention. However, besides the more obvious specific operational needs such as acquisition of helicopters for medevac and improved armour for protection from improvised explosive devices, it is difficult to directly link these strategic changes to the Afghan intervention in and of itself.

In terms of organization and practices of the Armed Forces, Sweden has over the past 10 years gone from a conscript-based organization relying upon partial or full mobilization in case of war to a professional all-volunteer force. As well as reintroducing non-commissioned officers, it has also – for the first time in its history – made large swathes of officers redundant. Sweden has transformed its Armed Forces from an organization focused on mass and low technology to one that consists of a mere 14,000 soldiers (in the late 1980s, during the period of conscription, it was over 800,000) and is heavily reliant upon high technology and specialized capabilities (Petersson 2015). It even abandoned and then restarted long-term defence planning and has introduced NATO planning procedures for operational planning despite not being a NATO member. Instead of supplying its Armed Forces with Swedish-made weaponry and equipment, it has started to buy off the shelf or initiated close collaboration with other countries to develop equipment (Britz 2008). Still, the movement towards increased international cooperation has its limits. Some parts of Swedish strategic behaviour are remarkably consistent. Although a member of the European Union (EU) and a partner to NATO, full membership in the latter organization seems a political impossibility, with support for membership polling at around 30 per cent of the electorate.

In terms of use of force, Sweden has started to use force actively, internationally and for purposes other than national defence. Indeed, since the end of the Cold War, Sweden has been three times as intervention-prone with its Armed Forces as it was during the Cold War (Angstrom 2015). It has collaborated with all major powers, except China, in international missions abroad. The contribution to the International Security Assistance Force (ISAF) mission in Afghanistan is a prominent case of Swedish intervention.

The official strategic narrative of the Swedish participation in Afghanistan is best described as a catch-all (Noreen & Angstrom 2015). According to the Swedish Government, Sweden participates for short-term security reasons, for long-term interests, for short-term ideals about equality and democracy and for long-term ideals about a just international order and the strength of the UN. Hardly any political view on the legitimacy of the use of force is left behind. It would be misleading to suggest that Swedish participation in Afghanistan caused all of the aforementioned quite dramatic strategic, organizational and practical changes mentioned. Moreover, it is extremely difficult to sort out and systematically isolate which (if any) of the changes drove the strategic development, or if they happened haphazardly and in interaction. However, attempting to disentangle these trends is still a necessity if we want to understand Swedish strategy and how it has influenced and been influenced by the Afghan intervention.

So far, two interpretations stand out. First, the transformation of Swedish security policy and strategy has been presented as a more or less linear development from neutrality to solidarity (for example, Engelbrekt forthcoming, Dalsjo 2015). This interpretation relies heavily upon the declaratory politics of the Swedish Government; admittedly, it is possible to draw a convincing picture of a slowly declining policy of neutrality, coupled with a gradually increasing commitment to participate actively in the defence of others should security be threatened. For example, the Cold War formula of Sweden being 'non-aligned during peace, aiming for neutrality during war' (for example, Government Bill 1982, p. 4) has been replaced with a self-proclaimed:

> Sweden will not remain passive if a catastrophe or attack would occur in another membership nation [of the EU] or Nordic country. We expect that these countries act similarly should it happen to Sweden. Hence, Sweden shall be prepared to give and receive military support.
> (Government Bill 2009, p. 9).

The Defence Committee of 2014 further reinforced these policies and maintained that: 'The Armed Forces shall alone *and in collaboration with others* be able to defend Sweden' (Defence Committee 2014, p. 38, emphasis added). This statement is usually understood in light of an increasing Europeanization of Swedish defence and security policies (Holmberg 2010). It is the membership of the EU and its gradually increasing role in foreign and security issues that has influenced Swedish policies. According to this framework of understanding, the Swedish participation in Afghanistan is evidence of Sweden trying to reinforce and project the image of a country willing to bear costs in solidarity with its partners in NATO and its fellow members of the EU.

Second, the transformation of Swedish security policy and strategy has been described as a more or less linear development from a passive–nationally-oriented strategy during the Cold War; over a passive–international strategy during the first post–Cold War years; through an active–international strategy commencing in the early 2000s, and then to an active–national strategy as the Afghanistan mission is winding down (Edstrom & Gyllensporre 2014). This, too, is a convincing story in which not only the declaratory policies of Swedish Government are included but also patterns of Swedish strategic behaviour such as interventions. According to this framework of interpretation, Swedish participation in Afghanistan is evidence of a growing role as a state using large-scale force actively internationally for the first time in a few hundred years. Similarly, it is also a state using an international mission as a vehicle for transformation of its military organization and its defence doctrine. The Afghan mission was not only evidence of a growing impetus toward solidarity, but it also reconfigured the Armed Forces.

Although convincing at first glance, both of these interpretations of Swedish strategy suffer from the assumption of unitary rational actors. This does not mean that the two previous interpretations are wrong, but rather that they can be slightly misleading in portraying the development as neat and straightforward. Instead, we suggest that Sweden has pursued a strategy of unintended ambiguity. Ambiguity has several advantages for a small state surrounded by major powers with uncertain futures. In the mid to late 1990s, it was not, for example, certain whether NATO would continue to exist; whether Russia would develop into a Western benign modernized stable democracy; whether the US would remain a European power, or whether the EU would develop military capabilities. Putting all eggs in one basket in such an uncertain period is unwise for a small state such as Sweden. What started out as a typical 'hedging strategy' (Tunsjo 2011), however, soon developed into an unintended strategy. This analysis draws upon Agrell's (2010, p. 241) claim of the decline of the Swedish Armed Forces as the result of a non-active decision: 'The national defence was not discarded intentionally, it just happened to be abandoned one day'.

The reason, we claim, is the absence of a particular body specifically charged with shaping Swedish strategy. There are strategic processes, including both long-term and short-term defence planning. There are also strategic actors: the military leadership of the Armed Forces; the Ministry of Defence, the Government and the Parliamentary Defence Committee. But, critically, none of these actors has the responsibility of shaping national strategy. Indeed, Sweden is one of few states in Western Europe in which the military headquarters of the Armed Forces and the Ministry of Defence are not located in the same place and the Ministry of Defence is constitutionally prevented from directly controlling the Armed Forces. Although the impact of this should not be overestimated – the Government collectively controls the Armed Forces – there is still a coordination gap between the actors in which shaping national strategy can be ignored. Since strategy by definition involves choice (for example, Angstrom & Widen 2015), there is a political cost attached to shaping strategy. In silent agreement, the strategic elites can now choose to ignore the cost by ignoring strategy.

One could, of course, argue that the structural processes of reform were present regardless of the non-existence of a separate strategic decision-making body. This would certainly be true to some extent. However, had there been a strategic decision-making body in the Swedish strategic process, it would not have been possible to ignore aligning political aims with reasonable and credible military capabilities. If the political advantages were gained through action rather than shirking responsibility (as in some other political domains), we would expect that the structural pressures caused intentional decisions.

One could even think that this suggests a country void of strategic thought. A country, in short, that during the Cold War stagnated in its strategies and bureaucratized the use of force to such a degree that clear, concise thinking was replaced with routines much like those of other states in the similar position (for example, Angstrom & Honig 2012). Once the strategic situation thawed and choice became more open-ended, Swedish strategic elites were both inexperienced in pursuing strategy and unsure of what political ends to pursue. What followed was not the absence of strategy but rather overlapping, non-synchronized processes; ad hoc, pluralist and unintentional. It was not absence of strategy, but a multitude of tacit strategies.

We build this analysis around three aspects of Swedish strategy that have been accentuated by the Afghan intervention. First, the Afghan mission reinforced the principle of domestic political consensus regarding security policy and the use of force. This manifested itself most clearly in the catch-all strategic narrative of the intervention. The narrative then served as a prime tool of ambiguity, legitimizing the use of force for a whole host of reasons. Second, the Afghan mission yet further strengthened the internationalization of the Swedish Armed Forces – short of alliance membership. This manifested itself through an ever-increasing number of Swedish officers serving in NATO staffs and NATO headquarters and increasing harmonization with NATO standards; but, crucially, Sweden has yet to expand on its NATO partnership and seek membership. Thus Sweden has actively pursued an ambiguous policy of military non-alignment – and, although stressing 'solidarity', left a vast room for interpretation of exactly what this solidarity entails. Third, the Afghan mission has not fundamentally changed the main discursive divide of home and away – national and international – in Swedish strategy. Instead, both these policy domains are intact in separate spheres in which the use of force is legitimized differently. The overarching ambiguity inherent in attempting to combine ideals of peaceful conflict resolution, while retaining the capability of the use of force, is thus still an integral part of Swedish security policy and strategy.

Our analysis, furthermore, is based on close readings of parliamentary debates, Government Bills, after-action reports from the Armed Forces and a series of interviews with key individuals – political and military – in Swedish strategic decision-making. Even though this approach has its advantages, it is difficult to infer exactly how the overlapping processes of change in Swedish strategy are related to the participation in the Afghan intervention. One would need to make cross-case comparisons in order to do so, but this partly falls outside the framework of this book and partly carries its own weaknesses due to the particularities of the Swedish case. To reiterate, our main claim is that the strategy of ambiguity was not a consequence of the Afghan intervention only. However, the Afghan intervention fuelled the strategy of ambiguity; it fitted neatly into it and reinforced its basic premises.

The catch-all strategic narrative in Afghanistan: ambiguous political ends

Ambiguity was not a result of the Swedish participation in the Afghan intervention, but the presence of Swedish troops under ISAF command contributed to further ambiguity as the leading principle of Swedish post-Cold War strategy. It did so emphatically by generating a catch-all strategic narrative (Noreen & Angstrom 2015). This narrative was created and – on an annual basis – recreated by the Swedish Government in crafting its bills for continued participation in ISAF. By including all potential reasons to participate in Afghanistan, the bills (arguably) tried to satisfy as many target audiences as possible. In doing so, they created ambiguity regarding the reasons why Sweden intervened in Afghanistan and for what purposes it wielded military force. As a result, there is growing street-level resistance towards the intervention among the electorate. Indeed, one could even claim that the Swedish voters were left slightly confused by the Government narrative.

Strategic narratives enunciate political ends regarding the use of force. They shape the public perception of a particular policy and establish so-called interpretative dominance of how a particular event should be understood. In this, analogies and strategic narratives share common ground (for example, Angstrom 2011). In short, the contents of the story as well as the manner in which it is told open certain policy routes but forecloses others (Ringmar 1994). Or, in Finnemore's (2003, p. 15) terms, ideational frameworks do not cause interventions – but they enable them. For legitimizing the use of force (hence making such a strategy possible), a strategic narrative that appeals to critical support groups becomes imperative. One of the essential prerequisites of the alleged strategic utility of narratives is that they should be coherent, realistic, hold a promise of success and correspond with the reality on the ground; that is, the story needs to be upheld against public perception and it needs to be free of inconsistencies (for example, Freedman 2006, 2013; Betz 2011; Dimitriu 2011; Ringsmose & Borgesen 2011; Simpson 2013).

The catch-all narrative of the Swedish intervention in Afghanistan consists of a series of overlapping, sometimes contradictory signals. It stresses the need for Afghan security while maintaining that the mission is also about Swedish security. In stressing the need for security in Afghanistan it suggests that democratization, political stability, just governance and gender equality are central components of this security. While reinforcing the need of military forces, the narrative insists on holding up the ideals of peaceful conflict resolution and development as central objectives. Furthermore, while stressing more immediate security concerns, the narrative also embraces long-term interests such as the promotion of a just international order. Finally, it does not recognize that Sweden is fighting a war but still insists that the use of force is necessary.

In its 2010 Afghanistan strategy, the Government – tellingly – held that the Swedish troop contribution to ISAF in Afghanistan:

> is motivated by the Afghan people's vulnerability to violence, oppression and poverty, Sweden's self-interest in furthering security and stability in the region and globally, as well as our interest to contribute to a collective security regime and efficient international crisis management.
> (Ministry of Foreign Affairs 2010)

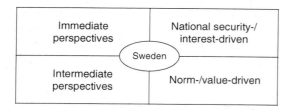

Figure 3.1 The Swedish catch-all narrative (Ringsmose *et al.* 2015).

Moreover, interventions within the NATO framework were particularly motivated by the need to transform the Swedish Armed Forces and increase their capabilities (Defence Commission 2007, p. 11). Hence in a few lines, the Swedish Government attempted to legitimize the use of force by appealing to humanitarian needs, egoistic self-interest and the importance of strengthening collective security organizations by participating in their actions. Considering that NATO is the major security organization in Afghanistan, it is difficult not to read the statement as being in support of NATO. As Figure 3.1 shows, the Swedish strategic narrative in Afghanistan combines immediate and intermediate perspectives, as well as national security/interest and norm/value drivers, thus attempting to accommodate multiple – if not all – political aims.

This catch-all solution has effectively limited the political space for competing narratives. Like a wet blanket, the Government's catch-all narrative has been extraordinarily successful in preventing other competing narratives from developing. In order to please as many domestic audiences as possible – partly a result of a domestic political culture favouring consensus, and partly a result of the functionalist aim of gaining the support of all the major political parties in Parliament in order to prevent sudden changes for the Armed Forces – the Government developed the catch-all narrative. Since the narrative cannot provide a clear political end for the troops in Afghanistan, it must be said to promote ambiguity. As such, the need for overall agreement created ambiguous political ends, which in turn furthered ambiguity in Swedish strategy. From the analysis of narrative, we can also conclude that we are not talking about an absence of strategy: there is definitely strategic behaviour by Swedish units in Afghanistan.

The downside of a resulting unintended strategy of ambiguity is, however, that there are great dangers of misinterpretation and confusion in the electorate. Polls show that Swedish public in general is highly supportive of participation in peace-support operations. The specific Afghanistan mission does not poll close to the general support of military participation – which, although decreasing over the past 20 years, remains over 50 per cent in favour. This also suggests that the catch-all narrative has not been successful in convincing the public of the need for Swedish participation in ISAF. Indeed, one possible interpretation of the data is that the catch-all narrative and the Afghan operations coincide with a quite dramatic downturn in public support: from regularly over 70 per cent to below 60 per cent. The narrative has not been successful in specifying one story of the goal of Swedish participation, either. Instead, the SOM institute (a reputable research institute at Gothenburg University) polls show that the public is split between considering support for NATO, increasing security for Sweden, preventing drugs trade and supporting Afghan democracy and economic development to be the relevant goals of the operation (Ydén & Berndtsson 2012, 2013) The public, furthermore, clearly disapproves of the NATO argument; it does not seem convinced that there is an imminent terrorist threat from Afghanistan, but it is highly supportive of the argument of supporting Afghan democracy. Perhaps the clearest sign of the confusion among the electorate is the increasing share of those who are 'undecided' since the beginning of the Afghan intervention with its catch-all narrative. From below 10 per cent to regularly over 20 per cent of 'undecided' respondents speaks volumes for how the public fails to be attracted and convinced by the catch-all political ends that Sweden pursues in Afghanistan.

In this decreasing support of Swedish international missions, we can witness the costs of elite political consensus. By not enforcing or creating a clear Swedish strategy, the Government has gained political support from the opposition, but has failed to send a clear signal to the public of why and how Swedish military forces take part in the Western intervention in Afghanistan. On the one hand, ambiguity may not be too bad a strategy under such circumstances, since all potential target audiences can relate to the strategy. However, on the other hand, target audiences will be uncertain of the Swedish Government's intentions. From this perspective – and especially under circumstances in which there appears to be a lack of coherent, explicit strategy – ambiguity may not be the most successful strategy.

In summary, the Afghan intervention has added new layers of complexity to Swedish political ends regarding its use of force. For various target audiences it becomes increasingly unclear – and therefore also less predictable – what political ends Sweden aims to pursue using military force. The Afghan intervention – and how the story of the Afghan intervention has been told by the Swedish Government – has therefore muddied the waters rather than sending a clear sign to the rest of the world that Sweden is moving from a policy of neutrality to one of solidarity. The target audiences cannot be unequivocally sure of Swedish commitments to a solidarity clause based on evidence from Afghanistan because the various motives mentioned throughout by the Swedish Government may not be reproduced elsewhere, and thus there is always the possibility that Sweden reneges.

Internationalization without commitment and professionalization without resources: ambiguous military means

The second major trend that has been furthered by (although not *caused* by) participation in the intervention in Afghanistan relates to the creation and organization of the Swedish Armed Forces. First, there is an increasing internationalization of the Swedish Armed Forces. This internationalization – understood as a growing degree of harmonization of Swedish Armed Forces' procedures, identity and Swedish officers being exposed to the military practices of other states – began in earnest when Swedish officers, free from the shackles of the neutrality policy, began to be integrated into multinational units or multinational staffs. Clearly the Afghan intervention created a need for further international coordination, but this process had started earlier. As such, it is difficult to claim that the Afghan intervention *caused* this process, although it certainly reinforced it. As we demonstrate below, the intervention in Afghanistan influenced the trajectory of internationalization insofar as it increased the number of Swedish officers exposed to NATO standards abroad but also provided incentives to adopt NATO planning procedures for operations on Swedish soil, thus further deepening harmonization with international actors.

Second, there is an increased professionalization of the Swedish Armed Forces. This professionalization relates to soldiers, to improved academic training of the officer corps and to the reintroduction of non-commissioned officers. This shift is related to the Afghan intervention in several ways, although the process started earlier. Creating academic training for officers, for example, began in the mid 1990s. Still, the Afghan intervention created an urgent need for readily available military units that were capable of and prepared for combat situations to a higher degree than the peacekeeping Swedish conscript army during the Cold War. The military needs in Afghanistan therefore seemingly propelled the process of professionalization. The professionalization trend contributed to ambiguity mainly by being underfunded and therefore generating what was – by Swedish standards and considering the size of the country – a very small military organization. This resulted in a situation in which surrounding states suddenly had difficulties 'reading' Swedish strategy, since it had reduced its Armed Forces significantly without seeking membership in NATO and with barely enough professional units to sustain a battalion-sized, long-term international intervention. Moreover, the Swedish Parliament did not decide to abolish conscription altogether, but maintained the right to call conscripts if need be. Conscription is dormant, but can be reactivated, which creates further ambiguity.

The internationalization meanwhile promotes ambiguity in military means in two ways. First, it signals that Sweden, in the way its Armed Forces operate, acts as a NATO member without actually being one, thereby trying to combine the advantage of being interoperable with NATO with the advantage of not being politically bonded to them. This has been recognized by (for example) the Swedish Armed Forces headquarters in 2003: 'Cooperation with NATO must be as close as Sweden's security policy line allows' (Hederstedt & Kihl 2003). Neighbouring states, therefore, cannot be sure of Swedish intentions. It either prepares for increased collaboration with NATO in case of war but prefers to free-ride during peace, or it has no intentions of joining NATO but harmonizes its procedures just to be interoperable in international missions. Second, it signals that Sweden tries to pursue a self-proclaimed strategy of solidarity – showing itself to be a member of a community of like-minded, rather than the alliance as such – but crucially cannot depend on the possibility of escalation dominance through reinforcements from alliance members.

Harmonization of Swedish Armed Forces' staff procedures with NATO standards began in the early 2000s at the Swedish National Defence College, but it was formally introduced in the field manual *Joint Operations* in 2005. When the formal decision was made, it was more a case of reinforcing something that was already implemented than the beginning of a reform process. Hence again, the Afghanistan mission did not cause this harmonization, but it did further accentuate its value. Turning to the Swedish collaboration with the NATO-led ISAF organization, the Swedish commitment has expanded and deepened – especially from 2006, when Sweden was given responsibility for the PRT area around Mazar-e-Sharif. When Provincial Reconstruction Teams (PRTs) were phased out and replaced by the Transition Support Teams, Sweden was appointed a 'framework nation' for one of these: the Nordic Baltic Transition Support Unit. In more concrete terms, this gave Sweden command over the present Finnish forces and those from the NATO members Norway and Latvia.

Swedish officers with central positions within the ISAF organization testified that multinational collaboration worked fairly smoothly. As one of the interviewees noted, he worked with colleagues of 'different characters, different histories, different cultural backgrounds, and different ways to solve problems', and although there were sometimes 'frictions' there was also a common professional understanding – an 'adhesive' – between the officers (interviews with Military Representative 5 2014, also Military Representative 4 2014, Military Representative 7 2014).[1] What is even more notable is that the Swedish policy of military non-alignment seemed to play such an insignificant role within the NATO-led organization. When we asked the officers whether they ever perceived themselves as restricted due to the fact that they represented a militarily non-aligned country, and whether and in what sense they were excluded from important information, nobody responded affirmatively (interview with Military Representatives 1–8).

According to one interviewee, officers within ISAF simply assumed that Sweden was a NATO member (Military Representative 4 2014). According to another interviewee, one of the representatives from Norway (a NATO member) did complain about the lack of transparency within ISAF, but the Swedes were essentially satisfied with the information that was supplied to them:

> No restrictions at all like that [...] I never felt excluded. Then there were, of course, some national cases in the US pipeline [...] Where I worked, I experienced no problems with it. However, I talked to a Norwegian colleague who worked with planning for the future [...] he then said that

sometimes the Americans did some side planning that he was not allowed to take part in [...] He was mightily annoyed that he did not get to know anything.

(Military Representative 5 2014)

There was a standard within ISAF that the number of officers from any country appointed to the more central staff units of the organization, such as the Headquarters in Kabul, should be proportional to the country's contribution in troop size. It is, therefore, interesting to note that Sweden held a relatively high profile in these contexts. Although the Swedish troop size in Afghanistan peaked in 2009, the number of appointments of Swedish officers to ISAF staff units continued to increase after these years and culminated in the early 2010s (see Figure 3.2). Swedes were, according to several interviewees, considered to possess special skills for these central positions within the ISAF organization. They were flexible, meticulous and expressed themselves fluently in English (the working language).[2]

In one evaluation study (Derblom et al. 2010, p. 49) of the Swedish-led PRT, it is stated that contemporary Western armies are very seldom organized with regard to the conflicts in which they actually have to serve. This summarizes, in a nutshell, not only the problem for the Swedish Armed Forces in organizing their activities within the PRT of Mazar-e-Sharif but also the entire ISAF mission. The mission was characterized by constant reorganizations and adaptations to new situations from 2002 until its end in 2014. As an example, the ambitious Counterinsurgency (COIN) doctrine that was introduced in 2006 has been considered as a bottom-up process, although originally based on British and American experiences of counterinsurgency in Southeast Asia since the 1950s and 1960s (Hunt 2010).

Sweden obviously had no problem adapting quite smoothly to the US-initiated COIN doctrine. Essential parts of the doctrine were already familiar to the staff of the PRT Mazar-e-Sharif before it was introduced in Afghanistan; that is, the ability to perform armed combat at different levels of engagement. It moreover suggests the possibility of practicing a 'firm–fair–friendly' approach, along with a strong emphasis on mission tactics (Derblom et al. 2010, p. 50). Reports from Swedish force commanders reveal that the Armed Forces indeed adapted to the central elements of the COIN doctrine: 'The planning of COIN principles has been initiated [...] through education and customized staff practices', the PRT force commander testified in 2009 (Swedish Armed Forces 2009a, p. 44, also Swedish Armed Forces 2010, p. 6 and Swedish Armed Forces 2009b, p. 23). Swedish ISAF soldiers were already enrolled in counterinsurgency courses in Kabul in 2007 and were, moreover, increasingly involved in counterinsurgency warfare, which culminated around 2010 (Military Representative 8 2014, Civilian Representative 1 2014, Swedish Armed Forces 2009a, p. 44, Swedish Armed Forces 2010, p. 6, Swedish Armed Forces 2009b, p. 23).

Swedish strategy and the Afghan experience 43

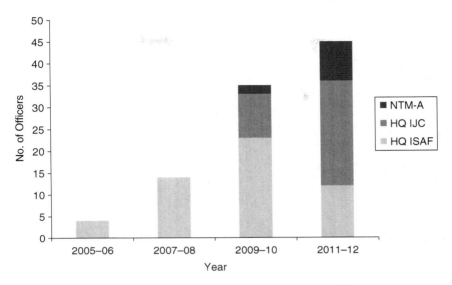

Figure 3.2 The number of Swedish officers appointed at NATO Training Mission in Afghanistan (NTM-A), Headquarters Joint Command (HQ IJC) and Headquarters ISAF (HQ ISAF), 2005–12. The diagram is based on tables compiled by Lieutenant Colonel Lars-Erik Laksjö, Swedish Armed Forces Headquarters, Stockholm, 2013. (Detailed tables are available at the Department of Peace and Conflict, Uppsala University.)

In addition to the immediate theatre of operations, over the last decade Swedish officers were increasingly sent to serve in NATO or EU staffs. Figure 3.3 shows how, beginning in 2006, the number of Swedish officers posted in NATO or EU staffs doubled – and then doubled again in 2007. The peaks in these numbers coincide with Sweden commanding the EU Battle Groups 6 months later. Hence the Battle Group in 2008 was preceded by 50 officers working in international staffs, and the Battle Group in 2011 was preceded by over 80 officers in international staffs during 2010. If the pattern holds we can expect a high increase during 2014, since Sweden takes over a Battle Group in 2015. Regardless of the reason behind the major peaks, the table also shows how, once established on a higher level, the figures do not drop to the levels of the early 2000s.

In summary, the military means designated to reach the political ends also send ambiguous signals. Again, this process was not *caused* by the intervention in Afghanistan, but the sharp increase of Swedish officers partaking in ISAF staffs coincides with a similar sharp increase of Swedish officers partaking in NATO or EU staffs outside the immediate theatre of operations. The last decade has also witnessed an increasing harmonization of Swedish staff and decision-making procedures with NATO standards. At

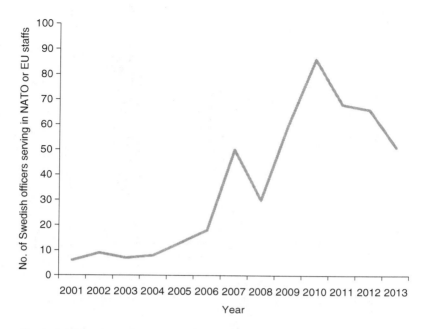

Figure 3.3 Number of Swedish officers serving in NATO or EU staffs outside the immediate theatre of operations (Swedish Armed Forces Annual Reports 2001–13).

the same time, Sweden has not attempted to take the step to full integration with NATO forces in Afghanistan (it rather contributed to ISAF escalation through creating a division of labour; see Angstrom & Honig 2012). Nor has it sought membership in the organization. This process also started before Afghanistan, but the intervention has accentuated it. The Afghan intervention also increased the pace of professionalization of Sweden's Armed Forces. However, the limited size of the forces entailed – rather confusingly – Sweden sending its best trained units abroad to do peacekeeping while retaining the territorial units to prepare for the more difficult task of defending the nation. All of these trends imply that the target audiences of Swedish strategy perceive mixed messages.

Home and away as two distinct domains: ambiguous methods

The third part of our analysis stresses the methods by which the Swedish Armed Forces utilizes its means in pursuit of the political goals. We have so far argued that the political ends and the military means of Sweden after the Cold War have furthered an ambiguity. When it comes to methods, this image is further reinforced. Again, it is not the Afghan intervention as such that has driven this development, but the Afghan intervention has rather confirmed an overall division of how Sweden uses force.

In earlier analyses (for example, Angstrom 2015, Angstrom & Honig 2012) it has been pointed out that in the Swedish strategic discourse there is a sharp divide between the national and the international. These analyses were based on the different ways in which force was legitimized in the national and international domains, as well as the differences between the domains regarding how training and units were organized. The divide between national and international was necessary to create in order to maintain a strategic identity that combined a robust national defence against the Cold War threat from the Soviet Union with a policy of stressing peaceful conflict resolution abroad. To solve the apparent contradiction between on the one hand, supporting peace initiatives abroad, and on the other hand preparing for national defence, two distinct policy domains were created. By keeping them apart, it is possible to pursue two different strategies. There is also, however, a strong claim to be made that the methods used nationally and internationally differ. The intervention in Afghanistan has, rather than breaking this mould, reinforced the discursive division. This creates further ambiguity regarding how force is wielded by the Armed Forces.

In an unambiguous, coherent strategy one would expect that force is used within the same discursive framework. In order to credibly project this unambiguous image, moreover, one would expect that training ground manoeuvres would reflect this strategy to maintain the integrity of age-old maxims such as 'train as you fight'. Furthermore, we would also expect that forces are kept intact and are trained in similar ways for both international and national tasks. Finally, we would expect that force is used in the same way at home and away. Even a cursory glance, however, makes these claims dubious. The fact that force is wielded differently suggests that Sweden's neighbours cannot be sure of its capabilities or its preferred way of using force.

First, there are different doctrines and strategic documents for international missions and national defence. For the defence of Sweden, there is a plethora of documents and procedures in which it is made clear how force should be used to defend the country. There are, however, a similar range of documents for international missions. These documents, critically, stipulate different tasks and ways of war. Hence, when Swedish units are deployed internationally, they operate with a different set of tasks to how they operate at home. For example, the main operational idea of how to use force in Afghanistan has been linked to the PRT. It is through combining and harmonizing aid and security in a comprehensive approach that political ends are met, according to Swedish military doctrine (Swedish Armed Forces 2011, pp. 84–7). In comparison, for the national defence of Sweden, the main idea is joint operations combining air, sea and land forces in manoeuvre warfare (Swedish Armed Forces 2011, pp. 147–8).

Furthermore, changes in the way that Sweden fights caused by the Afghan intervention should be visible by examining doctrinal change: from the 2002 doctrine to the 2011 doctrine. Although the doctrine from 2011 stresses expeditionary capabilities, availability and flexibility, these changes can be attributed to an ongoing political process since the end of the Cold War, rather than being derived from the Afghan mission in and of itself. Certainly, there is an interaction between a general trend and the specific Afghan mission insofar as the latter also influences the former. However following (among others) Dalsjo (2015) and Edstrom and Gyllensporre (2014), the strategic shift from focusing on territorial defence to focusing on deployable Armed Forces was a gradual one from the end of the Cold War to (perhaps at its peak) the 2009 Government Defence Bill – symptomatically titled 'usable defence forces'. Some aspects of the warfighting methods, such as being able to conduct a counterinsurgency campaign, are clearly a reflection of Afghanistan, but the overall picture is still that the additions to Swedish doctrine are concerned with international missions in general. For national missions, the basis for operations is still the same as it was before the Afghan intervention. Thus, the doctrine (Swedish Armed Forces 2011 p. 62) now identifies certain principles of war for national missions and others for international stabilization operations. This follows a longer tradition of separation. As recently as in 2002, for example, national and international operations even had different doctrinal documents. This is a clear signal that the Armed Forces are expected to behave differently in different contexts. And this means that although after Afghanistan international operations are a part of the main doctrine, they are still distinguished from operations such as they are understood in a national context.

Second, the organization of the units sent out to Afghanistan has been different from how the defence of the national territory is organized. In the last parliamentary bill on the defence in 2009, the Armed Forces implemented a new organization in which the army was organized in seven so-called manoeuvre battalions of professional, all-volunteer soldiers. These units were intended to serve as the basic building blocks and to act as the 'fighting unit'. However, although the core of some of the rotations in Afghanistan has been recruited from the same unit, the composition of the Swedish forces in Afghanistan at large comes from different units (see Chapter 5 in this volume for further discussion). Again, this hardly amounts to a credible train-as-you-fight capability. Moreover, the reorganization cannot be understood as a result of the Swedish–Afghan mission, since the Government identified the battalion-sized Battle Group as the main fighting unit in 2006: before the need for such battle-prepared forces emerged in Afghanistan. The causal arrow rather goes in the opposite direction. The Government, as part of its responsibilities within the EU and the creation of EU Battle Groups, saw the opportunities for increased harmonization and efficiency if the Swedish Armed Forces were organized and fought in a way that the EU expected. There would then be no need for further resources or retraining of units if they already were organized in this way. What was sent to Afghanistan was thus not necessarily tailor-made for the needs of the mission, but rather what was available.

This being said, the Afghan intervention has certainly reinforced some things, such as the need for expeditionary capabilities. As such, it is fair to conclude that while the Afghan mission did not cause a change in the way in which Swedish forces are trained, equipped and organized, it certainly reinforced some trends while downplaying others.

Third, training for territorial defence and training for international operations have been kept apart during the entire post-Second World War era. Since the Swedish Army launched its special international missions training organization and training ground in 1948, the bulk of the army's main education and the training for international missions have been separate. The training and preparation of Swedish units slated for the intervention in Afghanistan is no exception. Again, it suggests that neighbouring states are sent mixed messages regarding Sweden's military capabilities and how it intends to use force.

Fourth and finally, there is the tricky issue of civil–military coordination, which characterized the entire ISAF mission and thereby also Sweden's contribution. On previous international missions, Swedish units have operated in a distinctly military setting, not harmonizing their efforts with the Swedish International Development Cooperation Agency (SIDA). However, in Afghanistan the Swedish mission ostensibly became more similar to the old Cold War idea of how Sweden was to defend itself using 'total defence'. Harmonizing the use of all potential sources of power towards one common goal was very much the idea of defending Sweden against foreign invasion. Civil–military coordination efforts in Afghanistan were direct consequences of NATO's concept 'comprehensive approach', and to some extent the COIN doctrine. Although one can make comparisons with Swedish 'total defence' ideas, the influences from NATO and the US were far more important. A lesson learned from this gigantic ISAF experiment in civil–military coordination was that it did not work smoothly, especially not when it concerned the military's relationship with SIDA. The military preferred so-called 'quick impact projects'; that is, small, 'more flexible and immediate' projects that are quite different from the traditional development projects offered by SIDA (Johansson & Sigurdsson 2011, p. 12, also Derblom et al. 2010, pp. 73–5). According to the force commanders of the Swedish-led PRT, the soldiers 'had more benefit from American advisers in development issues than from Swedish SIDA advisors.' (Military Representative 3 2003) Apparently, there was a shared system of understanding between the Swedish military and USAID personnel of the crisis in question – and, most importantly, of the concrete problems that were connected to the crisis.[3] In this context one should note, however, that USAID's huge resources were channelled through military authorities, which was definitely not the case concerning SIDA's relation to the Swedish Armed Forces. These were two strictly separate organizations with very different missions that should not be intermixed (Civilian Representative 1 2014, Civilian Representative 3 2014).

A further indication that the increasing civil–military collaboration internationally is not the old national defence concept of 'total defence' is that the

Swedish Armed Forces doctrine (2012, p. 86), makes clear that 'total defence is a national solution aimed at furthering the defence of Swedish territory', while the so-called comprehensive approach in international missions is not regulated by law, but should be understood as an aspiration to more efficient civil–military coordination. Moreover, even if this suggests fragments of similar warfighting concepts in the national and international realms, this harmonization surely cannot be said to be inspired by the Afghan intervention, since the Cold War concept of total defence obviously predates the Afghan war.

The officers who had to implement the Government's overly vague ideas behind the Swedish mission in Afghanistan had a difficult task. This was revealed in the force commanders' reports from PRT Mazar-e-Sharif. Annoyance became especially evident when they had to try to coordinate civilian and military efforts, initially in the absence of any civilian representatives, and the force commanders had to improvise (for example, Military Representative 8 2014). However, when the missions according to the Government discourse became more extensive, the force commanders' criticism diminished. A catch-all strategy gave the military the leeway to interpret the mission in their own way according to their military profession and experience. As a consequence, the behaviour of Swedish units in Afghanistan has varied significantly. This suggests that there are, even when given the same task, great variety and freedom of action for individual force commanders in Afghanistan to choose how they use force (Honig & Kaihko 2012). As Magnus Johnsson (forthcoming) shows, moreover, the use of force has varied from armoured battles to peacekeeping. Both of these studies reinforce the image of a military organization without clear strategic guidance. Hence, the variation in military behaviour suggests that neighbouring states face greater uncertainty and ambiguity about how Sweden uses military force.

In summary, Swedish participation in the Afghan War has accentuated ambiguity in how Sweden intends to use force. Most importantly, it has confirmed rather than eased the tension between, and separation of, national and international missions inherent in Swedish strategic discourse. There seems to be a lack of a coherent strategic guidance, making it difficult for various target audiences, be they friends or foes, to interpret Swedish strategy. Ends, means and ways in Swedish strategy, therefore, seem to have been pushed towards ambiguity by the Afghan experience.

Conclusions: Afghanistan, ambiguity and its consequences for Swedish strategy

How has participation in the Afghanistan intervention influenced Swedish strategy? It is beyond doubt that Swedish strategy has seen some dramatic developments over the past 15 years. It is, however, misleading to suggest that these changes are a direct result of participation in ISAF in Afghanistan. Political ends, military means and methods – the contents, organization and practices of strategy – have varied in a way that suggests that the Afghan intervention should be seen both as evidence of strategic change and as a driver of further change. The Afghan experience, in other words, has *reinforced* certain trends in Swedish strategic behaviour without necessarily *causing* them in the first place.

The strategic consequences of Swedish participation in ISAF are probably still difficult to grasp in their entirety. Still, there is enough early evidence to cast a shadow on early interpretations of Swedish strategy as moving from neutrality to solidarity. This overall interpretation may be correct, but focusing on the Afghan mission has highlighted conflicting tendencies that rather point to a highly complex picture of several overlapping ends, means and ways that – taken together – paint a picture of Swedish strategy as unintended ambiguity. The Afghanistan intervention, in short, has pushed Sweden towards increased ambiguity in its strategy. We suggest that the multitude of seemingly unrelated strategic trends is evidence of a lack of strategic coordination, resulting from the absence of a decision-making body with the specific task of formulating and pursuing strategy. While the broader political ends and strategies of the Afghan intervention were formulated in New York, Washington, Kabul and Brussels, the Swedish Government in Stockholm still had to decide its contribution. It could have done so coherently and unambiguously through, for example, seeking membership in NATO and fully integrating its forces with the Western allies, much like Denmark did. Sweden, however, chose differently.

What are the strategic consequences of the transition to ambiguity? Ambiguity, if it were intentional, may not be the worst strategy to pursue for a small state wedged between great powers. Indeed, ambiguity could be sign of a very opportune strategy of not choosing sides in advance (which, of course, can lead to trouble later), but rather maintaining freedom of action to balance between the great powers. Indeed, this would follow a longstanding theme of Swedish strategy. The Cold War neutrality doctrine, of course, aimed to further and maintain the country's freedom of manoeuvre in the event of superpower war. However, this relies upon possessing independent military capabilities that can credibly deter or – in the worst case – be actively used in such a balancing war. At the moment, there are grave doubts about Sweden possessing such military capabilities.

Ambiguity can also work as a successful strategy if one possesses military capabilities that can punish an aggressor. By creating a degree of uncertainty in the opponent's decision-making, ambiguity can prevent escalation. Israel, for example, has never admitted possessing nuclear weapons, but the fact that it does not say that it does not possess such weapons either, or where the line to use them is drawn, creates a situation in which neighbouring states cannot be sure how far they can escalate in a potential conflict with Israel. Paradoxically, from this perspective the danger for Egypt and Syria in the Yom Kippur war was not about their armies being defeated by the Israeli defence forces, but rather that they would be too successful in their offensive and that this could trigger a nuclear response from Israel. The logic is flawed in the case of Sweden, however, since it does not possess such a strong coercive military capability.

Ambiguity, furthermore, could potentially operate as a successful strategy and enhance stability if predictions of future behaviour could be made from estimates of military capabilities. However, as offense–defence theory (Herz 1950, Jervis 1978, Brown *et al.* 2004, Booth & Wheeler 2008) teaches us, offensive military capabilities cannot be distinguished from defensive ones, which suggests that ambiguity in political ends, military means and methods do not aid stability. On the contrary.

Where ambiguity instead has advantages is partly domestically and partly diplomatically. For domestic political reasons, it certainly made good strategic sense to include all pet-political projects of the political parties. Effectively, no alternative narrative of the Afghan war was told in Sweden since everyone became a stakeholder in the official narrative. Moreover, also in relation to other states, being ambiguous can be successful in negotiations; it does not provoke anyone, but rather creates more potential outcomes that can be agreed upon by the actors (Putnam 1988). Henry Kissinger even made so-called 'constructive ambiguity' the focus in his monumental *Diplomacy* (Kissinger 1994).

Ambiguity can, however, also be outright flawed as a strategy. The over-a-decade-long Afghan intervention has – instead of chiselling out a transparent, coherent strategy – made Swedish strategy more uncertain and difficult to read for insiders and outsiders. First, partners may doubt commitments if strategy is pursued with ambiguous political ends. Second, opponents may judge preparedness to escalate as non-credible. Third, ambiguity is also a sign of a domestic democratic deficit. Hence, the pursuit of increased political freedom of manoeuvre through ambiguity is a high-risk undertaking.

Notes

1 Eleven semi-structured interviews were conducted with Swedish military and civilian representatives in 2012–14. They were all employed by the Swedish Armed Forces or by Swedish Government agencies, and were concurrently involved in various ways in the ISAF mission. All interviews were conducted in Sweden by Erik Noreen. For a full list of interviews and codes, see References.
2 It is notable, however, that we do not find any Swedish officer in these central ISAF staff units with higher rank than Colonel (OF 5). The reason given was that the highest posts were reserved for NATO Generals. There was thus a fairly clear restriction that affected the non-aligned Sweden (Military Representative 7, 2014).
3 Also: 'The projects undertaken have essentially been aimed at Force Protection, regardless of from where money has been received. Essentially, measures have been taken to improve accessibility, enhance the security of our own and ANSF forces and restore damaged property. Proposals of more humanitarian nature have either been rejected and/or handed over to appropriate NGO. *Great support and assistance have been received from USAID representative* at PRT MeS.' (Swedish Armed Forces 2010, p. 54, italics added).

References

Agrell, W. (2010) *Fredens illusioner: Det svenska nationella forsvarets nedgang och fall 1988–2009* [The illusion of peace: The rise and fall of the Swedish national defence]. Stockholm: Atlantis.
Agrell, W. (2013) *Ett krig har och nu: Fran svensk fredsoperation till upprorsbekampning i Afghanistan 2001–2014* [A war here and now: Sweden's road to armed conflict in Afghanistan 2001–2014]. Stockholm: Atlantis.
Andrén, N. (1996) *Maktbalans och alliansfrihet: Svensk utrikespolitik under 1900-talet* [Balance of power and non-alignment: Swedish foreign policy during the twentieth century]. Stockholm: Norstedts Juridik.
Angstrom, J. (2011) 'Mapping the competing historical analogies of the war on terrorism: The Bush presidency' *International Relations* Vol. 25 No. 2 pp. 224–42.
Angstrom, J. (2015) 'Forsvarsmaktens internationella insatser: I den svenska sakerhetens eller identitetens tjanst?' [International missions: In the service of Swedish security or identity?] in Engelbrekt, K., A. Holmberg & J. Angstrom (Eds) *Svensk sakerhetspolitik i Europa och varlden* [Swedish security policy in Europe and the world] 2nd edition. Stockholm: Norstedts, pp. 233–64.
Angstrom, J. & J. Willem Honig (2012) 'Regaining strategy: Small powers, strategic culture and escalation in Afghanistan' *Journal of Strategic Studies* Vol. 35, No. 5, pp. 663–88.
Angstrom, J. & J.J. Widen (2015) *Contemporary military theory: The dynamics of war.* London: Routledge.
Arreguin-Toft, I. (2007) 'How to lose a war on terror: A comparative analysis of counter-insurgency success and failure' in Angstrom J. & I. Duyvesteyn (Eds) *Understanding victory and defeat in contemporary war.* London: Routledge, pp. 142–67.
Betz, D. (2011) 'Communication breakdown: Strategic communications and defeat in Afghanistan' *Orbis* Vol. 55, No. 4, pp. 613–30.
Bjereld, U., A.W. Johansson & K. Molin (2008) *Sveriges sakerhet och varldens fred: Svensk utrikespolitik under kalla kriget* [Swedish security and peace in the world: Swedish foreign policy during the cold war]. Stockholm: Santérus.
Booth, K. & Wheeler, N. (2008) *The security dilemma: Fear, cooperation, and trust in world politics.* London: Palgrave Macmillan.
Britz, M. (2008) *Europeanization of defence industry policy in the 1990s.* Saarbrücken: VDM Verlag Dr. Müller.
Brown, M.E., O.R. Cote Jr, S.M. Lynn-Jones & S.E. Miller (Eds) (2004) *Offense, defence and war.* Cambridge, MA: MIT Press.
Dalsjo, R. (2006) *Life-line lost: The rise and fall of 'neutral' Sweden's secret reserve option of wartime help from the West.* Stockholm: Santérus, pp. 165–90.
Dalsjo, R. (2015) 'Fran neutralitet till solidaritet: Omgestaltningen av Sveriges sakerhetspolitik efter det kalla kriget' [From neutrality to solidarity: The reframing of Swedish security policy after the end of the cold war] in Engelbrekt, K., A. Holmberg & J. Angstrom (Eds) *Svensk sakerhetspolitik i Europa och varlden* [Swedish security policy in Europe and the world] 2nd edition. Stockholm: Norstedts.
de Graaf, B., G. Dimitriu & J. Ringsmose (2015) 'Conclusion' in de Graaf, B., G. Dimitriu & J. Ringsmose (Eds) *Strategic narratives, public opinion, and war: Winning support for foreign military missions.* London: Routledge, pp. 351–67.
Derblom, M., J. Frelin, K. Lindén, C. Nilsson & J. Tejpar (2010) *Utvardering av Prt Mes. Slutrapport* [Evaluation of Prt Mes Final report]. Stockholm: Swedish Defence Research Agency.

Dimitriu, G. (2011) 'Winning the story war: Strategic communication and the conflict in Afghanistan' *Public Relations Review* Vol. 38, pp. 195–207.
Edstrom, H. & D. Gyllensporre (2014) *Svensk forsvarsformaga efter det kalla kriget: Forlorade decennier eller vunna insikter?* [*Swedish defence capability after the cold war: Lost decades or gained insights?*]. Stockholm: Santérus.
Engelbrekt, K. (forthcoming) 'From neutrality to solidarity: Swedish security policy after EU accession' in Sperling, J. & V. Papacosma (Eds) *Europe's neutrals and European security in the 21st century.* London: Routledge.
Eriksson, J. (2004) *Kampen om hotbilden: Rutin och drama i svensk sakerhetspolitik* [*The struggle for the threat perception: Routine and drama in Swedish securitypolicy*]. Stockholm: Santérus.
Finnemore, M. (2003) *The purpose of intervention: Changing beliefs about the use of force.* Ithaca, NY: Cornell University Press.
Freedman, L. (2006) *The transformation in strategic affairs.* London: Routledge.
Freedman, L. (2013) *Strategy: A history.* Oxford: Oxford University Press.
Gray, C.S. (1999) *Modern strategy.* Oxford: Oxford University Press.
Herz, J. (1950) 'Idealist internationalism and the security dilemma' *World Politics* Vol. 2, No. 2, pp. 171–201.
Holmberg, A. (2010) 'Sverige och europeiseringen av forsvarspolitiken' [Sweden and the Europeanization of defence policy] in Engelbrekt, K. & J. Angstrom (Eds) *Svensk sakerhetspolitik i Europa och varlden* [*Swedish security policy in Europe and the world*]. Stockholm: Norstedts, pp.131–46
Holmstrom, M. (2011) *Den dolda alliansen: Sveriges hemliga Natoforbindelser* [*The secret alliance: Sweden's secret NATO connections*]. Stockholm: Atlantis.
Holsti, K. (2004) *Taming the sovereigns: Institutional change in international politics.* Cambridge: Cambridge University Press.
Honig, J.W. & Kaihko, I. (2012) 'Challenges of command: The rise of the "Strategic Colonel"' in Haas H. (Ed) *Authentic leadership in extreme situations.* New York: Peter Lang, pp. 89–108.
Hunt, D. (2010) 'Dirty Wars: Counterinsurgency in Vietnam and today' *Politics & Society* Vol. 38, No. 1, pp. 35–66.
Jervis, R. (1978) 'Cooperation under the security dilemma' *World Politics* Vol. 30, No. 2, pp. 167–214.
Johnsson, M. (forthcoming) *Peacemakers or warlords? Understanding the discretion of Swedish commanders in the Afghanistan campaign* Ph.D. Dissertation. Uppsala: Uppsala University.
Kissinger, H. (1994) *Diplomacy.* New York: Simon & Schuster.
Kronvall, O. & M. Petersson (2012) *Svensk sakerhetspolitik i supermakternas skugga 1945–1991* [*Swedish security policy in the shadow of the super powers 1945–1991*] 2nd edition. Stockholm: Santérus.
Noreen, E. & J. Angstrom (2015) 'A catch-all strategic narrative: Target audiences and Swedish troop contribution to ISAF in Afghanistan' in de Graaf, B., G. Dimitriu & J. Ringsmose (Eds) *Strategic narratives, public opinion, and war: Winning support for foreign military missions.* London: Routledge, pp. 282–99.
Petersson, M. (2015) 'Forsvarstransformeringen efter det kalla krigets slut: klassificering, forklaring, karakteristik' [Defence transformation after the end of the cold war: Classification, explanation, characteristic] in Engelbrekt, K., A. Holmberg & J. Angstrom (Eds) *Svensk sakerhetspolitik i Europa och varlden* [*Swedish security policy in Europe and the world*] 2nd edn. Stockholm: Norstedts, pp. 209–33.

Putnam, R. (1988) 'Diplomacy and domestic politics: The logic of two-level games' *International Organization* Vol. 42, No. 3, pp. 427–60.
Ringmar, E. (1996) *Identity, interest and action: A cultural explanation of Sweden's intervention in the Thirty Years' war.* Cambridge: Cambridge University Press.
Ringsmose, J. & B. Borgesen (2011) 'Shaping public attitudes toward the deployment of military power: NATO, Afghanistan, and the use of strategic narratives' *European Security* Vol. 20, No. 4, pp. 505–28.
Simpson, E. (2013) *War from the ground up: Twenty-first century combat as politics.* Oxford: Oxford University Press.
Tunsjo, O. (2011) 'Geopolitical shifts, great power relations and Norway's foreign policy' *Cooperation and Conflict* Vol. 46, No. 1, pp. 60–77.
Ydén, K. & J. Berndtsson (2012) 'Nar kriget kommit – svenskarna och den nya forsvarspolitiken' [When the war arrived – the Swedes and the new defence policy] in Weibull, L., H. Oscarsson & A. Bergstrom (Eds) *I framtidens skugga.* Gothenburg University: SOM Institute, pp. 501–12.
Ydén, K. & J. Berndtsson (2013) 'Efter Afghanistan? Forsvaret, kriget och svenskarna' [After Afghanistan? The defence, the war and the Swedes] in Weibull, L., H. Oscarsson & A. Bergstrom (Eds) *Vagskal [Crossroads].* Gothenburg: Gothenburg University SOM Institute, pp. 617–30.

Primary Sources

Defence Commission (2007) *Sakerhet i samverkan* [Security in collaboration] Ds 2007: 46 Stockholm.
Defence Commission (2014) *Forsvaret av Sverige: Starkare forsvar for en osaker tid [Defence of Sweden: Stronger defence for an uncertain time]* Ds 2014: 20 Stockholm.
Government Bill (2009) *Ett anvandbart forsvar [A useful defence]* Regeringens proposition, 2008/09: 140 Stockholm.
Government Bill (1982) *Om sakerhets- och forsvarspolitiken samt totalforsvarets fortsatta utveckling [About the security and defence policy and the countinued development of the total defence]* Regeringens proposition, 1981/82: 102, Stockholm.
Hederstedt, J. & J. Kihl (2003) Arsrapport Fran Perspektivplaneringen 2002–2003; *Malbildsinriktningar Infor Forsvarsbeslutet 2004* [Yearly report from future planning 2002–2003; Goals in front of the defence decision 2004] Rapport 7 edited by Swedish Armed Forces. Stockholm: Hogkvarteret.
Ministry of Foreign Affairs (2010) *Strategi for Sveriges stod till det internationella engagemanget i Afghanistan* [Strategy for Swedish support for the international engagement in Afghanistan] Available online at www.regeringen.se/contentassets/62 84170ece4f493cad8960d2369bbcf6/strategi-for-sveriges-stod-till-det-internationella -engagemanget-i-afghanistan (accessed 25 August 2015).
Swedish Armed Forces (2009a) 'Fs 18 Slutrapport' [Fs 18 Final report] SWECON bet H/R 09 500:81524, 24 August 2010. Stockholm: Swedish Armed Forces.
Swedish Armed Forces (2009b) 'Slutrapport Fs 17' [Fs 17 Final report] HKV bet H/S 09 500:81422, 18 December 2009. Stockholm: Swedish Armed Forces.
Swedish Armed Forces (2010) 'Slutrapport Fortsattningsstyrka 19 (Fs 19)' [Final report continuity mission 19 (Fs 19)] SWECON bet H/R01 800:80093, 12 January 2011. Stockholm: Swedish Armed Forces.

Swedish Armed Forces (2011) 'Slutrapport FS 21.' [Final report FS 21] HKV bet H/R 09 500:96993, 14 December 2011. Stockholm: Swedish Armed Forces.

Swedish Armed Forces Annual Reports (2001–13) Stockholm: Swedish Armed Forces, Available online at www.forsvarsmakten.se/sv/om-myndigheten/dokument/arsredovisningar/ (accessed November 2014).

List of Interviews

(Interviews were conducted in Stockholm and Enkoping between December 2012 andMay 2014. Transcripts of all the interviews are available at the Department of Peace and Conflict, Uppsala University).

Civilian Representative 1. Swedish Ambassador. Kabul. Interviewed 2014.

Civilian Representative 2. Senior Civilian Representative. PRT MeS. Interviewed 2014.

Civilian Representative 3. Senior Civilian Representative. PRT MeS. Interviewed 2014.

Military Representative 1. Colonel, Chief of Staff. RC North. Interviewed 2012.

Military Representative 2. Training Commander, Lieutenant Colonel. Armed Forces Headquarters, Stockholm. Interviewed 2013.

Military Representative 3. Colonel, Force Commander. PRT MeS,. Interviewed 2013.

Military Representative 4. Colonel. ISAF Headquarters, Kabul. Interviewed 2014.

Military Representative 5. Lieutenant Colonel, ISAF Joint Command, Kabul. Interviewed 2014.

Military Representative 6. Major. RC North, International Training Centre, Livgardet, Stockholm. Interviewed 2014.

Military Representative 7. Colonel. ISAF Hadquarters, Kabul. Interviewed 2014.

Military Representative 8. Colonel, Force Commander. PRT Mes. Interviewed 2014.

4 Swedish use of force and the international legal framework
The legacy of Afghanistan

Inger Osterdahl

Introduction

This contribution deals with the Swedish understanding of some of the international legal issues involved in the use of force by the international community in Afghanistan. The international legal issues involved pertain to the law of war (the *jus ad bellum*) and the law in war (the *jus in bello*). The international institutional framework within which the military force is exercised is also of interest; for Sweden, primarily and traditionally the UN and the UN Security Council (UNSC), but also – and relatively more recently – NATO.

Within the law of war, the Swedish view of different justifications of the international use of force is in focus. The attitude toward whether Swedish troops should be involved in the use of force internationally at all is also an issue. With respect to both conceivable justifications and preparedness to use force internationally, there has been a considerable Swedish development during the last 20 years – climaxing in the extensive and intensive Afghanistan experience, but beginning before and continuing after.

The international experiences that have affected conceptions of the justifications and use of international force have all been made within operations based on a UNSC mandate; but, more importantly for our purposes, practically every case has been in close cooperation with NATO. The NATO connection is a potentially very significant aspect of the Swedish involvement in the International Security Assistance Force (ISAF) in Afghanistan, and is arguably closely intertwined with the developing Swedish view of the legitimacy of the international use of force based on a broadening range of justifications.

Several issues with respect to the law in war also arose in Afghanistan. Sweden had to tackle these – somewhat reluctantly at times, since it had not intended to wage war in Afghanistan. The participation in robust international peace operations, of which ISAF was the most robust so far, almost necessarily gives rise to considerations of international humanitarian law (IHL). In Afghanistan, the issue of whether there was an armed conflict in the sense of IHL arose, as did such issues as who should be considered a party to the armed conflict (in the case that there was one) and how to handle the detention of persons threatening the security of the ISAF mission. The Swedish position on these issues, which were heavily politically charged, is dealt with below.

Finally, we analyze how the experience of Afghanistan, as *primus inter pares* among Sweden's international experiences in recent decades, continues to affect the identity shift that Sweden is going through regarding its role in international use of military force. Here, we return to the issue of how the use of force is legally justified and the institutional framework within which force will potentially be exercised. On both counts, exciting developments unfold in Swedish policymaking in the wake of the ISAF experience. If military force were to actually be exercised, issues pertaining to IHL will make themselves felt again – including the vexed question as to whether Sweden is or is not involved in armed conflict or war.

An evolving Swedish view of the legitimacy of the use of force

Sweden's position on the international use of military force has traditionally been restrictive – at least since 1814, when Sweden's latest war ended – and, since the creation of the UN, fully consistent with the collective security system under the UN Charter. The international use of force has only been considered acceptable either in self-defence or pursuant to an authorization by the UNSC. This is in line with the UN Charter, which basically prohibits the international use of force by states, except in the case that an armed attack occurs (Article 51) or the use of force has been authorized by the Security Council (Articles 39 and 42).

From the late 1990s the traditional position seemed to be gradually shifting and Sweden seemed to become more tolerant towards the use of force even without a Security Council mandate, on condition that the force was used for humanitarian purposes and that action by the Security Council had been made impossible through the use of the veto (compare Engdahl & Hellman (Eds) 2007, pp. 61–66). The veto was beginning to be considered a drawback rather than a benefit of the collective security system from the Swedish point of view (compare Bring *et al.* 2014, pp. 185–7). Developments in the official rhetoric on the issue of the use of force during the 2000s were quite remarkable. Changes in the Swedish attitude towards humanitarian intervention – the first sign of an evolving Swedish view of the legitimate international use of force – corresponded in time with the internationalization and activation of the Swedish Armed Forces (see generally Osterdahl 2009, 2010, 2011). This was manifested most importantly in relatively large troop contributions to NATO-led operations, first in ex-Yugoslavia and then in Afghanistan. This activation consisted of officially transforming the Swedish defence from being guided by threat scenarios (that is, passively reacting to threats against the Swedish territory) to being guided by active will (Defence Commission 2007, p. 48).[1]

Debates in the Parliament illustrate the shift in attitude toward the international use of force for humanitarian purposes in exceptional cases, even without a UN mandate. The shift can be observed across the political spectrum, with the exception of the leftists and the environmentalists, and later on (from 2010) the Swedish Democrats. The Swedish official position on the NATO intervention in Kosovo in 1999 without a UNSC mandate, which spurred much of the debate in Parliament on humanitarian intervention, was that there was no 'unequivocal basis' for it in international law (Preliminary report of the proceedings in Parliament 1998/99:110 Intervention No. 138, see also 1998/99:100 and 1998/99:109). The specific terms used to characterize the legality of the intervention bear witness to a certain measure of ambivalence on the part of the Swedish Government; Sweden did not close the door entirely on unilateral humanitarian intervention.

The idea of a responsibility to protect constitutes a chronological and conceptual continuation of the debate on humanitarian intervention (compare ICISS 2001, UN General Assembly 2005). The author considers the concepts to be closely related and basically synonymous, although in principle the responsibility to protect has a much wider reach than humanitarian intervention (Engdahl & Hellman (Eds) 2007, pp. 15–26, pp. 41–60; Amnéus 2008). The responsibility to protect fits nicely into the Swedish political debate and Sweden has participated in its development (compare Government Communication 2008, p. 9).

In its *National Strategy for Swedish Participation in International Peace and Security Support Activities*, the Government states its view on the responsibility to protect, and the use of force potentially without a mandate, from the UNSC (Government Communication 2008). This was the first National Strategy of its kind ever drawn up by a Swedish Government. It was drafted at the height of internationalization and activation of the Swedish defence. The overarching political goal expressed is that Sweden will take a greater and more coordinated responsibility in operations for peace and security (Government Communication 2008, p. 5). This potentially implies a more frequent use of international force. The increased level of ambition shall be attained through active engagement in which the multilateral system's opportunities are taken advantage of to the fullest extent (Government Communication 2008, p. 6). The Swedish effort will principally take place within the framework of the UN, the EU, NATO and the OSCE (Organization for Security and Cooperation in Europe) (Government Communication 2008, p. 6).

On the subject of the use of international force and the responsibility to protect, the Strategy is fairly explicit. The central premise is that operations must have a clear basis in international law (Government Communication 2008, p. 8). The use of force within the framework of peace support operations must also have a solid international legal basis (Government Communication 2008, pp. 8–9). As far as peace-enforcement operations are concerned, under Chapter VII in the UN Charter a mandate from the Security Council shall always be sought, and the choice of wording can be noted (Government Communication 2008, p. 9). The mandate shall be sought, not necessarily granted.

As far as peacekeeping operations undertaken under Chapter VI are concerned, clear support from the UNSC shall be sought. In the case of such operations, however, the Strategy states that international law admits that these take place with the agreement of the host state and other relevant parties (Government Communication 2008, p. 9). In a nebulous passage, which will merely be reproduced and not further analyzed here, the Government presents a surprisingly flexible view of the possibility and legitimacy of the use of military force in different kinds of international peace support operations:

> A military peace support operation can use force in all these situations [peace enforcement and peacekeeping] and in self-defence, but the use of force can also be allowed in other situations where it would be lawful under international law. This view is shared within the EU.
> (Government Communication 2008, p. 9)

The Strategy concludes that the UNSC has the primary responsibility for international peace and security. But what if there is a humanitarian emergency and the UNSC is unable to agree on intervention? This question is labelled *the* big challenge as far as international law and the use of force is concerned (Government Communication 2008, p. 9). This prophecy might turn out right or wrong in retrospect, but in any case it is interesting for our purposes since it illustrates the evolving Swedish view on the use of force.

The Strategy enumerates the circumstances in which this question could arise and at the same time slightly expands the four categories of situations in which the responsibility to protect – in its reactive aspect – would be triggered in the Security Council: genocide, crimes against humanity, war crimes and ethnic cleansing or other widespread violations, including systematic rape of women and use and exploitation of children in armed conflict (Government Communication 2008, p. 9; UN General Assembly 2005, para. 138).

The UN Summit in 2005 did, according to the Strategy, determine that the international community has a common responsibility to prevent serious human rights crimes, genocide and ethnic cleansing (Government Communication 2008, p. 9). The strategy states that it is the 'international community' that has the common responsibility, whereas the World Summit Outcome says that it is 'the international community, through the United Nations' that has this responsibility – at least when it comes to international action – in case the individual state to whom the original responsibility to protect belongs does not manage to protect its own population (UN General Assembly 2005, paras. 138–9).

The strategy never discusses the responsibility to protect as exercised by the Security Council. Since it immediately proceeds to the situation in which it is *not* able to shoulder its responsibility, it seems as if the Government views the responsibility to protect not as something that in practice will necessarily be channelled through the UN, but rather as an instrument for others to use once action through the Security Council has proven impossible (Government Communication 2008, p. 9). It states: 'In a situation of emergency, when the Security Council does not shoulder its responsibility, Sweden must, after *careful evaluation*, consider what may still be done to minimize human suffering' (Government Communication 2008, p. 9; italics added). The author suspects that this is as close as we get for the moment to a Swedish doctrine on unilateral humanitarian intervention or unilateral exercise of the responsibility to protect.

The 'careful evaluation' must, according to the strategy, always take place with the particular situation as a point of departure and pay regard to international legal, political and humanitarian aspects (Government Communication 2008, p. 9). If Sweden foreclosed armed intervention – or any other measure involving interference with the sovereignty of the state in which human suffering was occurring – then the statement would have little meaning, since passive non-interventionist measures to relieve human suffering would be neither legally nor politically controversial. According to this author, the statements made on the responsibility to protect in the strategy signify that Sweden is prepared to intervene by military force in situations of humanitarian emergency, even when lacking a UNSC authorization. This would no doubt require a multilateral setting, but nothing is said on this aspect.

Since the early 2000s, the responsibility to protect has figured in the debates on Swedish participation in international peace support operations (compare Preliminary report of the proceedings in Parliament 2005/06:140, 2007/08:19, 2008/09:53). There is no obvious dividing line between the two principal political blocs. In the debates on Libya and the Swedish contribution to the NATO-led Operation Unified Protector, the responsibility to protect formed an important component (Government Bills 2011a, 2011b, 2011c; Preliminary report of the proceedings in Parliament 2010/11:81, 2010/11:118, 2011/12:5; UN Security Council resolutions 1970 & 1973). In this case as well as in the case of ISAF in Afghanistan, there was a UNSC authorization – and in the case of Libya, this explicitly referred to the responsibility to protect – so the issue of potentially intervening without a UNSC mandate did not have to be tackled.

Although the question has not presented itself so directly in actual practice, it is the impression of the author that, by the end of the 2000s, the ground was prepared for the acceptance by a broad majority in the Swedish Parliament of the possibility to intervene in extreme circumstances of human suffering in the name of the responsibility to protect – even without UNSC authorization. In 2015, Sweden decided to participate in a US-led international coalition fighting the Islamic State in Iraq and the Levant (ISIL) in Iraq, without a UN mandate but at the invitation of the Iraqi Government. The cause cited, interestingly, is not even the responsibility to protect but rather the fight against ISIL. In the multidimensional process of the evolving Swedish view on the legitimacy of the international use of military force, the long and solid experience of the use of force in ISAF surely worked as a decisive catalyst.

Was Sweden at war in Afghanistan?

The question of whether or not Sweden was at war in Afghanistan was raised in the political debate when the fighting intensified (see, for instance, Preliminary report of the proceedings in Parliament 2008/09:52, 2009/10:32, 2010/11:35, 2011/12:46; see also Agrell 2013). It was asked not primarily from a *jus ad bellum* perspective – that is, whether there was a tenable legal justification for the use of military force in Afghanistan – but rather from a more general perspective: whether Sweden was involved in military fighting, and if so whether Sweden was engaged in war for the first time in 200 years. The fact that the use of military force had a solid basis in international law was generally not disputed (with a marginal exception: see Preliminary report of the proceedings in Parliament 2010/11:35, Intervention No. 1. (Swedish Democrat); compare further Preliminary report of the proceedings in Parliament 2001/02:54, 2001/02:123, 2002/03:37, 2003/04:121, 2005/06:45, 2006/07:116, 2008/09:52, 2009/10:32, 2011/12:46, 2012/13:46, 2013/14:47). The Swedish official position on the original US intervention in Afghanistan in 2001 was that it constituted a legitimate act of self-defence (Aftonbladet 2001, Swedish Official Inquiry 2003, p. 213).

Neither was it generally disputed that war or armed conflict of some kind and intensity was ongoing in parts of Afghanistan between the international forces of different kinds, including ISAF and the Taliban among other oppositional groups (in addition to the armed conflict between the Government of Afghanistan and the Taliban, among others). Although an outright war between the international forces and the Afghan Government on the one hand and the Taliban (among others) on the other was not recognized, references were often made in the debates to the latent war in Afghanistan risking eruption if international forces were to leave. What was disputed and highly sensitive was whether or not it could rightly be claimed that Sweden was at war.

The question of whether Sweden was at war in Afghanistan is multidimensional. It has an obvious *political* dimension, which is probably the main reason why the question was posed in Parliament. That the question came at all illustrates the development sketched earlier whereby Sweden gradually has become more prepared to use military force internationally and for wider purposes. This is likely to eventually result in participation in military combat.

Being involved in actual military fighting anywhere except in self-defence of the Swedish territory would be controversial. In Sweden, the general understanding is that what is regarded as some form of peacekeeping mission almost by definition does not – and definitely *should* not – involve armed conflict, much less 'war'. This applies even if the peace support operation has been granted a robust mandate involving the use of military force if necessary. The sensitivity of being involved in military fighting could only be augmented by the fact that NATO has been a driving force in many of the international peace operations in which Sweden would participate. If Sweden were to participate in NATO-led peace operations, the concept of crisis management would have to be kept far apart from self-defence in order for no one to associate Sweden with NATO as a collective defence organization (Wedin 2008).

Once the internationalization and activation of the Swedish Armed Forces was under way, it was stated in official documents that the defence of Swedish values and Swedish interests – arguably, of Sweden itself – could take place in different parts of the world (Government Bill 2009a sections 3–5 passim, Defence Commission 2008, pp. 11–12). According to a generally accepted Swedish view, if military force can legitimately be used in self-defence only, and Sweden can be defended anywhere in the world in principle, then Swedish soldiers can legitimately use force in Afghanistan for the (self-) defence of Sweden. If so, the claim that Sweden was at war in Afghanistan would lose some of its controversial essence. No participant in the official debate ever put the self-defence argument precisely in these terms, it should be added. However, the terms in which Mr Allan Widman of the Liberal Party put his argument in favour of the continued Swedish contribution to ISAF in 2007 are not radically different. He argued that the Swedish troops participated in the mission with the understanding that the value of every human being is equal and that it is equally important to protect defenceless children in Nuristan as it is to protect Swedes along the Morjarv line (here, Mr Widman made a romantic and heroic allusion to the Swedish war history) (Preliminary report of the proceedings in Parliament 2006/07:116).

The question of whether Sweden was at war in Afghanistan has several *legal* dimensions as well, of which the lawfulness of the international intervention under the *jus ad bellum* has already been dealt with. Another legal dimension of the question – intertwined with the political dimension – is the fact that, if there is a war (which in modern international legal terminology is translated into 'armed conflict'), then IHL (part of the *jus in bello* more generally) applies. And vice versa: if IHL is applied, this is a sign that an armed conflict (a war, in more everyday language) exists (compare O'Connell (Ed.) 2012).

Because it would be highly inopportune to concede that Sweden might in fact be involved in an armed conflict – 'at war' – in Afghanistan, the Government remained unclear on the issue of whether armed conflict reigned where the Swedish troops were located (Engdahl 2013, pp. 236–7). This was despite the fact that ISAF had the indisputable, and in itself largely uncontroversial, mandate to use armed force on a wide and intense scale (UNSC resolutions 1386, 1510, 2120). The language changed over time into being a little more indicative of the possible existence of an armed conflict: not only in the southern and eastern parts of the country but also in the northern part of Afghanistan in which the Swedish troops were located (see Government

Bill 2007, pp. 6–8, Government Bill 2008, pp. 6–7, Government Bill 2009b, pp. 8–9, Government Bill 2010, pp. 8–10, Government Bill 2011d, pp. 10–12). From the end of 2009, the Government talks of the 'non-international armed conflict' in Afghanistan in its bills to Parliament. From 2012, the Government bill uses the term 'armed resistance' to denote the rebel forces, but de facto the non-international armed conflict in Afghanistan still seems to reign. The 'armed conflict' (doing much harm to the civilian population) is referred to once in the bill of 2012 (Government Bill 2012 p. 7). From 2013 there is no longer any mention of 'armed conflict' in the Government bills; but judging from the description of the security situation, the situation gradually worsens (Government Bill 2013, Government Bill 2014).

The Government wanted to emphasize the clear and strong basis in international law of the ISAF operation through the consecutive UNSC resolutions, but it did not want to detail the international humanitarian legal aspects of the activities of the Swedish troops in its bills to Parliament. Except for the political dimension of whether Sweden was 'at war' or not in Afghanistan, the legal consequences in the form of the applicability of IHL and any further legal consequences following from that were not debated.

Presuming that the Swedish troops were in fact involved in armed conflict, at least at times – a presumption that is probably no longer disputed – this raises a few further issues from the international humanitarian legal point of view. Whether 'Sweden' technically should be considered to have been involved in armed conflict depends on what entity should be considered party to the conflict: 'the Afghan government supported by international military presence' on the one hand or 'the Taliban and other oppositional groups' on the other (compare Government Bills 2009b, p. 8, 2010, pp. 8–9, 2011d, p. 10). There is no clear-cut legal answer to whether 'Sweden' was party to the conflict: that is, in some sense at war. The issue of international peace operations becoming involved in armed conflict is rather new, and the legal doctrine has not settled on definitive answers to the question of who should be considered party to a potential armed conflict arising.[2]

As discussed in detail by Engdahl, Sweden (and Germany) never considered themselves party to the conflict in Afghanistan in the sense of IHL, whereas Norway and Denmark did (Engdahl 2013, pp. 234–7). The entity that should most reasonably be considered party to the conflict in the legal sense (on the side of the Afghan government against the Taliban and other oppositional forces) is NATO, according to Engdahl – not the individual states contributing to the NATO-led ISAF peace operation, or ISAF, or the UN (Engdahl 2013, pp. 254–6). In that case, Sweden in its own right would technically not be a party to the conflict, in line with the Swedish official view. Swedish troops, however, could still be involved in armed conflict as members of the ISAF, led by NATO (and mandated by the UN). The 'command and control' factors deciding which of many possible parties to a conflict should be considered *the* party (or possibly the par*ties*, in the case of ISAF: the UN, ISAF, NATO and/or the individual troop-contributing states) have been widely discussed in the international legal literature, and for Sweden's part primarily by Engdahl with respect to ISAF, among other operations.

Furthermore, as pronounced by the International Criminal Tribunal for the Former Yugoslavia (ICTY) in the Tadic case, armed conflict reigns (and IHL consequently applies) in the entire territory under the control of a party to the conflict – whether or not actual combat takes place there – until a general conclusion of peace is reached (or, in the context of (NATO-led) ISAF, the party withdraws from the territory) (Prosecutor v. Tadic 1995 para. 70).[3] This means that according to relatively settled international legal opinion, armed conflict reigned in Afghanistan and NATO was party to it (in the sense of IHL on the side of the Afghan Government) in the entire territory under the control of ISAF – whether or not actual combat took place there. This means that the implicit argument in the Swedish Government bills – that there was not an armed conflict (in the legal sense) going on in the Northern region in which the Swedish troops were located, because there was less actual fighting between the international troops and the oppositional forces – is not tenable.

A key reason for the question of whether it is the troop-contributing nations or ISAF/NATO/UN that should be considered party to the conflict (in the international legal sense) arising is that it is states, not international organizations, that are bound by the international legal instruments making up the IHL (Engdahl 2013, p. 254). Some fear that, if the organizations rather than the troop-contributing nations are considered party to the armed conflict, compliance with the IHL will decrease. However, Engdahl argues that the troop-contributing nations cannot evade their obligations under IHL when their military forces participate in an armed conflict, even though the military forces are under the command of another state or an international organization (Engdahl 2013, p. 254, compare also Greenwood 1998, p.18). The view that Engdahl puts forward probably coincides with as official a Swedish view of this particular issue as is possible to find; the same view of the continuing obligations of troop-contributing states under IHL is put forward in the Swedish Official Inquiry, which investigated the applicable law with respect to the use of force in international peace operations, and is mirrored in the proposed changes in the Swedish legal regulation (which have not been adopted so far) (Swedish Official Inquiry 2011, pp. 35–6, 23–4).[4]

In the new Law on the Use of Force by Personnel of the Swedish Armed Forces in International Military Operations suggested by the Official Inquiry, a provision saying that personnel of the Swedish Armed Forces shall respect Sweden's obligations under IHL, irrespective of whether Sweden is formally a party to the armed conflict or not (Swedish Official Inquiry 2011, p. 42, p. 261). It seems to be the view of the Official Inquiry that such a provision would merely codify and clarify for Swedish purposes what already constitutes the existing international law, although the latter is unclear and not yet precisely codified (Swedish Official Inquiry 2011, pp. 197–200, pp. 201–3).

IHL applies in armed conflict; that is, most immediately, the four Geneva Conventions and their Additional Protocols. In the case of Afghanistan (among other cases involving multinational peace operations) the question arose as to whether the conflict to which the international forces were party should be considered a non-international conflict or an international conflict (for which different sets of IHL apply) (Hampson 2012, Lubell 2012). The concept of armed conflict – fundamental to the application of IHL – is not defined in the Geneva Conventions or the Additional Protocols. An international conflict has been defined by the ICTY as 'a resort to armed force between states' (Prosecutor v. Tadic 1995, para. 70). This definition is relatively undisputed in international law. A non-international armed conflict has been defined by the ICTY as 'protracted armed violence between governmental authorities and organized armed groups or between such groups within a state' (Prosecutor v. Tadic 1995, para. 70, see also International Committee of the Red Cross 2008, p. 5). This definition is also relatively uncontested in international legal opinion.

Some argue that the involvement of multinational peacekeeping forces inevitably makes the conflict(s) international. In the case of Afghanistan, the conflict between the NATO-led ISAF and the opposition forces (irrespective of whether the ISAF/NATO/UN and/or the troop-contributing nations legally constituted party/parties to the conflict) would be considered an international conflict in the sense of IHL, as would the original conflict between the Afghan Government and the opposition forces (David & Engdahl 2013, pp. 659–6, 675–9). Others, like Engdahl, argue that it is the classification of the opponent that decides whether an armed conflict should be classified as international or non-international (David & Engdahl 2013, pp. 667–74, Engdahl 2008, p.109; for the largely corresponding view of the International Committee of the Red Cross, compare Ferraro 2013).

According to the latter view (David & Engdahl 2013, p. 672), irrespective of whether UN/ISAF/NATO and/or the troop-contributing states would be considered party/parties on the international side, their opponents in Afghanistan would be insurgents or non-state actors and consequently the conflict should be considered a non-international (non-interstate) armed conflict. The original conflict between the Afghan Government and the insurgents would also remain non-international. If the multinational forces hypothetically had also become involved in armed conflict with the Afghan Government this would have been an international armed conflict according to Engdahl, who compares Afghanistan with the case of Libya, whereas the conflict between the multinational forces and the opposition forces would remain non-international (David & Engdahl 2013, p. 672). As Engdahl points out, however, from the point of view of IHL the classification of the armed conflict as non-international or international is becoming gradually less important, since large parts of the (much more developed) IHL pertaining to international armed conflicts is today arguably also applicable in non-international armed conflict via the development of customary law through practice on the ground (David & Engdahl 2013, p. 673, compare also Henckaerts & Doswald-Beck 2005 and Swedish Official Inquiry 2010).

The rules contained in IHL are not disputed in principle – although their exact scope and content might be debated in a particular case – nor is it controversial in principle that IHL should be applied in armed conflict. IHL largely enables the Armed Forces to carry out acts that would be forbidden under peacetime law; on the other hand, the forces become lawful targets themselves. The Swedish troops in Afghanistan did apply IHL when the situation so required, Engdahl writes (Engdahl 2013, p. 237). It is usually in the interest of multinational peace operations to apply international humanitarian law carefully in case they participate in armed conflict. One reason for this is the goodwill generated among the population in the area of operation and among the international and home audiences. It is the fact that the application of IHL gives evidence of the existence of an armed conflict that makes IHL a potentially sensitive topic; after all, the Swedish Government wanted to avoid the impression that Sweden was 'at war', almost at any price. As Engdahl writes, the different positions taken by Sweden, Norway and Denmark on whether the respective states were formally party to the conflict in Afghanistan depended less on differing views on the applicable law (that is, IHL) than on differences of opinion concerning how to identify a party to an armed conflict (probably among other, political, considerations) (Engdahl 2013, p. 237).

Another issue that arose in the wake of Afghanistan (among other robust multinational peace operations in the 2000s) was the issue of the detention of persons threatening the security of the operation and what law would apply to these detentions. This issue is also closely dealt with in the aforementioned Swedish Official Inquiry on the Use of Force in International Military Operations (Swedish Official Inquiry 2011, pp. 130–6, 234–44). After a series of international conferences and seminars within the framework of the so-called Copenhagen Process on the Handling of Detainees in International Military Operations launched by the Danish Government in 2007, The Copenhagen Process Principles and Guidelines were adopted in 2012 (see Hartmann 2013, Johnson 2013, Mahnad 2013). The experiences of the multinational forces in Afghanistan formed an important backdrop to the Copenhagen Process. According to paragraph IX, the Copenhagen Process Principles and Guidelines are intended to apply to international military operations in the context of non-international armed conflicts and peace operations; they are not intended to address international armed conflicts. In non-international armed conflicts (and situations not amounting to armed conflicts) there are, by definition, no prisoners of war. Tellingly, the Commentary annexed to the Copenhagen Process Principles and Guidelines in paragraph 3 states that persons not detained will be released (that is, not killed).

The issue of the applicable law in these situations is extremely complex and involves, among other things, considerations of IHL, human rights law and the domestic law of the host country and the troop-contributing state(s).

International human rights law is applicable in times of peace (or, at least, times not amounting to armed conflict) as well as in times of armed conflict or war. The human rights obligations of peacekeeping troops, as well as the intricate relationship between IHL and human rights law, has been the subject of a vast debate in international legal doctrine and practice (compare Larsen 2012, International Court of Justice 2004). The Swedish Official Inquiry basically finds that it is unclear what international law implies on the subject of detention during international military operations in non-international armed conflict situations. Therefore, the Official Inquiry suggests clarification and codification of the basic normative parameters for Swedish purposes, as in the case of Sweden's continuous obligations under IHL mentioned earlier. Concerning detention within the framework of the ISAF in Afghanistan, the Swedish approach is illustrated in the Government bills from late 2009 on, which state that it may be necessary to detain persons threatening the security of ISAF and that a condition for the transfer of a detained person to the Afghan authorities is that the transfer can take place with full respect for international law, including human rights and IHL (Government Bill 2009b, p. 12, Government Bill 2010, p. 15, Government Bill 2011d, p. 15, Government Bill 2012, p. 16, Government Bill 2013, p. 15). The Swedish Official Inquiry on the Use of Force in International Military Operations notes that, in the case of Afghanistan, several troop-contributing states felt compelled to enter into bilateral agreements with Afghanistan on the treatment of detainees transferred to the Afghan authorities (Swedish Official Inquiry 2011, p. 131, compare also Larsen 2012, pp. 404–6, 414–16). At the time the Inquiry was finished in late 2011, Sweden had sought, but not yet achieved, a similar agreement with Afghanistan.

The risk of Sweden becoming involved in a war in Afghanistan radically decreased once the ISAF concluded its mission at the end of 2014. The international military presence continues in the form of a non-combat Resolute Support Mission (RSM), established by NATO to train, advise and assist the Afghan National Defence and Security Forces (UNSC resolution 2189). Sweden contributes to the NATO RSM with 50 personnel (see Government Bill 2013, Swedish Armed Forces 2015). The NATO RSM does not have an explicit UNSC mandate, but is legally based on a status of forces agreement between NATO and Afghanistan and the invitation of the Afghan Government to NATO to establish RSM (UNSC resolution 2189, preambular para. 13). The Security Council finds that the bilateral agreement between NATO and Afghanistan and the invitation of the Government of Afghanistan provide 'a sound legal basis for Resolute Support Mission' (UNSC resolution 2189, preambular para. 13).

Continuing identity shift reinforced by the ISAF experience

As if developments during the 2000s had not been sweeping enough, Swedish security and defence policy seemed to undergo further remarkable transformations during the first half of the following decade. The more recent changes are partly similar to and partly different from those that could be perceived during the 2000s. On the whole, the changes complement and reinforce each other.

The internationalization and activation of the Swedish defence forces, as conceptualized in the 2000s and as manifested by the ISAF experience, have been toned down. Due to developments in the 'near abroad', the focus on the defence of the Swedish territory has been strengthened (as opposed to expeditionary operations), but this does not imply that the general direction of the larger reform of the Swedish defence begun in the 2000s will be altered (Defence Commission 2013, p. 227, Defence Commission 2014, p. 13, Government Bill 2015b, p. 9). In this section, two current developments of legal significance are commented upon.

The first is the continuously developing Swedish attitude with respect to legal justifications of the use of force. The Swedish experience in Afghanistan was not legally controversial, since it was safely based on consecutive UNSC resolutions. The Afghan experience, however, made the Swedish defence forces and the Swedish general public more familiar with the thought and practice of the international use of force. Afghanistan stands out because the Swedish engagement in ISAF was so important for Swedish circumstances, both in terms of quantity (number of troops and length of mission) and quality (the robustness of the mission and the relative intensity of the use of force). The newly-won familiarity with the international use of force on expeditionary missions arguably makes it easier to accept not only the (traditional Swedish) very limited use of force strictly contained within the limits of UNSC mandates, but potentially also the more extensive international use of force based on other, less obviously solid, legal justifications. In the first current development discussed next, it is the nature of the legal justification rather than the foreseen intensity of the use of military force that is in focus.

We have discussed the possibility that Sweden would go along with an international decision to intervene abroad for humanitarian reasons in an extreme case without a UNSC mandate. This situation has never arisen in practice. However, in 2015, Sweden joined the US-led international coalition fighting ISIL in Iraq and Syria without a UNSC mandate (Government Bill 2015a). Against the backdrop of the discussions during the 2000s on the possibility of intervening without a UNSC mandate in extreme cases, the current course of action could not be said to be unexpected. However, it is not primarily for humanitarian reasons – or in the name of the responsibility to protect – that the international coalition's military intervention in Iraq and Syria takes place; it is in order to fight ISIL.

The second current development of legal significance in the Swedish security and defence policy – which likewise cannot be said to be unexpected against the backdrop of the developments in the 2000s, but which has become a little more acute in 2014 and 2015 – is the ever-closer relationship of Sweden with

NATO. From the international legal point of view, this relationship has to do with the institutional framework within which Sweden will potentially exercise international force, and hypothetically the institutional framework within which Sweden will seek legitimacy for the international use of force – depending on the future development of the UNSC and its legitimating capacity. The closer relationship of Sweden to NATO arguably constitutes one of the most important legacies of the Swedish experience in Afghanistan. The significance of the NATO aspect of the Swedish ISAF experience, as with the new-found Swedish familiarity with the international use of military force, can also be put in terms of quantity and quality: the breadth of issues involved on which cooperation could take place, and the intensity or intimacy of the cooperation. At the NATO Summit in 2014, by the time of the close of the ISAF mission Sweden was promoted to Enhanced Opportunities Partner with NATO. The second current development (which will be discussed shortly) concerns continued – potentially quantitatively and qualitatively significant – cooperation by Sweden with NATO closer to the Swedish territory.

As far as the first development is concerned, the Swedish Government wanted to send 35 personnel to participate in the military training operation carried out in Northern Iraq by the international coalition against ISIL (Government Bill 2015a, p. 7). In case of need, an additional number of personnel can be sent to Northern Iraq, although the maximum number in total may never exceed 120 (Government Bill 2015a, p. 7). The international military operation carried out in Iraq and Syria is led by the US (Government Bill 2015a, p. 7). According to the Government Bill, the coalition aims initially to stop ISIL's advances (among other things) by means of educating and training security forces in Iraq (Government Bill 2015a, p. 7). The Swedish troop contribution will work in Northern Iraq and its main task is advising and educating the Iraqi security forces. The Swedish troops will remain under Swedish national command and control (Government Bill 2015a, p. 7). From the point of view of IHL, this means (among other things) that – contrary to the case in Afghanistan – if Swedish troops hypothetically were to become involved in fighting in Iraq, Sweden should probably be regarded as a party to the ongoing conflict in her own right (compare Engdahl 2013, pp. 254–6).

At the time of the original Swedish decision to participate, there was no UNSC mandate for the international military operation in Iraq or Syria. The Government Bill refers to a number of Security Council resolutions instituting different kinds of international non-military sanctions against ISIL and other terrorist movements (Government Bill 2015a, p. 4, p. 8; UNSC resolutions 2161, 2170, 2178). The Government Bill furthermore refers to two letters from Iraq – one to the UN Secretary-General and one to the Security Council – asking for military training (among other things) and welcoming air cover in coordination with the Iraqi Armed Forces respectively (letter dated 25 June 2014 from the Permanent Representative of Iraq to the United Nations addressed to the Secretary-General, letter dated 20 September 2014 from the Permanent Representative of Iraq to the United Nations addressed to the President of the Security Council). The Government Bill states that the international legal basis of the military training operation is Iraq's invitation to the international community to help with support for the fight against ISIL and the bilateral international agreements entered into by Iraq with the participating states concerning the tasks of the troops, among other things (Government Bill 2015a, p. 8).

The right to use military force is based on the agreement by Iraq, according to the Government Bill (Government Bill 2015a, p. 8). There are no common rules of engagement for the international coalition (Government Bill 2015a, p. 8); any coordination necessary will take place through collaboration with other actors in the area of operation (Government Bill 2015a, p. 7).

On the face of it, the justification of the use of force invoked by the Swedish Government is irreproachable: the agreement, or invitation, by Iraq. In the Swedish context, the most noteworthy aspect is that the justification is used at all; that is, that Sweden is prepared to use military force internationally without a UNSC authorization. In the Swedish context, it is also noteworthy from a political point of view that Sweden participates in an international military coalition solely led by the US. Furthermore (and again from the point of view of the law), if the issue is dug into a little further, intervention by invitation is far from uncomplicated and is in fact the subject of an extensive international legal debate (compare Gray 2008, pp. 67–113).

As for the task of the Swedish troops, the Government Bill states that it is to instruct and that the troops in principle will not have armed tasks within the operation (Government Bill 2015a, p. 9). There is a risk however, the Government Bill continues, that the Swedish personnel or other personnel within the coalition are subject to armed attack and that the situation is such that the Swedish personnel needs to act in a way that exceeds self-defence of one's own person; for instance, in order to protect another person or an object (Government Bill 2015a, p. 9). This is an interesting and extensive interpretation of the inherent right to self-defence of one's person on the part of non-combat troops in peaceful missions. The extent of the right to self-defence fundamentally of one's own person, but potentially extending to other persons and objects, has been widely debated in the international legal literature with respect primarily to UN peacekeeping forces (compare, for Sweden's part, Swedish Official Inquiry 2011).

As far as the second development is concerned, and turning our attention to Sweden's ever-closer relationship to NATO, there are several interesting developments in the home arena complementing the formative international experience in Afghanistan (and then in Libya). In line with the Swedish so-called declaration of solidarity, which had developed during the 2000s and was confirmed by Parliament in 2009 (Government Bill 2009a, p. 9, Preliminary report of the proceedings in Parliament 2008/09:133 § 11, Preliminary report of the proceedings in Parliament 2008/09:131 § 5), the Swedish Ordinance with Instruction for the Defence was changed in 2010; among other changes, the following passage was inserted: 'The defence forces shall be able to give and receive support' (Government Ordinance 2010 § 3 a, see also Government Bill 2015b pp. 7–8, passim).This implies that Sweden shall be able to give and receive support in dealing with NATO and other international actors, including individual states, should the case arise. The new passage in the Instruction for the Defence clearly shows the redirection of the Swedish defence towards cooperation with others. The Swedish Government concluded a host nation support agreement with NATO in 2014, but the treaty will have to be accepted by the Swedish Parliament before it enters into force (compare Government Bill 2015b, pp. 37–8). This is planned for 2016.

In 2014, a thorough Official Inquiry was carried out on behalf of the Ministry of Defence of Sweden's international cooperation in the area of defence policy (Report from the Inquiry on Sweden's International Defence Cooperation 2014). The Inquiry recommends that the question of Swedish membership in NATO be analyzed in a further Official Inquiry in cooperation with Finland (Report from the Inquiry on Sweden's International Defence Cooperation 2014, p. 71 *et seq*; a further Inquiry is projected in Government Bill 2015b, p. 8, 48).

Another recent Official Inquiry of great significance for the issue of the relationship of Sweden to NATO is 'Participation with armed force in training abroad – Extended decision-making power of the government' (Swedish Official Inquiry 2015). From the title of the report the political significance of its content is not obvious. From the point of view of the law, the report is interesting but not overly controversial. Normally, the Parliament has to agree to any dispatch of Armed Forces abroad by the Government (Instrument of Government 1974, Ch. 16 Art. 15). However, by means of the Act on Training for Peace Support Operations (1994), Parliament has delegated to the Government to make decisions as to the dispatch of Swedish armed troops abroad in order to participate in training for peace support activities within the framework of international cooperation. The suggestion now by the Official Inquiry is to delete 'peace support activities' from the text of the law in order for it to read: '[t]he government may send Swedish Armed Forces to other countries in order to participate in training – within the framework of international cooperation' (para. 1 of the suggested revised Act).

The Inquiry, which carefully goes through the developments in Swedish security policy in the post-Cold War period, finds that the Swedish defence forces need to be able to participate in multinational exercises that aim at high conflict levels, exceeding peace support scenarios (Swedish Official Inquiry 2015, p. 66). The Inquiry states that NATO currently develops its capacity for high-intensity fight against qualified enemies with capacities from all arenas (Swedish Official Inquiry 2015, p. 66, compare Government Bill 2015b, pp. 43, 46, 70). In order to arrive at a quick Swedish decision-making procedure, the Act should be changed so as not to limit the independent decision-making power of the Government to 'peace support activities'; if the Act remains unchanged, the Parliament has to be involved in the decision-making procedure every time Sweden is supposed to participate in an exercise going beyond peace support scenarios – which, judging from the Inquiry, can be expected to happen quite frequently, or else it would not be a problem (compare also Government Bill 2015b, p. 38).

The Inquiry says that exercises with a component of collective defence undertakings (under Article 5 in the NATO treaty) are beginning to be clearly prioritized, and NATO aims at an expansion of this type of exercise activities (Swedish Official Inquiry 2015, p. 66). This in its turn means that Sweden will need and want to participate in such activities. However, Sweden is not involved in the collective defence under the NATO treaty.

Conclusion

Three dimensions of the shift in Swedish identity in the field of security and defence policy have been investigated in this contribution: the law of war, the law in war and international institutional arrangements. These three dimensions are closely interrelated. The ISAF experience has significantly contributed to the shift in the Swedish identity both directly and indirectly.

As to the law of war, this was the least directly formative aspect of the Afghanistan experience, from the perspective of this contribution. The ISAF had a mandate from the UNSC throughout, and the consequent solid basis of ISAF action in international law was emphasized in the Swedish Government bills and debates in Parliament. Developments before and in the wake of ISAF indicate that a broadening of the range of acceptable justifications, or legal bases, of the international use of force is taking place in the Swedish official perception. Humanitarian intervention and the responsibility to protect, potentially without a mandate from the UNSC, seem to be evolving conceivable justifications of the international use of military force – judging from the Swedish official debate spurred by different international operations with or without Swedish participation. Intervention based on an invitation from the host state, and not on a Security Council resolution, is becoming a more common component of the Swedish legal justification for its contribution to international military missions. The indirect implications of the ISAF experience for the Swedish view of the legitimacy of the international use of force have probably been significant. The readiness to use force generally on international missions was strengthened; this opens the door for the use of force based on an increasing range of legal justifications. Both the use of international military force and the slight relativization of the importance of a UNSC mandate as a legal basis for the international use of force are perceptible in the Swedish official debate and mark radical departures from the formerly peaceful stance of Sweden.

As to the law in war, the ISAF experience gave rise to a lot of questions because Sweden had become involved in rather violent action at times. The question of whether an armed conflict reigned where the Swedish troops were located, and thus whether IHL should apply, must be answered with 'yes'; furthermore, the conflict was non-international but Sweden did not consider itself party to it – and probably rightly so – although none of these issues are undisputed. In case of armed conflict, the Swedish troops arguably remain bound by Sweden's obligations under IHL, irrespective of who is to be formally considered party to the conflict. Despite the robust mandate given by the UNSC and the ready Swedish contribution of troops to ISAF, the issue of whether Sweden was at times involved in an armed conflict in Afghanistan was domestically very sensitive. The detention of persons threatening the security of ISAF and the question of what law would regulate such detention caused Sweden (as well as other troop-contributing states) a lot of concern. The acute issue was solved through bilateral agreements between the troop-contributing states and the Afghan authorities to which the detainees would be transferred. Efforts have been made to clarify and codify the international normative parameters in a Swedish law on the use of force (including coercive measures) in international military operations – so far, to no avail.

As to the institutional context in which Sweden contributes to international military missions, the ISAF experience is illustrative of an important development since the end of the Cold War: the ever-closer cooperation with NATO. This may be one of the most important politico–legal legacies of the Swedish experience in Afghanistan and also marks a radical departure from its former stance in security and defence policy. The close relationship to NATO arguably influences both the readiness to use international force at all – Sweden is prone to contribute to NATO-led international military missions – and the attitude towards possible justifications of the international use of force. With the move toward NATO, in practice Sweden moves away from its earlier strict allegiance to the UN and its Charter in matters of international peace and security. In the most recent international military undertaking projected by the Government, Sweden will contribute non-combat personnel to the US-led international coalition in Iraq and Syria without a Security Council mandate under Swedish national command and control. Closer to home, Sweden is preparing to participate in NATO exercises beyond the traditional peace-support scenario, implying a highly intensive fight against a qualified enemy. However, one crucial aspect of the Swedish identity in security and defence policy that still remains after Afghanistan is non-participation in NATO's formal collective defence undertaking.

Notes

1 All translations from Swedish have been made by this author unless otherwise indicated.
2 The UN peacekeeping operation in Congo (ONUC) in 1960–64 was an exceptional instance of an early peacekeeping operation becoming involved in armed conflict.

3 Bosnian Serb, Duško Tadić, was indicted by the ICTY in 1995 for crimes committed in 1992 in the Prijedor municipality in Bosnia-Herzegovina. In 1999, Tadić was convicted of grave breaches of the 1949 Geneva Conventions, crimes against humanity and violations of the laws or customs of war. In 2000, he was sentenced to a maximum 20 years' imprisonment. In 2008, Duško Tadić was granted early release.
4 It can be noted that whereas the Swedish authorities (in this case, the Ministry of Defence) want to talk about 'international peace and security-building operations', the Inquiry simply talks about 'international military operations' (compare Swedish Official Inquiry 2011, pp. 44–5, 53).

References

Act on Training for Peace Support Operations (1994) [Lag om utbildning for fredsframjande verksamhet] (1994: 588).
Aftonbladet (2001) 'Goran Persson: Jag tycker det var ratt' [Goran Persson: I believe it was right] Available online at www.aftonbladet.se/nyheter/article10237427.ab (accessed 23 August 2015).
Agrell, W. (2013) *Ett krig har och nu: Sveriges vag till vapnad konflikt i Afghanistan* [*A war here and now: Sweden's road to armed conflict in Afghanistan*]. Stockholm: Atlantis.
Amnéus, D. (2008) *Responsibility to protect by military means: Emerging norms on humanitarian intervention*. Stockholm: Department of Law, Stockholm University.
Bring, O., S. Mahmoudi & P. Wrange (2014) *Sverige och folkratten* [*Sweden and international law*], 5th edition. Stockholm: Norstedts Juridik.
David, E. & O. Engdahl (2013) 'How does the involvement of a multinational peacekeeping force affect the classification of a situation?' *International Review of the Red Cross* Vol. 95 No. 891/892 Autumn/Winter, pp. 659–79.
Defence Commission (2007) *Sakerhet i samverkan – Forsvarsberedningens omvarldsanalys* [Security in cooperation – The international analysis of the Inter-parliamentary commission on defence], Departementsserien [Ministry series] (Ds) 2007:46.
Defence Commission (2008) *Forsvar i anvandning* [*Defence in use*], Departementsserien [Ministry series] (Ds) 2008:48.
Defence Commission (2013) *Vagval i en globaliserad varld* [*Choice of path in a globalized world*], Departementsserien [Ministry series] (Ds) 2013:33.
Defence Commission (2014) *Forsvaret av Sverige – Starkare forsvar for en osaker tid* [*The defence of Sweden – Stronger defence for uncertain times*] Departementsserien [Ministry series] (Ds) 2014:20.
Engdahl, O. (2008) 'The status of peace operation personnel under international humanitarian law' *Yearbook of International Humanitarian Law (YIHL)* Vol. 11, pp. 109–38.
Engdahl, O. (2013) 'Multinational peace operations forces involved in armed conflict: who are the parties?' in Larsen, K. M., C. Guldahl Cooper & G. Nystuen (Eds) *Searching for a principle of humanity in international law*. Cambridge: Cambridge University Press, pp. 233–71.
Engdahl, O. & C. Hellman (Eds) (2007) *Responsibility to protect: Folkrattsliga perspektiv* [*Responsibility to protect: Perspectives of international law*] The chapter 'FN–stadgans regler och skyldigheten att skydda – en teoretisk oversikt' ['The rules of the UN Charter and the responsibility to protect – a theoretical outline'] (no particular author is indicated for that chapter). Stockholm: Forsvarshogskolan [National Defence College] pp. 15–26.

Engdahl, O. & C. Hellman (Eds) (2007) *Responsibility to protect – Folkrattsliga perspektiv* [*Responsibility to protect – Perspectives of international law*] the chapter 'Kriterier for en humanitar intervention' [Criteria of a humanitarian intervention] (no particular author is indicated for that chapter). Stockholm: Forsvarshogskolan [National Defence College], pp. 41–60.

Engdahl, O. & C. Hellman (Eds) (2007) *Responsibility to protect – Folkrattsliga perspektiv* [*Responsibility to protect – Perspectives of international law*] The chapter 'Svensk installning till humanitara interventioner' ['The Swedish position on humanitarian intervention'] (no particular author is indicated for that chapter). Stockholm: Forsvarshogskolan [National Defence College], pp. 61–6.

Ferraro, T. (2013) 'The applicability and application of international humanitarian law to multinational forces' *International Review of the Red Cross* Vol. 95 No. 891/892 Autumn/Winter, pp. 561–612.

Government Bill (2007) *Regeringens proposition 2006/07:83 Fortsatt svenskt deltagande i den internationella sakerhetsstyrkan i Afghanistan* [*Continued Swedish participation in ISAF*], 15 March.

Government Bill (2008) *Regeringens proposition 2008/09:69 Fortsatt svenskt deltagande i den internationella sakerhetsstyrkan i Afghanistan (ISAF)* [*Continued Swedish participation in ISAF*], 13 November.

Government Bill (2009a) *Regeringens proposition 2008/09:140 Ett anvandbart forsvar* [*A useful defence*], 19 March.

Government Bill (2009b) *Regeringens proposition 2009/10:38 Fortsatt svenskt deltagande i internationella sakerhetsstyrkan i Afghanistan (ISAF)* [*Continued Swedish participation in ISAF*], 22 October.

Government Bill (2010) *Regeringens proposition 2010/11:35 Fortsatt svenskt deltagande i den internationella sakerhetsstyrkan i Afghanistan (ISAF)* [*Continued Swedish participation in ISAF*], 4 November.

Government Bill (2011a) *Regeringens proposition 2010/11:111 Svenskt deltagande i den internationella militara insatsen i Libyen* [*Swedish participation in the international military operation in Libya*], 29 March.

Government Bill (2011b) *Regeringens proposition 2010/11:127 Fortsatt svenskt deltagande i den internationella militara insatsen i Libyen* [*Continued Swedish participation in the international military operation in Libya*], 9 June.

Government Bill (2011c) *Regeringens proposition 2011/12:5 Fortsatt svenskt deltagande i den internationella militara insatsen i Libyen* [*Continued Swedish participation in the international military operation in Libya*], 15 September.

Government Bill (2011d) *Regeringens proposition 2011/12:29 Fortsatt svenskt deltagande i den internationella sakerhetsstyrkan i Afghanistan (ISAF)* [*Continued Swedish participation in ISAF*], 9 November.

Government Bill (2012) *Regeringens proposition 2012/13:41 Fortsatt svenskt deltagande i den internationella sakerhetsstyrkan i Afghanistan (ISAF)* [*Continued Swedish participation in ISAF*], 8 November.

Government Bill (2013) *Regeringens proposition 2013/14:33 Fortsatt svenskt deltagande i den internationella sakerhetsstyrkan i Afghanistan (ISAF) och framtida deltagande i Natos utbildningsinsats (RSM) i Afghanistan* [*Continued Swedish participation in ISAF and future participation in the NATO training mission RSM in Afghanistan*], 7 November.

Government Bill (2014) *Regeringens proposition 2014/15:13 Svenskt deltagande i Natos utbildnings- och radgivningsinsats Resolute Support Mission (RSM) i Afghanistan* [*Swedish participation in the NATO training mission RSM in Afghanistan*], 6 November.

Government Bill (2015a) *Regeringens proposition 2014/15:104 Svenskt deltagande i den militara utbildningsinsatsen i norra Irak* [*Swedish participation in the military training mission in Northern Iraq*], 9 April.
Government Bill (2015b) *Regeringens proposition 2014/15:109 Forsvarspolitisk inriktning: Sveriges forsvar 2016–2020* [*Defence policy direction: Sweden's defence 2016–2020*] 23 April.
Government Communication (2008) *Nationell strategi for svenskt deltagande i internationell freds- och sakerhetsframjande verksamhet* [*National strategy for Swedish participation in international peace and security support activities*], Regeringens skrivelse 2007/08:51 13 March.
Government Ordinance (2010:650) *Forordning (2010:650) om andring i forordningen (2007:1266) med instruktion for forsvarsmakten* [*On change in the ordinance (2007:1266) with instruction for the defence*].
Gray, C. (2008) *International law and the use of force*, 3rd edition. Oxford: Oxford University Press.
Greenwood, C. (1998) 'International humanitarian law and United Nations military operations' *YIHL* Vol. 1, pp. 3–34.
Hampson, F.J. (2012) 'Afghanistan 2001–2010' in E. Wilmshurst (Ed) *International law and the classification of conflicts*. Oxford: Oxford University Press, pp. 242–79.
Hartmann, J. (2013) 'The Copenhagen process: Principles and guidelines' *YIHL* Vol. 16, pp. 3–32.
Henckaerts, J-M. & L. Doswald-Beck (Eds) (2005) *Customary international humanitarian law.* Cambridge: International Committee of the Red Cross; Cambridge University Press.
Instrument of Government (1974) [Regeringsformen] (1974:152).
International Commission on Intervention and State Sovereignty (ICISS) (2001) The Responsibility to Protect: Report of the International Commission on Intervention and State Sovereignty. Ottawa, ON: International Development Research Centre.
International Committee of the Red Cross (2008) 'How is the term "Armed Conflict" defined in international humanitarian law?' *International Committee of the Red Cross Opinion Paper.* Available online at www.icrc.org/eng/assets/files/other/opinion-paper-armed-conflict.pdf
International Court of Justice (2004) *Legal consequences of the construction of a wall in the occupied Palestinian Territory* Advisory Opinion, I. C. J. (International Court of Justice) Reports 2004, p. 136.
Johnson, J.T. (2013) 'A dialogue: Ethics, law, and the question of detention in non-international conflicts' *YIHL* Vol. 16, pp. 53–68.
Larsen, K.M. (2012) *The human rights treaty obligations of peacekeepers* Cambridge: Cambridge University Press. Letter dated 25 June 2014 from the Permanent Representative of Iraq to the United Nations addressed to the Secretary-General, UN Security Council Doc. S/2014/440.
Letter dated 20 September 2014 from the Permanent Representative of Iraq to the United Nations addressed to the President of the Security Council, UN Security Council Doc. S/2014/691.
Lubell, N. (2012) 'The war (?) against Al-Qaeda' in E. Wilmshurst (Ed.) *International law and the classification of conflicts.* Oxford: Oxford University Press, pp. 421–54.
Mahnad, R. (2013) 'Beyond process: The material framework for detention and the particularities of non-international armed conflict' *YIHL* Vol. 16, pp. 33–51.
O'Connell, M.E. (Ed) (2012) *What is war? An investigation in the wake of 9/11*. Leiden/Boston: Martinus Nijhoff Publishers.

Osterdahl, I. (2009) 'The neutral ally: The European Security and Defence Policy and the Swedish constitution', *Nordic Journal of International Law (NJIL)* Vol. 78 No. 1, pp. 95–132.

Osterdahl, I. (2010) 'The use of force: Sweden, the Jus ad Bellum and the European Security and Defence Policy', *NJIL* Vol. 79 No. 1, pp. 141–88.

Osterdahl, I. (2011) 'Challenge or confirmation? The role of the Swedish Parliament in the decision-making on the use of force', *NJIL*, Vol. 80 No. 1, pp. 25–93.

Preliminary report of the proceedings in Parliament 1998/99:100 26 May 1999.

Preliminary report of the proceedings in Parliament 1998/99:109 14 June 1999.

Preliminary report of the proceedings in Parliament 1998/99:110 15 June 1999.

Preliminary report of the proceedings in Parliament 2001/02:54 18 January 2002.

Preliminary report of the proceedings in Parliament 2001/02:123 12 June 2002.

Preliminary report of the proceedings in Parliament 2002/03:37 16 December 2003.

Preliminary report of the proceedings in Parliament 2003/04:121 25 May 2004.

Preliminary report of the proceedings in Parliament 2005/06:45 6 December 2005.

Preliminary report of the proceedings in Parliament 2005/06:140 13 June 2006.

Preliminary report of the proceedings in Parliament 2006/07:116 30 May 2007.

Preliminary report of the proceedings in Parliament 2007/08:19 31 October 2007.

Preliminary report of the proceedings in Parliament 2008/09:52 18 December 2008.

Preliminary report of the proceedings in Parliament 2008/09:53 19 December 2008.

Preliminary report of the proceedings in Parliament 2008/09:131 12 June 2009.

Preliminary report of the proceedings in Parliament 2008/09:133 16 June 2009.

Preliminary report of the proceedings in Parliament 2009/10:32 18 November 2009.

Preliminary report of the proceedings in Parliament 2010/11:35 15 December 2010.

Preliminary report of the proceedings in Parliament 2010/11:81 1 April 2011.

Preliminary report of the proceedings in Parliament 2010/11: 118 17 June 2011.

Preliminary report of the proceedings in Parliament 2011/12:5 21 September 2011.

Preliminary report of the proceedings in Parliament 2011/12:46 12 December 2011.

Preliminary report of the proceedings in Parliament 2012/13:46 18 December 2012.

Preliminary report of the proceedings in Parliament 2013/14:47 16 December 2013.

Prosecutor v. Tadic (1995) (IT–94–1–AR72), International Criminal Tribunal for the Former Yugoslavia (ICTY), Appeal on Jurisdiction, 2 October 1995.

Report from the Inquiry on Sweden's International Defence Cooperation (2014) *International defence cooperation: Efficiency, solidarity, sovereignty* Fo 2013:B October 2014.

Swedish Armed Forces (2015) Afghanistan – RSM Available online at www.forsvarsmakten.se/en/about/our-mission-in-sweden-and-abroad/current-missions/afghanistan-isaf/ (accessed 13 August 2015).

Swedish Official Inquiry (2003) *Var beredskap efter den 11 september* [*Our preparedness after 11 September*], SOU 2003:32.

Swedish Official Inquiry (2010) *Folkratt i vapnad konflikt* [*International law in armed conflict*], SOU 2010:72.

Swedish Official Inquiry (2011) *Vald och tvang under internationella militara insatser* [*The use of force in international military operations*], SOU 2011:76.

Swedish Official Inquiry (2015) *Deltagande med vapnad styrka i utbildning utomlands – En utokad beslutsbefogenhet for regeringen* [*Participation with armed force in training abroad – Extended decision-making power of the government*], SOU 2015:1.

UN General Assembly (2005), 2005 World Summit Outcome, Doc. No. A/res/60/1, 24 October.
UN Security Council resolution 1386 20 December 2001.
UN Security Council resolution 1510 13 October 2003.
UN Security Council resolution 1970 26 February 2011.
UN Security Council resolution 1973 17 March 2011.
UN Security Council resolution 2120 10 October 2013.
UN Security Council resolution 2161 17 June 2014.
UN Security Council resolution 2170 15 August 2014.
UN Security Council resolution 2178 24 September 2014.
UN Security Council resolution 2189 12 December 2014.
Wedin, L. (2008) 'The case of Sweden' in C. Archer (Ed.) *New security issues in northern Europe: The Nordic and Baltic States and the ESDP.* London and New York: Routledge 2008, pp. 38–55.

5 MOTs, Juliette and omelettes

Temporary tactical adaptations as the postmodern, interoperable force awaits the anticipated operation?

Magnus Johnsson

Introduction

Throughout the Afghanistan campaign, Sweden has deployed and employed organizational units that have not been part of its regular force structure. Despite a pronounced national strategy to develop and maintain a standing force structure of readily deployable units usable for operations in Sweden and abroad, several unique unit types have played a central role in Sweden's largest military effort of the last decade. For example, in the beginning of the Provincial Reconstruction Team (PRT) era, small military observation teams (so-called MOTs) were not only the eyes and ears of the Swedish PRT commander in the remote provinces of his area of operations, but also his mouth and hands. Monitoring – the activity that the MOTs performed in their provinces and districts – actually defined the business of the PRT for several years, even though the MOT concept was something new and unfamiliar. Similarly, during the latter part of the campaign, operational monitoring and liaison teams (OMLTs), also an organizational novelty, were responsible for the core task of raising the proficiency of the Afghan National Army. None of these unit types were part of the Swedish Armed Forces force structure, yet they constituted core components of the contribution.

While Sweden has spent tremendous efforts on developing its national defence force and two EU Battle Groups, in practice irregular MOTs, OMLT, provincial offices and advisory teams have done the job in its major military engagement. Such organizational adaptations at the tactical level constitute a somewhat puzzling contrast to the strategy of producing versatile, deployable and usable military units. They also accentuate a possible gap or tension between strategic military capability development and actual (or subjectively perceived) requirements in the field. And ultimately, they put into question the ability of the nation state to develop military capabilities for future wars.

The purpose of this chapter is to further our understanding of such tactical, organizational adaptations. Through a structured focused comparison of the genesis, rationale, tactical effects and strategic imprint of such units, light is shed on an aspect of military capability that falls outside the regular institutions of military capability development. The results of the analysis suggest that the dogma of strategic force transformation has somewhat limited prospects of providing a versatile and readily usable force structure, and that the state's focus on top-down development prevents it from being sensitive to tactical needs and from initiating responsive adaptations.

Understanding military change

Military organizations change. For various reasons they alter their organizational structure, their equipment and the way they use their equipment. They also change the way they think about their assumed or actual opponents and what mechanisms of warfare that will make the opponents yield. Changes can be big or small and take place in different parts of the organization. The literature offers different terms to theorize about such change – for example, development; adaptation; transformation, innovation and change – and as is the case in so many other fields of social science, the conceptual clarity and consensus is far from perfect.

A common way to arrange these concepts is by creating a conceptual pair or a dichotomy on some dimension. In an analysis of *tactical change*, Sorenson and Widén use the term *tactical adaptation* to signify short-term alterations in response to the opponents' immediate actions and *tactical development* to signify long-term alterations caused by other factors such as technological, social and organizational (Sorenson & Widén 2014, p. 402). With such a construction, adaptation and development become two instances or subclasses of change in the short- and long-term; that is, a matter of duration.

In another example, Theo Farrell writes about two kinds of *military change*. He uses the term *military adaptation* to signify military change that is of less significance[1] and that has the character of adjustments 'in response to operational challenges and campaign pressures', and *military innovation* to signify change on a larger scale that 'involves developing new military technologies, tactics, strategies, and structures' (Farrell 2013, pp. 6–7): a phenomenon that is sometimes called *military transformation* or *force transformation* (Farrell & Terriff 2010, p. 4). Consequently, in Farrell's construction, adaptation and innovation – or change – is a matter of scale.

What Sorenson and Widén imply, and what Farrell mentions, is another possible dimension: organizational level. This dimension is pertinent with regards to both the origin of the change – that is, where (at what organizational level) the drivers of change occur – as well as where the actual alteration is realized. For example, in Sorenson and Widén's concept of tactical adaptation, the change is both initiated and realized at the tactical level since the cause of change is the actions of the opponent and the change itself is tactical alterations. However, Farrell suggests that adaptations can also be realized at the strategic level and the innovations that he writes about, for example change of strategy, can be assumed to be initiated at the strategic level. These examples together imply a number of combinations of the change's place of origin and place of realization, shown in Figure 5.1.

		Place of realization	
		Strategic	Tactical
Place of origin	Strategic		
	Tactical		

Figure 5.1 The relationship between place of origin and place of realization in military change.
Source: the author.

To illustrate, the implementation of a Senior Gender Advisor at the Directorate for Operations in the Swedish Armed Forces Headquarters can be seen as the result of a focused development effort at the strategic level, derived from and fuelled by UN Security Council (UNSC) Resolution 1325 (Egnell *et al.* 2014, pp. 76–7). The Senior Gender Advisor can therefore be seen as a function initiated and realized at the strategic level. Parallel to that, gender functions have been developed at the (operational and) tactical level; for example, in the shape of gender advisors in multinational staffs at the tactical level (Berts *et al.* 2013, pp. 40–1, 46). Consequently, these positions can be seen as functions initiated at the strategic level but realized at the tactical level. Regarding change at the strategic level that originates at the tactical level, Farrell exemplifies with the US COIN strategy originating in tactical experiences in Iraq (Farrell 2013, p. 18). And finally, an example of tactical change[2] initiated at the tactical level is the US counterinsurgency tactics employed in the Iraqi Anbar province in 2006, which preceded both the Counterinsurgency Field Manual (United States Dept of the Army 2007) and the strategically-driven 'surge' (Russell 2011, p. 2).

When juxtaposing military organizational change during operations with long-term military planning, another dimension of a temporal–logical character becomes relevant. This dimension distinguishes between alterations of the military enterprise – big or small, tactical or strategic – that are driven by *a priori* ideas of war as compared to those driven by *a posteriori* experiences of war. In practice, these two processes are known under terms such as *military capability building* (or *force transformation*, to use a modern term) and lessons learned. In Western countries, military capability building is a rational, institutionalized process that attempts to design military capabilities based on assumptions of future conflicts. Ideally, such top-down processes also include mechanisms for organizational learning that pick up experiences from actual military deployments and operations.

The purpose of this investigation requires concepts that can isolate initiatives and changes that occur in the field and relate them to more regular, strategic development processes. However, the dichotomies mentioned here are not clear-cut enough, so with the risk of adding conceptual obscurity, I choose two concepts that serve this purpose.

To signify operation-specific organizational changes at the tactical level, which the three cases can be categorized as, I use the term *tactical adaptation*. This term points to the tactical level and also suggests something reactive rather than proactive. By tactical adaptation, I refer to organizational changes at the tactical level that directly or indirectly have their origin at the tactical level as well. They are changes that affect the deployed units in the field as a result of some perceived need or requirement in the field. For the contrasting concept, the term *force transformation* is used. By force transformation, I refer to changes at any level of the military hierarchy that result from development efforts at the strategic level. Unfortunately, these two concepts fail to account for all possible instances of military change. There are, for instance, examples of tactical adaptations in ongoing operations that are *not* initiated at the tactical level. However, the concepts are good enough for the purpose of isolating and describing the cases at hand. Although the theory surrounding these two concepts are not the core issue of this chapter, a brief review is deemed useful for placing the issue of in-the-field organizational adaptation in theoretical context.

Force transformation and tactical adaptation

All states struggle to develop their military capacities in order to meet their own perceived requirements of future wars. The idea of technology-driven revolutions in military affairs (RMA) of the 1970s and 1980s originated in the Soviet Union and spread to the United States, where they were institutionalized in the Air Land Battle Doctrine. After the fall of the Soviet Union, the West's need for standing forces diminished, and a growing hesitance began to permeate many if not all Western states' thinking about military development. However, the idea of *network-centric warfare* provided a compelling narrative of how modern Western states could downsize their militaries but at the same time develop them, and still maintain the upper hand in armed conflict (Alberts *et al.* 1999). This continuous process of adaptation came to be known as *force transformation*: a business that was quickly institutionalized within both the United States Department of Defence and NATO (Cohen 2004, Farrell & Terriff 2010, pp. 2–3, Farrell & Rynning 2010, pp. 676–7, NATO 2003, Onley 2006, Terriff *et al.* 2010).[3] In recent years, however, *transformation* has become something of a catch-all phrase (Hamilton 2004, pp. 3–4), signifying the continuous change and adaption of the military forces of Western states in general – something that, of course, is nothing new at all.

Regardless of the term, this strategic development effort is almost deductive in nature in that it relies on best guesses of future wars. It is a rational (albeit fearful and hesitant), bureaucratic, top-down affair (for example, Cohen 2004, p. 400, Russell 2011, pp. 23–53, Grissom 2006). In Sweden, as well as in many other Western countries, transformation is institutionalized in a complex process containing studies, experiments, plans and directives that straddle the border between the political sphere and the military sphere. Based on the requirements that the state stipulates, with the resources made available and with the support provided by other parties, the military bureaucracy conducts a process of defining, developing and integrating doctrine; organization; training; equipment, support and so on. The US Marine corps' *Expeditionary Force Development System* (USMC 2009, p. 3) can be seen as an example of such an institutionalized force transformation process. Perspectives are long, usually measured in decades, which means that lead times as well as life cycles are too. The time between conception and operation for a complex weapon system such as a fighter aircraft or an armoured vehicle can therefore be around 20 to 40 years. Naturally, with those kinds of perspectives, it is difficult (if not impossible) to predict relevant operational requirements with any precision.

A less salient view on force transformation is the bottom-up perspective. Research on military innovation has focused on top-down processes and bureaucratic inertia, while there is a 'conceptual void to be filled regarding bottom-up innovation' (Grissom 2010, pp. 919–20, 925). According to Farrell, there is even a need for 'a theory able to explain bottom-up change by organizations at war' (Farrell 2010, p. 569).

By *tactical adaptation*, we here refer to in-the-field changes, adaptations and innovations that alter or replace organizational force structures, equipment, tactics, techniques and procedures that have resulted from force transformation. A concrete example is the Swedish purchase of BAE Systems RG-32 patrol vehicles (Swedish Defence Materiel Administration 2013),[4] which illustrates the Armed Forces' unpreparedness for particular operations in certain types of terrain. An example of another type of adaption is the British continuous change of tactics in the Afghan Helmand province in 2006 and 2007. Believing that the campaign was failing, each successive British commander chose a new and different tactical approach than his predecessor, altering the force's behaviour with each rotation (Farrell 2010).

These two examples illustrate the blurring of top-down and bottom-up perspectives. Tactical adaptation is defined as bottom-up per se, in that it originates in the field and the tactical level. However, as the RG-32 example illustrates, a tactical need may spur strategic efforts, such as the procurement of new vehicles. Nevertheless, the procurement of the RG-32 was clearly not an outcome of force transformation but rather of a tactical experience that strategic force transformation had failed to encompass. The British example, on the other hand, illustrates a more pure tactical phenomenon, since the force commanders in theatre stood for the initiative.

Reasonably, an actual, real-life force structure – as well as the practices of those who staff the force structure – is some form of resultant of repeated clashes between the ideals of top-down design on the one hand and the lessons of bottom-up experiences on the other. Deployed units, materiel and practices are used by operatives in the field, and their experiences are (perhaps) fed back to a more or less receptive design process. Hence tactical adaptations may lead to force transformation; new tactics and techniques may in time be captured in doctrine or lead to a change to organizational structure or the acquisition of a new enabling technology (Farrell 2010, p. 596). However, as the analysis here will show, there is a potential tension in the vertical relation between adaptors in theatre and transformers back home, and various institutional obstacles may obstruct both feedback and sensitivity to feedback from the tactical level. Ultimately, such tension may lead to anomalies in the field that put into question the mainly two-dimensional models of military change discussed above. Farrell's explanation for such potential tension, and organizational proneness to change in general, is that military organizations are both rational and routine-bound:

> They are rational in that they monitor their performance and their environment, and respond to under-performance and environmental change. But they are bound by routines in [...] *how* they measure performance and perceive their environment, and *how* they generate and select appropriate responses.
> (Farrell 2010, pp. 569–70, italics in original)

This leads military organizations to favour the exploitation of existing competencies, organizations, tactics and technologies over exploring new ones (Farrell 2010, p. 571). As we shall see, this theory may be a competitive explanation to the findings in this investigation.

The study

In the following three sections, three cases of organizational adaptation at the tactical level are analyzed through a structured focused comparison. The underlying empirical question here is how these organizational adaptions have affected the regular force structure. To investigate this, five aspects of each case are investigated using the analytical questions shown in Table 5.1.

For the empirical and theoretical aspects of this volume, the issue of *origin* and *imprint* is of greatest relevance, while *rationale*, *operation* and *effect* are more relevant for the description of the cases and the understanding of the underpinning reasons for the adaptation initiatives. However, together they form a coherent whole.

The main method of data elicitation is a series of interviews with strategically selected individuals who have been directly involved in the particular processes at various levels of the military organization. These include commanders in the field, development officers in the Armed Forces Headquarters and elsewhere, personnel responsible for and involved in pre-deployment training of Afghanistan contingents and personnel involved in lessons learned, totalling 11 respondents. The number of respondents may appear small, but it should be noted that Sweden is a small country and the number of individuals

Table 5.1 Analytical scheme

Origin	The emergence of the organizational unit	How did the unit come about? What were the drivers and where did they originate? Were particular individuals and/or organizations active in advocating and realizing the units?
Rationale	The purpose of the organizational unit	What problem was the invention supposed to solve? What was the organizational shortcoming that they were supposed to mend?
Operation	The operational conduct of the organizational unit	How did the organizational unit function in terms of structure, skill and equipment? What did it do and to whom?
Effect	The effects of the organizational unit's conduct	What tactical effect did the organizational unit have? What strategic effect did the organizational unit have?
Imprint	The institutional organizational imprints of the development of the organizational unit	What institutional imprints has the organizational unit had on the enterprise in terms of organization; institutions; field manuals; equipment; lessons learned, organizational spillover/heritage and training?

that are involved in these processes are few. In fact, one individual may well play many different parts in the same process throughout the campaign: a circumstance that may be exploited by the researcher. The interviews play the main role in this study, but are complemented with data from written sources. It should be noted, however, that this type of written data is limited in volume and restricted or classified. Therefore, the accounts of the respondents weigh heavily in this investigation, which may be regarded as an empirical strength and an important contribution since such stories are fairly seldom captured.

The cases have been chosen from a range of alternatives that can be found within the Swedish contingents in Afghanistan. The Swedish contribution to ISAF has evolved over time. The first two contingents, which were deployed shortly after UN resolution 1386 in December 2001, were drawn from two special operations units and operated out of the Kabul area. During 2002, these where followed by a smaller force consisting of staff officers and CIMIC teams: a constellation that constituted the bulk of the Swedish contribution for the next couple of years. In 2004, the Swedish contribution changed shape again and redeployed to Mazar-e-Sharif as a part of the British-led Provincial Reconstruction Team (PRT). The operational core of the British PRT was the so-called Military Observation Team (MOT), and Sweden participated with two MOTs and one Quick Reaction Force (QRF). In 2006, the British redeployed to the Helmand province in southern Afghanistan and Sweden assumed responsibility of PRT Mazar-e-Sharif (PRT MeS), continuing with the MOT concept. During this time, a new construct emerged in ISAF: the Operational Mentoring and Liaison Team, abbreviated OMLT and pronounced 'omelettes' in military jargon. These were cells of ISAF officers that were attached to staffs at various levels of the Afghan National Army and tasked with mentoring their Afghan counterparts. Beginning in 2007, the MOTs where successively phased out of the PRT order of battle and replaced by regular mechanized companies. And since 2012, as a part of ISAF's transition process, the mechanized companies have also been phased out, thereby reducing the Swedish contribution to a few advisory teams, staff members and logistic elements (Johnsson Forthcoming 2016).

MOTs and OMLTs have been of particular significance to the Swedish contribution. First, they have no organizational equivalents in the regular force structure, and second, they have – in combination with the rifle companies – constituted the operational core of the Swedish contribution during a significant part of the Swedish participation in ISAF. They also constitute two very different organizational instances, one being a type of intelligence unit and the other more of a mentoring force. They therefore constitute worthy cases for the analysis of adaptation at the tactical level. The third case can be seen as a variant of the MOT. In 2006, the Swedish PRT suddenly had a MOT with only female operatives, designated MOT Juliette (MOT J). Generalized, MOT J can be seen as an instance of what later came to be called Female Engagement Teams, or FET but since MOT J emerged before the FET concept was established and therefore is not the result of the force transformation process, it deserves particular attention. Therefore, MOT J constitutes the third case of this analysis.

Military observation teams: the capillaries of the Provincial Reconstruction Team (PRT)

The military observation team, or MOT, was the core operational unit of PRT MeS from its establishment until around 2010. They were the capillaries of the PRT; the units at the edge of the organization where the exchange between ISAF and the Afghan society took place. Initially, each MOT was subordinate to the PRT commander, but subsequently provincial offices (PO) were established in the provinces of Jowzjan, Sar-e Pul and Samangan in order to coordinate MOT activities in these vast and remote areas. Each PO was stationed in a safe house in the province capital and operated as a MOT in and around the capital, while the regular MOTs operated in the other districts of the province (Interview 1). In this sense, the PO and its MOTs became the de facto PRT representatives in each province. When Sweden engaged in the Afghanistan campaign, military observation teams were not part of its force structure. The MOT concept was inherited from the British PRT, developed over time and subsequently replaced by more regular mechanized infantry units.

In the summer of 2003, the Swedish Government and the Swedish Armed Forces Headquarters were looking for ways to adapt their contribution, as ISAF was planning its expansion beyond the Kabul area. In this process, staff officers from the Armed Forces Headquarters J5 section and the Land Component Command's G3 section developed three courses of action for a Swedish PRT, recommending a single nation deployment in Jalalabad. However, circumstances – in particular the choices made by other actors such as Germany and Britain – led to the recommendation that Sweden should contribute to the British PRT in Mazar-e-Sharif and assume responsibility for one of the four provinces of that PRT. The Swedish political–military attitude was to participate all-in, which entailed adapting to the existing British force structure and modus operandi. Hence staffing one or more MOTs was a given for Sweden, since the MOT system was the backbone of the British PRT (Interview 2).

The Swedish contingent commander at the time, Lieutenant Colonel Olof Schylander, was tasked with phasing out the Swedish CIMIC force in Kabul and to *reconnoitre* in Mazar-e-Sharif. There, he came in contact with the MOT concept in discussions with a Danish MOT commander. In the words of a former British PRT commander:

> military observation teams (MOTs) are teams of eight men assigned to each province. They are the eyes and ears and often the voices of the PRT – fundamental to its situational awareness and influence, both for the military and civilian parts of it.
>
> (Brittain 2008)

However, this is not how the contingent commander understood the concept from his discussions with the Danish MOT commander. Instead, his understanding lay much closer to the more familiar CIMIC concept, and subsequently his recommendation was to recruit from the pool of individuals who had served in CIMIC teams in Kosovo and Kabul (Interview 3).

However, the staff officers planning for the deployment were instructed to use a military police readiness unit, designated MP02, for deployment. Since the task was not to deploy any regular unit such as a mechanized battalion, the MP readiness unit was seen as highly suitable (Interview 2). This led to Major Frederick Westerdahl, the commanding officer of MP02, getting involved in the preparation process. His unit was designed especially for international operations. The average age of the unit's personnel was over 30, half of which had both military and civilian police training. After a reconnaissance trip to the area of operations, Westerdahl assessed the mission to be 'challenging and feasible'. The major hurdle was to assemble a team with the right competences (since the whole team would not deploy) and the right equipment. To be able to communicate with the British, new radios were procured, for example. After the reconnaissance trip and discussion with his British partners, Westerdahl perceived the mission to be 'to enable the Afghan national police', a task that he and the British PRT commander thought was perfect for a MP unit. Subsequently, MP02 deployed one MOT, one logistics and communications detail, one MP platoon and a few staff officers. The second MOT was deployed a few months later from a ranger readiness unit of the Norrland Dragoon regiment in Arvidsjaur (Westerdahl 2006, Interview 4).

Schylander's vision of CIMIC-like operations in the PRT was never realized. First, the MOTs had no resources to conduct CIMIC activities. The PRT concept was to monitor the situation in the provinces and districts, to assess the needs of development, security and governance and to initiate or support activities to address those needs. However, many PRTs that lacked the resources to address the needs of the Afghans were to be accused of not accomplishing any change. Second, the purpose of the MOTs was to gather information for the aforementioned purposes, not to facilitate military–civilian relations (as is the purpose of CIMIC); but as the predominantly military PRTs focused more on security issues than development and governance, the de facto task became intelligence gathering. And third, the Swedish attitude seems to have been different in Afghanistan than in the Balkans. The task of 'handing out blankets' had disappeared from the discourse, and a tougher attitude marked the engagement in Afghanistan. One indication of this is that MOTs were mainly recruited from ranger and security units in Sweden. Even though the approach in the beginning was to strive for 'a good conversation', and even though armed skirmishes were signs of failure (Interview 4), later MOTs often participated in what can be considered as combat missions, or at least missions that had a risk of ending up in fire fights. Whether this was the result of an attitude, increased insurgent activity or both remains to be discovered. As Westerdahl describes the development, Swedish units – as well as ISAF as a whole – went from a strategy to prevent and subdue to a strategy to defeat (Interview 4).

Between 2006 (when Sweden assumed responsibility of PRT MeS) and somewhere between 2008 and 2010 (when the MOT structure was successively replaced by a mechanized battalion structure), the MOTs were the main operative tool of the PRT. The MOTs fed the PRT command with information about the districts pertaining to matters of security, development and governance. Based on this information, the PRT command – consisting of the PRT commander and his staff, including political advisors, development advisors and police advisors – devised plans for action within these three areas. However, the Swedish PRT was purely military in composition and hence lacked relevant resources for reconstruction or development work, and the task of accomplishing change in the districts often bounced back to the MOTs, which had the same lack of resources. This meant that the MOT, which was the de facto PRT presence in the remote parts of the four provinces of the area of responsibility, had little or no potential to match their monitoring with action (Interview 5). This limited the rationale of the MOT to surveillance, while by design it was implied to be something more: a shortcoming that seemed to generate unrealistic expectations in the districts as well as frustration within the force. Instead, PRT components, including the MOTs, attempted to *influence* various parts of Afghan structures at various levels (Brittain 2008). For a MOT, this implied engaging key leaders at the province, district and village levels. The operational meaning of influence was, and is, rather arbitrary and was left to the each unit in question to determine. This freedom led to very disparate behaviours in provinces and districts (Interview 5).

The Swedish force structure has never contained Military Observation Teams. Neither have there been units with such a name nor with the particular purpose and function that the MOTs in Afghanistan had. This is evidenced by the fact that Sweden sent other types of units to perform the role of MOTs in Afghanistan – for example, military police units, ranger units or just temporarily assembled units of 'buddies' – which were given MOT training at SWEDINT.

Typically, a MOT consisted of six (sometimes up to eight) soldiers riding in two vehicles. The team contained a commanding officer, a second in command, an interpreter and soldiers with various specialties: communications, medic, heavy weapons and so on. They resembled a light infantry squad that conducted short- and long-range patrols within their area of operations: typically one or two districts in one of the PRT's provinces. Initially the MOT operated in regular, white Toyota Land Cruisers. They were later painted in desert sand colour and equipped with IED protection, and eventually replaced with armoured vehicles. A stationary variant of the MOT was the provincial office, or PO, which was based in a safe house in the provincial capital and operated in and around the capital. The PO also had a coordinating role regarding all MOT activity within the province.

What distinguished a MOT from a light infantry squad, or a recon squad for that matter, were its tasks. Even though the unit was equipped and trained for small unit combat, its main task was to interact with the Afghan society and local population (Interview 6). This interaction derives from the PRTs' early role as a monitoring force. By representing the PRT throughout the area of responsibility at the provincial and district levels, the POs and MOTs became the PRTs' de facto tool for interaction with the surrounding society. To achieve interaction at the provincial and district levels, the MOTs where tasked to liaise (Westerdahl 2006), and the operationalization of this task was to conduct meetings. The MOT training at SWEDINT contained a large block of meeting and conversation technique, which taught operators how to plan, conduct and report meetings with key leaders. 'It was our thing', as one PO commander puts it (Interview 7). The training was conducted with the help of Afghan actors and contained elements of 'cultural awareness'. As one of the first MOT commanders (and later MOT trainers) describes it: 'All pre-deployment training is aimed at facilitating successful discussions' (Westerdahl 2006). Beyond that, the MOTs facilitated intra-community discussions. For example, one MOT in Sar-e Pul province, at its own initiative, arranged what it called 'mullah meetings': large gatherings with sometimes several hundreds of key community actors. On the one hand these events were mass meetings for influence, but they were also tools for facilitating interaction, coordination and networking between local players in the provinces (Interview 5). Finally, one commander describes the MOT as problem solvers in general. In areas in which both the Afghan Government and ISAF were weak or non-present, the MOT could be seen as a local power player that – through its wide mandate, firepower and many connections – had the ability and opportunity to deal with a wide range of societal issues, such as well digging, crime investigations, lost persons and arrests (Interview 6).

Respondents who have worked with the MOT concept express two main viewpoints regarding their tactical effects: that they were efficient, but non-effective. The first point probably rests on a widespread feeling of professionalism and professional pride. The Armed Forces most certainly took the MOT challenge seriously and recruited teams primarily from ranger and security units, and they were put through a separate pre-deployment training program (Interview 8). The teams that the Armed Forces sent out were well-trained, close-knit and self-confident. However, their chances of accomplishing any significant results in the area of responsibility were seen as slim. While official rhetoric often depicted the MOTs as peacemakers and reconstructors, the members themselves realized that the geographical areas were too large and that the needs and issues were too many for them to be able to even begin prioritizing. As many MOT members and others express it, there was a lot of tea-drinking and question-asking: skewed behaviours that left a lot of unrealized expectations in the districts and provinces (Interview 9).

Nevertheless, the MOT concept was eventually abandoned in the Swedish PRT. Beginning in 2008, various factors led to a successive change in force structure: from the PO/MOT structure to a mechanized battalion structure. FS15 (2008) was the first PRT to have a mechanized rifle company, designated *Quebec Lima*, based at Camp Northern Lights in Mazar-e-Sharif, with POs and MOTs still out in the more remote provinces of Jowzjan and Sar-e Pul (Interview 10). By the end of 2010, the PRT had three mechanized rifle companies and no POs or MOTs.

The Swedish Armed Forces' experience with the MOT concept between 2004 and 2010 has left very limited imprints. There were no MOTs in the force structure before or during the time period, and there are no MOTs in the force structure after – which perhaps cannot be expected if Afghanistan is seen as a unique operation. The MOTs that operated in Afghanistan during 6 years were temporary instances of something that had no place in the Armed Forces, and therefore had to lead an irregular organizational life in the field and at the training department. As one staff officer puts it, the MOTs lived a life of their own outside of the regular standing force (Interview 9). Ad hoc groups of individuals were assembled, trained for MOT operations and dissolved. Any residue is limited to unofficial training plans and equipment lists in the desks of the training officers (Interview 11), and perhaps as memories of the members of the teams.[5] Furthermore, the enterprise was not capable of handling experiences and lessons learned from the teams. As was also the case with the rest of the Swedish force, the learning processes were immediate and short. Empirical lessons were learnt in the field and often required instant attention, something that the long-term and rather rigid force transformation processes at home could not handle. Hence mission support, but also strategic transformation, suffered (Interview 9). If we assume that Sweden will or may participate in future operations of a similar character – not instead of, but as a complement to, the heavier type of operations that the Swedish Forces anticipate – then the Armed Forces should have admitted the MOT concept into an appropriate lessons-learned process, evaluated the field experiences and fed appropriate conclusions to the force transformation process. Such processes exist, but the MOT teams have not been treated with the same seriousness as have other, already-existing systems that have been deployed, such as various intelligence systems and vehicle systems that were already a part of the force structure.[6]

MOT Juliette: engaging the other half of Afghan society

The sudden emergence of an all-female MOT in 2006 was a personal initiative of Sweden's first PRT commander, Colonel Bengt Sandstrom. Two years earlier, Colonel Sandstrom commanded the Norrland Dragoon Regiment, which contributed rangers for one of the MOTs and the QRF of the British PRT. In that capacity he made regular duty trips to the area of operations in order to follow up on his deployed personnel and to learn about the PRT concept: something that he deemed necessary since Sweden had begun planning for its own PRT in Afghanistan and since he considered seeking the post of PRT Commander.

During one of these trips, he spent close to a day discussing the PRT concept and the MOT concept with the British Development Advisor. Among many things, they discussed aid projects targeted at women and the information, or intelligence, which such interaction generated. Realizing that tapping into this potentially huge intelligence source required female operators, Sandstrom began devising a female MOT: a team of 'women who could talk with women' (Interview 12). The team was designated *MOT Juliette*.[7] The rigidity of the PRT's ORBAT prevented any rearrangements before deployment, so Sandstrom constituted the female MOT in theatre by assembling three female officers who actually had other roles in the PRT. This move was communicated to the Army Tactical Command, which offered no objections.

The prime driver behind MOT Juliette was a perceived intelligence gap. The military and predominantly male nature of ISAF was seen by some as an obstacle in the effort to access and penetrate Afghan structures – also impaired by rather harsh and masculine traits – for intelligence. The revelation was that the many meetings of male soldiers failed to address any issues that could pertain to the female population. Thus, the concept claimed that if ISAF units could contain female operators, a whole new intelligence avenue of approach could be accessed, potentially resulting in a wealth of new intelligence (Interview 12). This was the opportunity that Colonel Sandstrom saw after his visit to the British PRT. Some, he says, thought that MOT Juliette was a gender project in terms of promoting or providing equal rights to female Swedish officers or to help Afghan women. This was never the intention, according to him. MOT Juliette was a tool that was supposed to deliver operational effect for the force (Interview 12).

Assembling the team in theatre had some draw backs. Most significantly, the team did not have time for full MOT training in Sweden, and they deployed without the standard issue equipment and vehicles that the regular MOTs had. Nor was it possible to conduct a handover/takeover process, since the team had no predecessor. This led to a relatively long start-up phase. Also, since there were no existing female MOTs to learn from (and indeed no concept to copy or adopt), MOT J had no clear mission statement and no modus operandi at the onset. This forced the three officers to develop, try and test methods on their own in the field. Furthermore, to be able to gain access to female Afghans they were in need of a female translator: an asset that was not realized until rather late into the deployment. This initial weariness generated some frustration within the team (Interview 12).

Consisting of only three persons, MOT J was significantly smaller than other MOTs. For a MOT, size is partly a matter of security, and hence MOT J was too small to be operationally autonomous. Consequently, they had to either tag along with another unit (such as another MOT or escort squad) or request close protection. Tagging along another MOT in effect created a male–female MOT: what was later to be called *Mixed Engagement Teams* (METs). This mix proved particularly useful when operating at the district level, since district councils were required to contain a minimum of 30 per cent women. The method of operating on their own with close protection was a behaviour that would later be institutionalized in *Female Engagement Teams* (FETs). With this approach, the team could approach other targets such as women's rights organizations, government agencies, female prisons and NGOs (Interview 13). In any event, MOT J did not become as operationally independent as hoped; not because of gender, but because of number.

MOT Juliette had slightly different effects than those that Colonel Sandstrom intended. The idea of gaining intelligence from the female population did not work as planned. Even though the female operators had unique capabilities and opportunities to interact with Afghan women, they rarely acquired any really useful or so-called 'actionable' intelligence. Colonel Sandstrom believes that societal structures such as family loyalty prevented this. Hence the anticipated direct intelligence effect never occurred (Interview 12).

However, the team did acquire large amounts of other types of information. As one MOT commander describes it, the meeting between ISAF units and Afghan locals is often very hard and 'masculine'. MOT J was able to open up a more humanitarian aspect of those intercultural meetings than geared-up Western soldiers and former Afghan *mujahedeen* could manage. By opening previously closed doors to Afghan society MOT Juliette provided new insight therein, which served as a new backdrop to traditional actionable intelligence and nuanced the otherwise masculine image of Afghan society that the PRT was usually fed. This gave a new and deeper understanding of the intelligence as well as of the society as a whole (Interview 13). As Colonel Sandstrom and other MOT commanders describe it, MOT Juliette contributed to a better situational awareness overall. Hence, it can be said that MOT J had an unintended, *indirect* intelligence effect.

The strategic impact of MOT J may well be the most difficult to assess. Being a personal initiative, the team effectively evaporated as FS11 rotated home. One year after that, FS14 also had a MOT J, but it was 'composed of voluntary women in FS14 who on their spare time engaged themselves in and pursued issues regarding UN resolution 1325, i.e. gender work' (Swedish Armed Forces 2009, p. 124). Nevertheless, MOT Juliette never became a part of the force structure. Colonel Sandstrom's initiative came almost 4 years after the United Nations Security Council adopted resolution 1325 (in October 2000), at a time when gender awareness was growing in the SAF (which was possibly one reason for his initiative) and implementation of the resolution was underway. However, the two primary sets of factors behind the process of implementing a gender perspective in the Swedish Armed Forces were political directives triggered by resolution 1325 and a growing understanding of the military utility of a gender perspective in the field, which was codified in the Military Strategic Doctrine of 2011 (Egnell *et al.* 2014, p. 50).

Did MOT Juliette have anything to do with this? Even if subsequent force structure developments cannot be directly traced to MOT Juliette of FS11, the team's symbolic impact can hardly be overestimated. It attracted considerable attention in Afghanistan, not only from Afghan officers, policemen and ordinary citizens but also from ISAF partners (Interview 12). Furthermore, since their return to Sweden, the three members of MOT Juliette have been the object of several news articles, seminars and academic papers. Therefore, even if the developments in the gender field after 2004 cannot be explained by the attention that MOT Juliette created (Interview 14), it can be argued that the developments that were underway in the gender field benefited from the good example that it constituted.

OMLT: training and fighting with the Afghan National Army

The build-up of Afghan National Security Forces has been an increasingly central effort since the US coalition toppled the Taliban regime in 2001. State-building, which inevitably followed the overthrowing of the Taliban, implies establishing a functioning police and military: an activity that is often discussed as part of so-called Security Sector Reform (Swedish Government

2007, p.8). Furthermore, the counterinsurgency strategy that ISAF adopted in 2009 also (allegedly) requires a functioning national security force. Hence, building and supporting ANSF has been an important task throughout the Afghanistan campaign. And after President Obama effectively made 2014 the final year of the Afghanistan campaign (Obama 2011) and NATO's exit strategy emerged, ANSF's build-up became a top ISAF priority (Hansen et al. 2012, p. 1).

A major tool for ANSF build-up has been the *Operational Mentoring and Liaison Teams* (OMLT). These have existed since 2006; the OMLT program has been coordinated as one of many within the NATO Training Mission for Afghanistan (NTM–A) and has focused on the Afghan National Army ANA (Hansen et al. 2012, p. 1). OMLTs operate at many levels of ANA, from corps through brigade and down to battalions, the latter known as *kandaks*.

The Swedish forces deployed to Afghanistan have conducted mentoring of Afghan security forces in various ways from the onset. After Sweden became lead nation for the Provincial Reconstruction Team in Mazar-e-Sharif in 2006, mentoring became a more structured operation as NATO requested Sweden to contribute with OMLTs (Interview 15). Initially, Sweden had smaller teams that mentored the staffs of ANA's 209th Corps and its 1st and 3rd brigades. In 2009, the effort expanded as the first Swedish OMLT Kandak began to mentor 2nd Battalion of 1st Brigade (Liander 2011). Unlike the emergence of MOTs, then, Swedish OMLTs were the result of NATO requests and a subsequent bureaucratic process within the SAF Headquarters.

The overarching purpose of OMLT mentoring was to 'coach, teach and mentor ANA units' in order to make ANA 'self-sufficient, competent and professional' (Nilsson 2013). Even though OMLT operations were relatively well-formalized, it is not possible to provide one general account of them. NATO's directive is interpreted and implemented differently not only by contributing nations but also by rotating contingents from contributing nations (Interviews 15, 14; Grissom 2010, pp. 507–8; Liander 2011, p. 15).

The structure of an OMLT has changed over time, so in order to provide an illustration, OMLT Kandak of Swedish contingent FS22 (2011–12) will be used as an example here. This 47-strong unit contained 21 mentors and a number of enabling sub-units, such as a staff squad, a rifle squad for close protection, a medical transportation squad and a TACP (Tactical Air Control Party) for directing close air support (Nilsson 2013). The mentors worked with assigned counterparts in the ANA Kandak, so that the commanding officer of the OMLT – a Lieutenant Colonel – mentored the commanding officer of the kandak – also a Lieutenant Colonel. Consequently, majors, captains and lieutenants of the OMLT mentored the majors, captains and lieutenants that worked in the staff and commanded the companies and platoons of the kandak. This infiltration of the kandak implied a very intimate relationship between mentors and mentees, and trust was identified as the key for success (Interviews 15, 14).

The tasks of the mentors were to 'guide, train, advise and mentor' their counterparts in ANA, to advise and support them in their planning processes, to participate in their operations and to liaise between the ANA unit and ISAF in joint operations (Hansen et al. 2011). This broad mission required what many mentors describe as 'living with the Afghans'. The role of the mentor was in many respects similar to the role as an officer in the Swedish Armed Forces. One of two main roles of a Swedish officer is instructor,[8] and a large part of basic officer training regards the training of soldiers. During formal training, he instructs soldiers in soldiering tasks (such as medical aid, marksmanship, tactics and so on) or officers during staff training – tasks similar to the first two tasks of an OMLT mentor, albeit under very different circumstances. Another related role of the Swedish officer is as a trainer during applied exercises. To participate in ANA operations was naturally very different from overseeing conscript soldiers during an exercise in Sweden, but the mentoring part would still have been familiar to the officer. As one mentor described it, 'mentoring in itself is not difficult, it is the combat situation that is demanding' (Interview 16). Hence the roles of the OMLT mentor can be described as instructor, trainer and battle buddy (Interview 16, Walldén & Gyhagen 2011).

Given that ISAF's exit is the goal and the development of ANA capabilities is one of the mechanisms for reaching that goal, evaluation of ANA capabilities can be assumed to be a priority. Hence, the effects of OMLT activities can be expected to be measured more stringently than those of other activities. As a part of NTM–A evaluation of ANA, each OMLT conducted continuous estimates of its dedicated ANA unit. One method was to document and rank observed shortfalls, design measures to mend them and then estimate the effects of the measures taken. Based on OMLT reports, NTM–A validated ANA units; at a certain threshold, the OMLT was detached from its ANA unit, indicating that the ANA unit held a required proficiency (Silwer 2012, p. 20). An ANA unit that reached the required level of proficiency would then be a measure of OMLT effect. However, without controlling for other factors (such as basic training, combat experience, unit cohesion and moral and so on), it seems difficult to isolate the effects of the OMLT. Furthermore, the mentors' role as liaisons between ANA and ISAF may add to this complexity. Some feared that, at a certain point, an ANA kandak might reach stipulated proficiency but still be dependent on the exclusive ISAF assets that the mentoring provided. This could have tempted the kandak to perform at a lower level of proficiency than they were actually at, in order to maintain mentoring and the assets that it comprised (Silwer 2012, p. 20).

Another complicating factor for equal evaluation was the freedom that each OMLT had to interpret and design their own mission (Interview 15): a circumstance that may imply that they also evaluated differently. Furthermore, the 6-month rotation schedule and each rotation's leave schedule, in combination with ANA vacancies (Silwer 2012), made it hard to conduct stable and continuous estimates. Nevertheless, accepting that mentoring 'at home' does lead to military proficiency of Swedish units during basic and applied training, it can be assumed that OMLTs did have effects on their mentee units. Having witnessed Swedish soldiers teaching basic medical skills to battle-experienced Afghan special operations soldiers, I am certain that *any* mentoring will have positive effects on ANA units of less proficiency. In conclusion, it can be assumed that the tactical effect of OMLT kandaks has been significant.

An indicator of potential strategic impact is the comprehensive lessons learned evaluation that the SAF Headquarters have completed regarding Swedish OMLT activities in Afghanistan. By compiling and analyzing reported experiences from the teams and conducting interviews with mentors, recommendations and directives have been given to relevant units of the SAF, particularly regarding training (Silwer 2012). Tactically, the SAF seem to have little to learn from OMLT experiences. Even though some units have had useful experiences of mountainous operations, for instance, 'the Afghan experiences still indicate that established knowledge prevails' (Walldén & Gyhagen 2011, p. 10). The recurring theme in evaluations of operational activities and combat in Afghanistan is that such experiences do not call for a reevaluation or reassessment of existing doctrine, tactics, training or force structure. And finally, there are no mentoring teams in the Swedish Armed Forces force structure. Sweden's previous experience of mentoring of this kind is limited to a modernization effort of the Ethiopian military in the late 1950s and a training and advisory mission in the Baltics in the end of the 1990s (Agrell 2013, pp. 195–6). It is perhaps the low frequency of such challenges that keeps Sweden from capturing such unique experiences and establishing a standing mentoring capability, which may be seen as unfortunate in light of the subsequent training and advisory mission in Iraq in which SAF participates (Swedish Armed Forces 2015).

Conclusion

The three cases in this brief investigation display several differences regarding tactical adaptation and organizational development at the tactical level. First, they originated in three different ways. The MOT concept was simply adopted as an existing force structure. With Sweden's acceptance of the lead nation role for one of ISAF's PRTs, it was presumably in the position to influence the design of its contribution. Yet the British model was adopted as was. In rather stark contrast, the particular MOT Juliette was the result of one individual's initiative, displaying not only the Force Commander's freedom to adopt his force but also suggesting an apparent indifference on the part of the Armed Forces regarding tactical requirements. And finally, the OMLT kandak came about as a result of international requests. It should be noted that none of these instances constitutes a strategic effort to adapt the organization at the tactical level as a result of requests or requirements from the tactical level. Nor are they the results of national strategic planning.

Second, the three cases came about for three different reasons. Adopting the MOT concept can be seen as accepting a fait accompli. While the seemingly undeterminable tactical effects of the MOT concept raises severe doubts regarding its utility, it can be questioned whether a more stringent force generation process was called for. MOT Juliette, on the other hand, emerged from a perceived intelligence requirement, while OMLT kandak was the outcome of compliance to international requests.

Yet in one respect, the three cases display a significant similarity. In all cases, the strategic level failed to incorporate the experiences made at the tactical level. In the end, this led to marginal imprints on the Armed Forces' force structure in terms of organizational development. The Government's Strategic Directive to the Armed Forces for 2014 displays no changes from previous years that can be traced to experiences from the Afghanistan campaign (Swedish Government 2013). However, smaller adjustments may be hidden in the design of single units of the force structure, and most definitely in the personal experiences of the many officers and soldiers who served during the campaign.

The results suggest a significant gap between the processes of strategic force transformation and tactical adaptation. A possible explanation for this gap is the difference in character between the two. While force transformation is an institutionalized, bureaucratic process of great political significance (not least for budgetary reasons) both in the Government and within the Armed Forces itself, the Armed Forces appears to be struggling with its 'lessons learned' concept. In the many interviews that I have conducted with officers who have served in Afghanistan, a recurring theme is a striking lack of interest regarding their experiences. As one previous Force Commander put it, when you rotate home and the after-action briefing is done, interest seems to vanish. It could be that there is simply no room for tactical experiences in the highly deductive process of force transformation. Another possibility is that participation in international operations is seen as something extracurricular, despite the Government's and the Armed Forces' explicit emphasis on international operations as a part of both Swedish foreign policy and the Armed Forces' core missions. Or in other words, international operations is something odd that certain parts of the Armed Forces have been occupied with, while other parts have been preparing for a future war on their own territory.

In this almost hostile environment, the Swedish forces in Afghanistan appear to have lived a separate and parallel life next to the regular, domestic Armed Forces, constituting something of a parenthesis in Swedish security policy. In no instance has tactical adaptation lead to bottom-up change of the force structure in the manner that Farrell envisions in his theory. This is not to say that no experience at the tactical level has led to more overarching and long-term change. Particular functional experiences, such as the use of the Tactical Air Control Parties or the very real battlefield work conducted by Mobile Medical Teams, have probably generated important insights into the training and equipping of their counterparts in the Swedish force structure.

The extensive experiences of the Improvised Explosive Device Disposal teams have continually fed the training and equipping of the mine-clearing teams of the Swedish Armed Forces: a development that has also benefited the force in Afghanistan.[9] Last but obviously not least, a significant number of the Armed Forces' future leaders has experienced their career-defining moments in Afghanistan.[10] However, the results of this investigation indicate that the experiences of the MOTs, MOT Juliette and OMLT kandak have had limited impact on force transformation.

Notes

1 Yet he points out that a small change (an adaptation) at the strategic level may well be very significant.
2 Which Russell unfortunately calls 'innovation'.
3 The US DoD *Office of Force Transformation* (OFT) was established in October of 2001, and NATO's *Allied Command Transformation* (ACT) was established in 2003.
4 Somewhat ironically, the RG-32M had to be 'mission adapted' after initial deployment in Afghanistan.
5 One MOT commander argues that some adjustments in the Swedish light infantry (ranger) units can be conceptually traced to individual MOT members' experiences; for example, the capability to liaison with local key leaders.
6 For example, electronic warfare systems and unmanned aerial vehicles, which have been continuously evaluated in theatre. Many officers that I have spoken to suggest that several such systems have been forced on the deployed force in order to seize a golden opportunity for battle testing.
7 According to Sandstrom, the label Juliette was merely a consequence of the letter J being the next available one for naming MOTs. Under slightly different circumstances it would have been called MOT Kilo or MOT Lima.
8 The other is Commander.
9 These observations were made in several interviews with operators of those units in a related research project.
10 I credit this insight to Dr Jan Willem Honig at King's College, London.

References

Agrell, W. (2013) *Ett krig har och nu: Fran svensk fredsoperation till upprorsbekampning i Afghanistan 2001–2014* [*A war here and now: From Swedish peaceoperation to insurgency fighting in Afghanistan*]. Stockholm: Atlantis.

Alberts, D.S., J.J. Garstka & F.P. Stein (1999) *Network centric warfare: Developing and leveraging information superiority*. Washington, D.C.: National Defense University Press.

Berts, H., R. Egnell & P. Hojem (2013) *Implementing a gender perspective in military organisations and operations: The Swedish Armed Forces model*. Uppsala: Uppsala University.

Brittain, J.R. (2008) 'Civil–military interaction: Practical experiences of a PRT commander' in Feichtinger, W. & M. Gauster (Eds) *Zivil–militärische zusammenarbeit am beispiel Afghanistan, civil–military interaction: challenges and chances*. Wien: Landesverteidigungsakademie, pp. 123–30.

Cohen, E.A. (2004) 'Change and transformation in military affairs' *Journal of Strategic Studies* Vol. 27, No. 3, pp. 395–407.
Egnell, R., P. Hojem & H. Berts, 2014. *Gender, military effectiveness and organizational change: The Swedish model.* New York: Palgrave.
Farrell, T., (2010) 'Improving in war: Military adaptation and the British in Helmand province, Afghanistan, 2006–2009' *Journal of Strategic Studies* Vol. 33, No. 4, pp. 567–94.
Farrell, T. (2013) 'Introduction: Military adaptation in war' in Farrell, T., F.P.B. Osinga & J.A. Russell (Eds) *Military adaptation in Afghanistan.* Stanford: Stanford University Press, pp. 1–23.
Farrell, T. & S. Rynning (2010) 'NATO's transformation gaps: Transatlantic differences and the war in Afghanistan' *Journal of Strategic Studies* Vol. 33, No. 5, pp. 673–99.
Farrell, T. & T. Terriff (2010) 'Military transformation in NATO: A framework for analysis' in Terriff, T., F. Osinga & T. Farrell (Eds) *A transformation gap? American innovations and European military change.* Stanford: Stanford Security Studies, pp. 1–13.
Grissom, A. (2006) 'The future of military innovation studies' *Journal of Strategic Studies*, Vol. 29, No. 5, pp. 905–34.
Grissom, A. (2010) 'Making it up as we go along: State-building, critical theory and military adaptation in Afghanistan' *Conflict, Security & Development* Vol. 10, No. 4, pp. 493–517.
Hamilton, D.S. (2004) 'What is transformation and what does it mean for NATO?' in Hamilton, D.S. (Ed) *Transatlantic transformations: Equipping NATO for the 21st century.* Washington D.C.: Johns Hopkins University, pp. 3–23.
Hansen, V.V., H. Luras & T. Nikolaisen (2011) 'Operational mentoring and liasion teams (OMLT): The Norwegian army and their afghan partners' *Policy Brief.* Oslo: Norwegian Institute of International Affairs.
Johnsson, M. (Forthcoming 2016) Strategic colonels. *The professional discretion of Swedish force commanders in Afghanistan 2006–2014.* Uppsala: Uppsala University.
Liander, M. (2011) 'Operational mentoring and liasion team (del 1)' *Arménytt*, 2011 No. 1, pp. 13–17.
NATO (2003) *New NATO transformation command established in Norfolk.* Available online at www.nato.int/docu/update/2003/06-june/e0618a.htm (accessed 17 March 2016).
Nilsson, R. (2013) 'Mentorering av afghansk infanteribataljon' [Mentoring of an Afghan infantry batallion] *Tidskrift i Sjovasendet.* Stockholm: Kungl. Orlogsmannasallskapet.
Obama, B. (2011) *Remarks by the President on the way forward in Afghanistan.* Washington, DC: The White House.
Onley, D.S. (2006) *DOD ends think-tank effort* Vienna, VA: GCN. Available from: http://gcn.com/articles/2006/09/08/dod-ends-thinktank-effort.aspx (accessed 7 March 2013).
Russell, J.A. (2011) *Innovation, transformation, and war: Counterinsurgency operations in Anbar and Ninewa, Iraq, 2005–2007.* Stanford: Stanford Security Studies.
Silwer, A. (2012) *Erfarenheter fran militar mentorverksamhet i Afghanistan* [*Experiences from military mentoring in Afghanistan*]. Stockholm: Forsvarsmakten.
Sorenson, K. & J.J. Widén (2014) 'Irregular warfare and tactical changes: The case of Somali piracy' *Terrorism and Political Violence* Vol. 26, No. 3, pp. 399–418.

Swedish Armed Forces (2009) *Minnesbok FS14. Afghanistan okt 2007–maj 2008* [*Memories from FS14. Afghanistan Oct 2007 – May 2008*]. Stockholm: Forsvarsmakten.

Swedish Armed Forces (2015) *Svensk militar insats i Irak* [*Swedish military mission in Iraq*]. Stockholm: Forsvarsmakten. Available online at www.forsvarsmakten.se/sv/aktuellt/2015/04/svensk-militar-insats-i-irak (accessed 9 June 2015).

Swedish Defence Materiel Administration (2013) *Terrangbilen Galten* [*Crosscountry truck Galten*]. Stockholm: Forsvarets materielverk. Available online at www.fmv.se/sv/Projekt/RG-32-M---Galten/ (accessed 19 August 2013).

Swedish Goverment (2007) *Regeringens proposition 2006/07:83. Fortsatt svenskt deltagande i den internationella sakerhetsstyrkan i Afghanistan* [*Continued Swedish participation in the international security force in Afghanistan*]. Stockholm: Regeringen.

Swedish Government (2013) *Regleringsbrev för budgetaret 2014 avseende forsvarsmakten* [Directions for the fiscal year 2014 SAF]. Stockholm: Forsvarsdepartementet.

Terriff, T., F.P.B. Osinga & T. Farrell (2010) *A transformation gap?: American innovations and European military change*. Stanford: Stanford Security Studies.

United States Dept. of the Army (2007) *The US Army/Marine Corps counterinsurgency field manual: US Army field manual no. 3–24: Marine Corps warfighting publication no. 3–33.5*. Chicago: University of Chicago Press.

USMC (2009) *US Marine Corps S&T strategic plan*. Quantico: United States Marine Corps.

Walldén, M. & P. Gyhagen (2011) *Rapport erfarenhetsspel 'OMLT – ANSF' V 115* [*Report from a training experience OMLT – ANSF*]. Kvarn: Markstridsskolan.

Westerdahl, F. (2006) 'Provincial reconstruction team: nagra erfarenheter' [PRT: some experiences] *Kungliga krigsvetenskapsakademins handlingar och tidskrift*, No. 2, pp. 111–19.

Interviews

Interview 1: Interview with MOT Commander of FS 19.
Interview 2: Interview with J5 Plans Officer at SAF Joint Command.
Interview 3: Interview with Lieutenant Colonel Olof Schylander, Commander of the Swedish ISAF contingent 2003–04.
Interview 4: Interview with Major Frederick Westerdahl, MOT Commander in 2004.
Interview 5: Interview with previous MOT Commander in Sar-e Pul province.
Interview 6: Interview with previous MOT Commander in Balkh province.
Interview 7: Interview with previous PO Commander in Jowzjan province.
Interview 8: Interview with previous MOT Training Officer at the Swedish Armed Forces International Center (SWEDINT).
Interview 9: Interview with Armed Forces Joint Command Staff Officer.
Interview 10: Interview with previous rifle company Commander.
Interview 11: Interview with Training Officer at the Swedish Armed Forces International Center (SWEDINT).
Interview 12: Interview with Colonel Bengt Sandstrom, Commander of FS11.
Interview 13: Interview with MOT Commander of FS11.
Interview 14: Interview with Staff Officer at the Nordic Center for Gender in Military Operations at SWEDINT.
Interview 15: Interview with Lieutenant Roger Nilsson, Commander of OMLT Kandak, FS22.
Interview 16: Interview with former OMLT Company Mentor.

6 Military–technological aspects of the Swedish mission to Afghanistan

Ake Sivertun

Background

In international peace support operations, the political goals must be clear, and only objectives consistent with international and humanitarian law are accepted in Sweden as rationales for the use of military force in such operations. With respect to military action, there are strategic, operational and tactical subgoals. These goals have to be flexible to some extent, since armed conflicts involve external as well as internal 'friction'. Military operations have an inner dynamic, with actions and counteractions leading to new situations and demands on the military personnel and equipment. External friction includes, for example, the physical conditions set by geography and climate (Sivertun 2012). Availability of resources, including basic material and industrial capacity, transport, energy and human resources are other important constraints. These factors, however, interact sometimes in compensatory ways so that, for example, high quality in equipment, education and training can make up for shortcomings in other areas. A capability to respond quickly and adapt to changing conditions and requirements also counts. As Lorber (2002) describes, a carefully designed, interdisciplinary process built on deep insights is important in deciding what systems of equipment to choose and how to use them. Learning organizations and processes for lessons learned, including the capacity to add or replace equipment and methods and introduce more suitable ones, are also important.

As stated in the introductory chapters in this book, the Afghanistan mission has been long, extremely complex and has gone through several major changes in focus over the years. This makes it a suitable object of study if we want to illuminate the responses to this kind of dynamic and friction. The purpose of this chapter is to analyze the consequences of the more than decade-long Swedish military engagement in Afghanistan for the development of central elements of Swedish military technology. It is a literature study that uses open sources. This created some problems, as, for example, causes for casualties in the Swedish contingent were not open. However, some figures – for example, from the Canadian contingent – could be used for illustration of the situation during different phases of the engagement, presuming that partly similar conditions were also valid for the Swedish forces.

The procedures for procurement are important in introducing new equipment and replacing old equipment. Sweden has a long tradition of developing and producing weapons and systems. This is the result of the desire to be independent that was inherent in the policy of neutrality, but it is also due to the fact that the defence sector has traditionally constituted a relatively high proportion of Sweden's industrial base. Furthermore, the system of military conscript service for all men demanded the acquisition of military systems that were relatively robust and easy to use by soldiers with limited military education and training. For these reasons, Sweden maintained its own military–industrial organization for development and production of various weapon systems on land, at sea and in the air.

During the last decades, however, the internationalization of the defence industry – together with political preferences and reductions in defence expenditures – have put Sweden in a position in which it now mostly procures military systems that are available on the market rather than producing its own. In addition, a Swedish desire to form alliances with others (mainly the Nordic countries) and demands for counter-purchase attached to the export of military systems (such as submarines, artillery and jet fighters) determine the sources for new materiel. Thus, Sweden's sale of SAAB JAS 39 GRIPEN fighter aircraft to South Africa entailed the counter-purchase of new armed vehicles as the situation in Afghanistan changed into more open battles – including the use of road bombs, also known as Improvised Explosive Devices (IEDs).

The road bombs led to some casualties, creating a demand for more robust vehicles. Multinational procurement of the NH Industries NH90 Helicopter (Swedish designation Hkp14) also had implications for the Swedish Afghanistan operation in that the procurement process was delayed – partly because of a complicated cooperation between four different helicopter industries, but also as a result of different (and sometimes changing) requirements formulated by the customers. In order to acquire important equipment in time, a special fast track was introduced in particularly sensitive cases of defence procurement (Pettersson 2012). Such a case was the weapon station ordered together with a reinforced version of the South Africa-produced BAE Land Systems OMC RG32M (Swedish designation Terrangbil 16 'Galten'). Another was the order for a number of Blackhawk UH-60M helicopters (Swedish designation Hkp 16) pending final delivery of the Hkp 14.

How are dynamics and frictions dealt with? Information and Communication Technology (ICT) facilities can improve the utility of physical objects and aid in substituting for numbers. They can also substitute for production and transport and facilitate cost-effective missions through the use of fewer resources within the same time and with lower losses. Knowing where, when and how an enemy is active makes it easier to allocate and use resources in an optimal manner to defeat it. With the help of sensors and computers to fusion data and analyze the information, it is possible to use different platforms and their systems together. Geographical intelligence and personnel building a Spatial Data Infrastructure, will be more important together with education in how to utilize this information in faster cycles of Command, Control and Communication (C3) (Brehmer 2005). This requirement for improved ICT skills in response to situations in which enemies are making greater use of modern ICT for coordinating their activities is evident in Afghanistan. Insurgents are also using ICT for their C3, as well as in placing IEDs. Rutgersson *et al.* (2011) claim that the window of opportunity for an artillery unit to engage an enemy is only approximately 6 minutes from the identification of a target. Modern weapon systems also require high-precision location coordinates for both the artillery unit and the target. All these factors increase the need for GEO intelligence and systems. In Afghanistan, a Geo Cell was established to produce digital maps that were fusioned with intelligence reports to form a base for plans and orders, and was vital for engagement.

ICT functions are dependent on military technology. Data capture depends on satellites, airplanes, unmanned aerial vehicles (UAVs) and land-surveying instruments as well as Global Navigation Satellite Systems (GNSS): for example, GPS satellites and positioning equipment. In making use of this hardware and software, it is necessary to handle, fusion, analyze and mediate the information. Several of the functions are now available in civilian applications such as low-cost smartphones. Advanced systems science skills must be employed to counter such threats, even those coming from low-tech enemies. In addition to running the systems and understanding how the information should be translated into relevant actions – for example, personnel with relevant education – training and exercises are needed (ISO/IEC/IEEE 42010 2011).

Tactics and technology in the Afghanistan mission

Military missions involve different tactics, and technology interacts with these in various ways. The defeat of an enemy can be achieved by decapitating him or hindering him from using his resources. Winning the hearts and minds of the people is another way to prevail, but in Afghanistan the operation developed in a negative direction, as the enemy managed to manoeuvre in a way that led the foreign forces to respond with more military power and protection.

In order to fight an enemy, it is necessary to know both the geographical and climatological conditions of the field and the game that is played there. Knowledge of the area and the mission is essential. A common problem concerning expeditionary missions like the one in Afghanistan is that familiarity with basic geographic data, as well as information about climate, weather and other conditions, is often missing. The equipment should, however, be suitable – for the region, the climate, the tactical situation and the trained personnel. Furthermore, the instructions given should be possible to follow and the results should be achievable.

In a speech on 12 February 2002 at the Department of Defense, the US Secretary of Defense, Donald Rumsfeld, remarked:

> as we know, there are known knowns; there are things we know we know. We also know there are known unknowns; that is to say we know there are some things we do not know. But there are also unknown unknowns – the ones we don't know we don't know.
>
> (Rumsfeld, 2002)

Perhaps only the last question remained unanswered when Swedish soldiers and officers were sent to Afghanistan to support the International Security Assistance Force (ISAF) beginning at the turn of the year 2001/02.

The Swedish Special Forces unit sent at that time had a very flexible procedure for procuring equipment and was trained to provide security in cities like Kabul, which was its first mission. Later on, the Swedish mission's task was to provide safety in Mazar-e-Sharif under British command. Its acquisitions were then partly coordinated with the British, and the choice of equipment was guided by the prevailing security and political situation. The vehicles chosen (Land Rovers) were unprotected according to common specifications related to the 'hearts and minds tactic', while also communicating that this was a peacekeeping action.

In March 2006, Sweden assumed the responsibility for security in Mazar-e-Sharif and four provinces in the North, and a joint Camp (Northern Lights) for the Nordic contingent in the area was built in the town. The assignment was to hand over the responsibility for security to the civilian authorities, but the situation changed significantly, with several attacks from insurgents and some casualties. This led to a discussion about a changed tactic and what military technological capabilities such a change would require.

As on most foreign missions, the number of soldiers wounded and killed in Afghanistan to a certain extent consists of various non-battle accidents, as shown in the figures appearing in Swedish and Canadian lists of wounded and killed. The total number of casualties in the civil war in Afghanistan is, however, relatively high, with tens of thousands of civilians, 4,000 ISAF soldiers and civilian contractors as well as over 10,000 soldiers of the Afghan National Security Forces killed (McChrystal 2011). Five Swedish soldiers have been killed in action since 2005: three in two separate IED incidents and two in an ambush by an insurgent wearing an Afghanistan National Police (ANP) uniform: a so-called 'Green on Blue' action. At least 13 soldiers were wounded (Swedish Armed Forces 2011). In addition, two local translators working with the Swedish Provincial Reconstruction Team (PRT) have been killed (Swedish Armed Forces 2014). Since there is no official Swedish statement on the causes of the Swedish casualties, Canadian statistics are used here to show the causes of deaths for a similar force. If we assume that the situation was similar for Swedish and Canadian soldiers, with the reservation that Canada was active in districts with a higher numbers of insurgents and reported fights, we at least have a rough picture of the situation and the need for suitable military equipment and applied tactics. This compilation of data shows that most of the Canadian deaths (n=97) were caused by explosives (IEDs), 22 by direct fire and 13 by suicide bombers. In addition, 26 soldiers were killed in accidents or died from other causes, including friendly fire (n=6). These figures could indicate the proportions between causes (Canada News Centre 2011).

What does this information tell us about tactics and materiel/military technology needs? One conclusion that can perhaps be drawn is that improved personnel protection – both on the individual and on the group levels – would have been beneficial to reduce the casualties, as well as better-protected vehicles and improved intelligence to make it possible to identify road segments and places suitable for attacks by insurgents (Woundable Points). In the US Army, there is a common practice among soldiers and officers to buy certain military equipment in so-called 'PX Shops' and on the internet. This habit of buying such equipment and using it in service to some extent spread to the Swedish personnel. The reasons behind it can be many. In some cases it is a method of obtaining items that is faster than the normal acquisition process. It can also be a way of acquiring equipment that is more suitable in size, shape and function. Unfortunately, the motives for buying equipment in PX Shops are also largely built on rumours, misunderstandings and fashion. Moreover, mismatches between equipment provided by the Armed Forces and equipment bought by the soldiers could increase the risk of injuries in case of enemy fire.

When it came to vehicles, things were a bit more complicated. Here, the acquisition of the armoured BAE Land Systems OMC RG32M offered some improvements for the operations. The experience indicated, however, that the vehicle had to be reinforced with additional protection, which was applied as heavy armour in the form of steel plates. This resulted in reduced payload and limited speed and range, thereby degrading the elements of protection provided by mobility and the ability to act militarily. The additional weight also had implications for service intervals and fuel consumption. A generally well-functioning vehicle had, in this case, to be used in a way different from that for which it was designed: limiting the capacity of the contingent to fulfil the political and military goals.

The Swedish force quite quickly had to ask for the heavier CV90 Battle vehicle in order to obtain the necessary protection and firepower. The Canadian contingent soon had to replace its Leopard 1 with new Leopard 2 A6 heavy tanks in the outposts that had earlier suffered from frequent attacks. Only when these tanks were introduced – together with improved systems for infrared (IR) detection of attacking insurgents – did it become possible to stabilize the situation and reduce the number of casualties (Canadian American Strategic Review 2011).

The German troops employed new UAVs with IR sensors flying in front of the vehicles to identify insurgents hiding and waiting to ambush German transports. However, after a short period of success some insurgents acquired heat-reflective survival blankets to hide under. In this way, the enemy managed to avoid detection by the IR sensors on the UAVs and was able to attack successfully when the area was no longer surveyed. This development occurred in very fast cycles of less than 6 months. However, the national acquisition process was longer and placed the enemy in favourable positions. This again indicates that, in many cases, the introduction of new equipment and new tactics must be much faster in order to retain the initiative.

Things that may seem trivial regarding equipment used in combat and other dangerous situations also matter. A previously well-suited rack for personnel weapons in the vehicles became impossible to use when a modified version of the personnel weapon (rifle) was introduced. Suddenly the rifles had to be placed on the floor until a new technical solution was found to mount the weapons more safely and make it easier to retrieve and use them under an attack (Anonymous, 2015). This is another example of how important it is to have a functional system for lessons learned in order to make professional and scientifically-founded evaluations and modifications of equipment and their tactical use.

Doctrine/strategy and equipment/military technology

During the Soviet occupation of Afghanistan, the Soviet Army had big problems with matching doctrine and equipment, as described by McMichael:

> Conventional Soviet doctrine ran aground in the DRA (Democratic Republic of Afghanistan) against two related obstacles: the physical environment and the threat. Instead of a moderate climate and the open terrain of Europe, Soviet forces found desert and highly restrictive, mountainous terrain, with severe extremes of weather and temperature. In addition, the local logistical infrastructure and road and rail networks were quite undeveloped. Besides severely restricting movement of heavy forces, these factors also created major problems in command and control. Vehicle breakdowns were frequent owing to inferior maintenance, shortfalls in repair, driver inexperience, and general wear and tear on the vehicles. Furthermore, the Soviet logistical structure for both the ground and air components initially proved unequal to the task of supporting such an unwieldy force in such inhospitable terrain.
>
> (McMichael 1990)

The Soviet solution to these problems was to switch from mainly ground-based operations to airborne ones. This was not an option for the Swedish forces in Afghanistan, but the coalition of forces soon got into a similar situation of relying on air transport and airborne missions. Sweden needed helicopters, but those were still under procurement and unavailable. Technology and tactics must be part of procurement, but must also influence achievable strategic goals! One lesson learned is perhaps that the political, strategic and tactical levels of decision-making must be more linked in order to ensure that needs are met and ambitions adjusted according to the changing situation. Seeing policies, strategies, organization and practices as separate entities is not fruitful; a systemic approach in which all of these factors correspond with each other is a necessity.

One example of the need for such a coordinated process is the procurement of helicopters for the Swedish Armed Forces. The Helicopter 14 (NH Industries NH90) is one of the most advanced helicopters available. It was not available on the market when Sweden, together with several other nations, ordered it in 2001. It has not been delivered yet (2015) but is estimated to be fully in service in 2020.

The deployment of two medical evacuation (medevac) helicopters in Afghanistan in 2011 was a direct initiative by the Swedish Minister of Defence. Due to a lack of suitable helicopters in the Armed Forces, two older HKP 10 (Super Puma) helicopters had to be modified as gap fillers for this specific task; however, they could not be fully operational because of their general configuration and were replaced after only one year by American MH-60 (Black Hawk) helicopters, which were more suitable for the extreme Afghan conditions. This is an example of an unusual political interference in the Afghanistan-related procurement process that unfortunately contributed in only a minor way to the military capacity in Afghanistan. Perhaps it had a political dimension not analyzed here. Anyway, the decision to modify these helicopters was not based on an analysis of what was optimal for the needs of the Swedish Armed Forces (Stensson 2009).

This affair was a catalyst for the procurement of a larger number of MH-60s to fill the gap after the HKP 10 and the new HKP 14. In the end, the delay in the procurement process resulted in the acquisition of very advanced and useful military equipment. Partly because of experiences from the Afghanistan mission, in which logistical aspects as well as the feasibility of defending and protecting the systems against different threats were important, these design specifications were emphasized and have been possible to satisfy to a high degree in the final version of the helicopter. When the process is evaluated, the negative experiences regarding time to design, order, deliver and register the vehicles (allowing them to fly also in civilian airspace) have to be weighed against the positive aspects of a very good flying system as the end result.

Systems for evaluating and sometimes redesigning military equipment are especially important, since most nations today have fewer but more sophisticated items of equipment. This is also the reason why it is necessary to draw the right conclusions from experiences in use and training. Information systems and procedures needed to record problems with equipment and adjust the subsystems, and/or the tactics must be present to get the most out of them. The analysis must also include enemy equipment, opportunities and threats, together with tactical considerations in planning and re-planning missions. Military Weapons Intelligence Teams (WITs), representing a military application of technology capacity, were deployed by the US military forces and their allies during the 2003 Iraq War and grew during the Afghanistan mission. Finding out in detail what equipment and methods were used by the enemy was often the key to identifying groups and individuals involved in terrorism and military attacks and to developing countermeasures. It was thus possible to speed up the processes, from identification of problems and mismatches with enemy systems to the drawing of correct conclusions. However, efficient systems to handle and correct them within the needed time frame are still lacking.

The mission context: managing both constants and change

It is important to weigh military practice against other circumstances. Sometimes the use of a sophisticated or powerful weapon can have a negative effect on public opinion or lead to desperate acts by the enemy. In addition to support through intelligence, planning, logistics and weapon systems, data from Information Systems (IS) can be used for simulations and training relating to a mission and for planning psychological operations within one's own forces and against enemy forces, as well as in civil society.

The geographical and climatological conditions in an area constitute the operational frame, encompassing the basic obstacles and opportunities for military operations at all command levels. In the 1830s, the Russian Foreign Minister, Count Karl von Nesselrode, described the battle with the British for the Afghan mountain passes Khyber and Khojak as the 'Great Game'. At that time, control of these areas was regarded as the key to controlling India. The British, however, failed three times to conquer Afghanistan. Certain technical advances, such as the development of sea transports, still made it possible to maintain the colonial control of India. The 'Great Game' chessboard was transformed into a game of controlling the sea transports through steamboats and by building the Suez Canal.

When the Soviet Union invaded Afghanistan in 1979 it was warned about the severe conditions in the country and that message was passed on by the Russians to the Western allies when they intervened in 2001. Although the fighting parties and the technologies with which the war was fought were different, the mountains were the same, and the ambushes and attacks occurred in almost the same places as during all previous wars in the history of Afghanistan. Moreover, it was still difficult to win the hearts and minds of the Afghan population.

Friction in war caused by geographical and climatological conditions can be overcome by technological and tactical adjustments. The question in the case of Afghanistan was whether the allied forces could make those adjustments in a successful way or whether there were other ways to meet the challenges. Civil means to achieve goals that are usually measured in military terms are sometimes more effective than military means, according to recent research (Ingelstam & Mellbourn 2014). However, law, order and stability must be enforced to provide an environment in which it is possible to build schools and infrastructure and to develop the economy as well as other elements of the civil society. The social and political landscape is another factor of importance in changing the incentives for fighting and supporting criminals or insurgents.

What is the most successful way to establish law and order in a country like Afghanistan according to prevailing experience? Several commentators, including the Swedish National Audit Office (2011), have criticized the Swedish engagement in Afghanistan. Their criticism was partly directed towards the political process that led at first to the decisions by the Swedish Parliament in 2001, to send a group of military personnel to participate in a peacekeeping mission, and then to the situation that lasted until the end of 2014, in which the soldiers were more or less involved in combat. Others have pointed out the different problems concerning the changes of command of the engagement in Afghanistan, in which the ISAF was initially formed with a weak UN mandate and, from 2003, was under NATO command. In parallel, the US Operation Enduring Freedom (OEF) worked to establish Hamid Karzai as an interim President and tried to build alliances with the different warlords and clan leaders in Afghanistan. As such, the political situation and mandate were not clear from the beginning, and changed significantly during the time of mission.

The goal of the mission also changed several times during the engagement. This situation has not been favourable, if we still consider war to be a continuation of *politics* by other means. Perhaps if we use the somewhat misinterpreted idea that war is *policies* by other means, we can understand the debate in which several authors claim that the whole engagement leaves Afghanistan in a worse state than it was in before (Ingelstam & Mellbourn 2014).

Others, such as former US Secretary of Defense Robert Gates (2014), claim that the tactical change towards counterinsurgent (COIN) operations was the reason for the decline in the number of victims of terrorist attacks. However, the new tactic could not be introduced until 2010, after the US deployment of Unmanned Combat Aerial Vehicles (UCAVs). This, together with forensic methods to identify the insurgents' command chain and those responsible for attacks against the allied forces, made it possible for the US forces to eliminate the enemy. The development of casualties from IEDs and other attacks during the period 2005–13 follow each other fairly well (Gates 2014), which could support the argument that technology and tactical moves must follow each other and be very carefully analyzed – both when one's own new technology is introduced and when new enemy technological applications occur as new use of old technology.

Changes at the national level and the Swedish policy of engagement in Afghanistan

Since the late 1990s, we have seen a new agenda for the Swedish Armed Forces. Previously there was a compulsory military service based on conscription of all men, but this system faded out because only a small portion of the cohort was recruited and those recruited received a very limited military training. Today, Sweden has a professional Army, Navy and Air Force with expeditionary capabilities that can be used under international mandate from, for example, the United Nations. The trend is, however, that the Armed Forces should again be more focused on defending Swedish territory.

The Swedish military doctrine has changed from acquiring military technological systems – mainly developed and produced in Sweden in accordance with the old policy of independence in peace and neutrality in war – to embracing a procedure in which equipment is procured 'off the shelf' on the international market. As exemplified here, the results of this shift are sometimes successful and sometimes controversial. Some of the new materiel is acquired as compensatory trade against airplanes from SAAB; submarines from Kockums (previously ThyssenKrupp, but recently SAAB); radar systems from Ericsson (now SAAB); artillery from Bofors/BAE Systems, combat vehicles from Hägglunds BAE Systems and so on. The current situation, in which huge weapon systems have been replaced with fewer and potentially smarter systems ('leaner but meaner'), has possibly influenced the opportunity for soldiers and officers to change or upgrade equipment according to new requirements and in this way fulfil their tasks.

The first Swedish unit deployed in Afghanistan belonged to a special protection force (Särskilda Skyddsgruppen or SSG, now SOG) within the Swedish Armed Forces. This force had its own procurement of equipment and was engaged in traditional military operations at the beginning of the mission. In the spring of 2002, the ISAF mission was taken over by NATO, with a widened mandate to operate in 2003. By 2008, it was clear that Swedish personnel – as a result of the inner military logic – was part of a counterinsurgency operation that went beyond the original mission formulation given in the decision by Parliament. The first unit worked under British command as a security force to support the Afghan authorities. Meanwhile, the US OEF and the United Nations Assistance Mission in Afghanistan (UNAMA) – supporting the Afghan Government's Disarmament, Demobilization and Reintegration program (DDR) – worked to demobilize the different armed fractions that remained after the war against the Taliban. UNAMA managed, according to its own statistics, to disarm 62,000 former Afghan soldiers during the period 2002–05. Whether this is correct is debatable, as several former soldiers let themselves be re-recruited by different warlords after the economic compensation for disarmament was paid. In 2009, the NATO/ISAF operation was merged with the American OEF operations under US command. During this period, the armed attacks from the insurgents and other groups escalated (Gates 2014).

A Swedish national audit in 2011 reported serious shortcomings with regard to Sweden's contributions to international efforts, not least participation in the UN-mandated NATO presence in Afghanistan, in which Sweden was in charge of one of the 25 Provincial Reconstruction Teams (PRTs). A review of this engagement makes it absolutely clear that there are interoperability problems between and within the various interested communities. One of the reasons on the Swedish side lies in a historically-grounded doctrine that the Government gives the state agencies directives on what to do, not how to do it. The implication is that ministers must not interfere with the work of the agencies, which as a consequence are very independent. Furthermore, there is no comprehensive architecture for Sweden's comprehensive approach to the engagement in the PRTs. Some corrective action lines were presented by the national auditors, with several points inspired by experiences in the Armed Forces. High-level architecture and systems thinking were two means suggested by which to solve the problems of coordinating the efforts regarding the PRT mission.

Lack of systemic thinking in e-Governance

In 2004, The Swedish National Audit Office (2004) found that there were serious shortcomings in the Government's management of the state agencies' use of information and communication technology (e-Gov): a fact that was detrimental to citizens and industry, as well as to the agencies themselves. These problems were also noted by several authors who had been working to promote a modern Swedish e-Gov strategy (Charas et al. 2007, Lind et al. 2009, Ostberg 2010). A further question that could be asked is whether the development of e-Gov could also have been beneficial for fast procurement processes in the Armed Forces.

In 2011, the Swedish National Audit Office (2011) again found that there were serious shortcomings in the Government's management, this time with regard to Swedish contributions to international efforts. Against the background of the e-Gov experience, Sweden's participation in the PRTs in Afghanistan was also criticized. In both cases, the focus is that the Swedish Government is using an extreme version of management via state agencies. The group of central offices is itself an agency, and every single contact between the Government and citizens, industry and society at large takes place within the perimeters of the 500-plus independent agencies, which act as isolated 'islands': some very big and some very small. Unless the agencies are specifically instructed to team up with other agencies – and are provided with a team-up-budget – cross-agency projects and services are few and far between. Swedish participation in international efforts is an area in which cross-agency involvement is a necessity but, as pointed out by the aforementioned 2011 audit, has yet to be implemented. Policy must in such cases be followed by politics in which the ideas are implemented in practice.

With respect to the PRT activity in Afghanistan, diplomacy was handled by the Ministry of Foreign Affairs; military action by the Ministry of Defence together with the Swedish Armed Forces; development cooperation by the Swedish International Development Agency (SIDA), and civilian operations by the Ministry of Justice, the Folke Bernadotte Academy, the Swedish Civil

Contingencies Agency and the Swedish National Police Board (Ingelstam & Mellbourn 2014). Operational problems with the bureaucracy also appear at the European level. Unclear roles and a deficit of competent staff in several areas can sometimes delay the process, making it difficult to act in time and to take advantage of a situation (Kusz 2014).

Conclusions

The Swedish decision to participate in the peace-support operation in Afghanistan was based on unclear goals. Moreover, the situation in Afghanistan changed substantially over time, precipitating new requirements and changes of policy but also affecting the strategies, organization and practices to implement the intentions and technologies needed to fulfil the mission. Afghanistan's geography and climate are so different fom Sweden's that equipment suitable and effective in a Swedish context does not fit very well. When it came to maps and other sources of geographical intelligence, this capability was gradually built up during the mission with Geo Cells. To what extent the experiences from that part of the engagement will spill over to the present situation, with a more national defence in Sweden, is unclear. However, updated and properly indexed geo-information is needed in modern military activities as well as in civil–military operations, since natural catastrophes sometimes cause more fatalities than combat activities. These resources must accordingly be maintained so as to provide both politicians and organizations with the tools and methods necessary to reach their goals. If the goal is to win 'hearts and minds', active participation in rescue operations can be important. If peacekeeping is regarded as the main objective, it is important that the military forces can protect themselves from attacks and find ways to avoid damage caused by environmental and climatological events. Distribution of resources is often a source of conflict. Roads and transport routes are essential both to civil society and to the military forces. In sparsely populated areas, such as those in Sweden, the possibility to move and act even in roadless terrain is important, and so are wireless communication capabilities.

In all environments, access to updated information about the Area of Operation (AOR) or the playground and about the manoeuvres of other players is important for decisions on how to move, act and protect. The geography is often quite stable and possible to include in C4 systems. Today, the German military forces and several others are cooperating with environmental protection and crisis management authorities in sharing synthetic aperture radar (SAR) and other satellite information that can be used to build up a digital base map of the most conflict-prone areas and those most susceptible to environmental emergencies. In case of an event in such an area, the situation and deviations from the normal state can be detected, and this information used as a basis for decisions, simulations and mission planning. Analysis of the demand for equipment and other resources can then be made with higher precision.

Scientifically and professionally evaluated lessons learned must be improved and fully implemented in the Armed Forces in general. Today, only the Swedish Air Force has a no-blame procedure for reports in cases of personal mistakes or reported problems with equipment. Technological intelligence must include not only knowledge about problems and mistakes in the design of systems in use, but also information on how potential adversaries use their weapons or make tactical adjustments to overcome Swedish systems and actions. System thinking has been a prominent endeavour for the Swedish Armed Forces for several decades, and here great improvements can be made through the development of computer systems – as well as other systems based on recent advances in simulations of systems and systems of systems. Combinations with lessons learned are here important for discovering mistakes in prevailing algorithms and models.

Closer cooperation between the political decision-makers and the military organizations is necessary to find the most suitable ambition and means for military defence. When civilian organizations are involved to achieve civil goals, there must be close cooperation that (at the very least) does not produce conflicting directives. Whether or not this is possible in the Swedish administrative culture is another question. The success of military and civil missions abroad is largely dependent on the technological systems used. Those systems must harmonize with the systems of other countries so that they can be used in joint missions. Such harmonization will also benefit missions in Sweden and its close neighbourhood. For improved productivity, the systems must also be understood as systems of systems. This involves the way in which they are used and mutual adjustments between technology, doctrines and tactical considerations – expressed conceptually in the terms *policies, strategies, organization and practices* – perhaps according to a TDOODA[1] decision loop and including military technology considerations (see Brehmer 2008).

Note

1 The Dynamic OODA loop, or DOODA loop (see Brehmer 2008), specifies that three different functions are needed in decision-making: data collection, sense-making and planning. That is, data must be collected via sensors and human observation, these data must be understood in terms of what needs to be done and this understanding must be worked into orders that achieve direction and coordination of the effort. The 'T' in the TDOODA acronym stresses the need to also include the analysis of technological aspects in the DOODA loop.

References

Abbaszadeh, N., M. Crow, M. El-Khoury, J. Gandomi, D. Kuwayama, C. MacPherson, M. Nutting, N. Parker & T. Weiss (2008) *Provincial reconstruction teams: Lessons and recommendations*. Woodrow Wilson School of Public and International Affairs, Princeton University.

Andersson, J., T. Evers & G. Sjöstedt (2011) *Private sector actors & peacebuilding.* Stockholm: Swedish Institute of International Affairs.

Anonymous (2015) Personal communication. April 2015.

Arnell, K *et al.* (2009) 'NATO and Sweden joint live experiment on NEC: A first step towards a NEC realization.' Reference Document DOPD12509. NATO Consultation, Command and Control Agency.

Brehmer, B. (2005) 'The dynamic OODA loop: Amalgamating Boyd's OODA loop and the cybernetic approach to command and control'. Paper presented at the 10th International Command and Control Research and Technology Symposium in McLean, VA.

Brehmer, B. (2008) 'Hur man åstadkommer en snabbare OODA-loop: överste Boyds syn på ledning' [How to aquire a faster OODA-loop: Brigadier general Boyds view of command] *Kungliga Krigsvetenskapsakademins handlingar och tidskrift* [Proceedings of the Royal Swedish Academy of War Sciences] No. 4, 2008, pp. 42–68.

Brehmer, B. (2014) *Insatsledning: Ledningsvetenskap hjälper dig att peka åt rätt håll* [*Command Leadership: 'Ledningsvetenskap' assists you in pointing in the right direction*]. Stockholm: Försvarshögskolan, Elanders.

Bygstad, B. (2010) 'Generative mechanisms for innovation in information infrastructures' *Journal of Information and Organization* Vol. 20, No.3–4, pp.156–68.

Canadian American Strategic Review (CASR) Background – Canadian Tanks to Kandahar – the Leopard C2 Available online at www.casr.ca/bg-leopard-c2-afghan.htm (accessed 3 February 2011).

Canada News Centre (2011) S 11.001 – January 12 Available online at www.forces.gc.ca/en/news/article.page?doc=canadian-forces-casualty-statistics-afghanistan/hie8w9c9 (accessed 5 June 2014).

Charas, P., P. Johannisson & O. Ostberg (2007) 'A philosophy of public service: Architectural principles for digital democracy' *International Journal of Public Information Systems* Vol. 3, No.2, pp. 89–99.

Checkland, P. (1999) *Systems Thinking, Systems Practice.* Chichester: John Wiley & Sons.

Egnell, R. & C. Nilsson, (2011) 'Swedish civil–military cooperation in international efforts: From promising concept to concrete action' *The Royal Swedish Academy of War Sciences Proceedings and Journal*, No.1, 75–93 (in Swedish; English summary).

Eronen, O. (2008) 'PRT models in Afghanistan: approaches to civil–military integration. CMC'. *Finland Civilian Crisis Management Studies*, Vol. 1, No. 5.

European Commission (2010) 'Towards interoperability for European public services'. *COM*, 744.

Frerks, G., B. Klem, S. van Laar & M. van Klingeren (2006) *Principles and pragmatism: civil-military action in Afghanistan and Liberia.* Utrecht: University of Utrecht, Bart Kleim Research Report.

Gates, R.M. (2014) *Duty: Memoirs of a secretary at war.* New York: Alfred A. Knopf.

Godsave, H. (2007) 'The Provincial Reconstruction Team (PRT) model of post conflict intervention: progress in Afghanistan and future Prospects'. M.A. Dissertation. London: King's College.

Gunner, G. & K.-A. Nordquist, (2011) 'An unlikely dilemma: Constructing a partnership between human rights and peace building' *Church of Sweden Research Series* No.4

Haskins, C., (Ed) (2007) *Systems Engineering Handbook: A Guide for System Life Cycle Prcesses and Activities*. Version 3.1. Revised by Forsberg K. & M. Krueger. San Diego, US-CA: INCOSE.

Holland Rose, J. (1915) *The Development of the European Nations, 1870–1914* (5th edition) Release Date: January 9, 2005 [EBook #14644].

Ingelstam, L. & A. Mellbourn (2014) *Fred Säkerhet, Försvar. Tyngdpunktsförskjutning i svensk politik. [Peace, Security, Defence. Changing Balance in Swedish Politics]*. Sveriges kristna råd [Sweden's Christian Council].

ISO/IEC/IEEE 42010 (2011) Systems and software engineering: Architecture description. December 2011.

Klang, M. & J. Nolin (2011) 'To inform or to interact, that is the question: The role of Freedom of Information'. *Social Media Policies, Information Science and Social Media International Conference*, Åbo/Turku, Finland.

Kusz, M. (2014) *Mänsklig säkerhet. Partnerskap 2014 rapport 2013. Fred Säkerhet Försvar. [Human Security. Partnership 2014 Report 2013. Peace Secuity Defence]*. Sveriges kristna råd [Sweden's Christian Council].

Lackenbauer, H. (2011) *Reflections on civil–military cooperation in Afghanistan: Experiences from a political adviser 2009–2010*. Swedish Defense Research Agency. FOI Memo 37093.

Lewin, K. (1951) *Field theory in social science; selected theoretical papers*. D. Cartwright (Ed.). New York: Harper & Row.

Lind, M., O. Ostberg & P. Johannisson, (2009) 'Acting out the Swedish e-Government action plan: mind and mend the gaps. *International Journal of Public Information System*, Vol. 5, No.2, pp. 37–60.

Lorber, A. (2002) *Misguided weapons: technological failure and surprise on the battlefield*. Washington, D.C.: Brassey's, Inc.

McChrystal, S. (2011) 'After 10 years, Afghan war only half done'. *The Guardian*, 7 October.

McMichael S. R. (1990) Soviet tactical performance and adaptation in Afghanistan', *The Journal of Soviet Military Studies*, Vol. 3, No.1, pp. 73–105.

Murray, R. (2011) *A new situation for the foreign service*. Stockholm: The Government Expert Group on Public Economics, ESO 2011: 1.

Norheim-Martinsen, P.M. (2009) *EU capabilities for a comprehensive approach: Broad interoperability as a comparative advantage*. Norwegian Defence Research Establishment, FFI-rapport 2009/01300.

O'Dwyer, G. (2013) 'Sweden's military spending to rise?' *DefenseNews*, February 1.

Ostberg, O. (2010) 'Swedish e-Gov 2010: Where is it coming from and where is it going'. *International Journal of Public Information Systems*, Vol. 6, No.2, pp.149–69.

Ostberg O., P. Johannisson & P.-A. Persson (2013) 'Capability formation architecture for provincial reconstruction in Afghanistan,' In Gotze, J. & A. Jensen-Waud (Eds), *Beyond Alignment: Applying Systems Thinking in Architecting Enterprises. Systems*, Vol. 3, pp 369–98. London: College Publications.

Pettersson, M. (2012) 'Erfarenheter av forcerad materielförsörjning av Vapensystem 01 in Swedish' [Experiences drawn from fast procurement of military equipment]) Examination paper. Stockholm: Swedish Defence University.

Rumsfeld, D. (2012) NATO HQ press conference by US Secretary of Defense, Donald Rumsfeld. Available online at www.nato.int/docu/speech/2002/s020606g.htm (accessed 17 March 2016). Brussels: Department of Defense, 12 February.

Runge, P. (2009) 'The Provincial Reconstruction Teams in Afghanistan: Role model for civil–military relations?' Occasional Paper IV. Bonn: International Centre For Conversion.

Rutgersson, L.-G., P. Eliasson & A. Sivertun (2011) 'Rapid mapping for precision targeting'. UGI 2011. Santiago, Chile, 14–18 November.

Sivertun, A. (2012) 'Militärgeografi och GIS som en del av Militärteknik', [Military geography and GIS as a part of Military technology]. *Kungliga Krigsvetenskapsakademiens Handlingar och Tidskrift* [*Proceedings of the Royal Swedish Academy of War Sciences*] No. 1.

SOU (2011) *A world-class Ministry of Foreign Affairs*. Stockholm: Government Central Offices, SOU 2011:21.

Stensson, C. (2009) 'Vi har inga helikoptrar i rätt skick' [We have no helicopters in the right condition] *Svenska Dagbladet* 19 November. Available online at www.svd.se/vi-har-inga-helikoptrar-i-ratt-skick (accessed 17 March 2016).

Strategy Page (2011) 'Murphy's Law: Afghanistan and the impossible scheme' *Strategy Page*, 7 June. Available online at www.strategypage.com/htmw/htmurph/articles/20110607.a spx (accessed 17 March 2016).

Svensson, S. (2011) 'Lessons still to be learned: interoperability between Swedish authorities in Northern Afghanistan'. Bachelor thesis. Gothenburg: University of Gothenburg (School of Global Studies).

Swedish Armed Forces (2011) 'Avlidna I utlandsstyrkan' ('Deceased in international service' Available online at www.forsvarsmakten.se/upload/dokumentfiler/internationellt/Avlidna_Utlandsstyrkan.pdf (accessed 15 December 2011).

Swedish Armed Forces (2014) Swedish Armed Forces website. Available online at www.forsvarsmakten.se (accessed 15 October 2014).

Swedish National Audit Office (2004) 'Who is in charge of the electronic administration?' (In Swedish). Stockholm: Swedish National Audit Office, RiR 2004:19.

Swedish National Audit Office (2011) 'Swedish Contributions to International Efforts' (In Swedish) Stockholm: Swedish National Audit Office, RiR 2011:14.

Tham, M., M. Lindell & C. Hull Wiklund, (2011) 'Chasing synergies: Civil–military relations in PRT Mazar-e-Sharif', FOI-R-3356-SE (in Swedish, English summary).

Wang, W., W. Yu, Q. Li, W. Wang & X. Liu (2008) 'Service-oriented high level architecture', European Simulation Interoperability Workshop. Edinburgh, Scotland: Simulation Interoperability Standards Organization.

7 Leadership lessons

New challenges for smaller nations in multinational, highly stressful missions

Gerry Larsson, Aida Alvinius, Maria Fors Brandebo, Peder Hyllengren, Sofia Nilsson and Alicia Ohlsson

Introduction

Sweden has a long history, dating back to before the First World War, of participation in international peace-support action. Afghanistan differs from other countries with which Sweden has had involvement as its context is more clearly characterized by irregular warfare and counterinsurgency. Recent behavioural and social science studies conducted in this type of context (notably Iraq, as well as Afghanistan) have mostly focused on psychological trauma and other mental health problems (Erbes *et al.* 2009, Friedman 2006, Hoge *et al.* 2004), but not on leadership aspects on both direct and indirect levels (Hannah *et al.* 2004).

Many stressors in irregular warfare operations are comparable to those in peacekeeping operations, but some aspects of stress can differ. Asnani *et al.* (2003) documented that, in areas distinguished by irregular warfare, the level of stress in soldiers is higher than in areas of peacekeeping. This is said to be due to the dangerous environment; firm discipline; insufficient social interaction, overload of risky tasks and emotional instability.

During the last decade, the authors have conducted a series of studies focusing on different aspects of leadership among Swedish military officers who have served in Afghanistan. Different hierarchical levels have been observed. In this chapter, most attention will be paid to studies focusing on Swedish Force Commanders, henceforth labelled 'the strategic level'. The common denominator is that the studies have highlighted leadership issues before, during and after highly stressful episodes. The present chapter summarizes key findings from this research with the aim of identifying generalizable knowledge related to military leadership, its antecedents and consequences in the kind of warfare encountered in Afghanistan. The chapter has little to say on policies and strategies, but hopefully more on practices and organization. The layout of the text will be structured according to a theoretical model of leadership. This conceptual map will hopefully add to the generalizability of the findings from the Afghanistan studies. Several references to the aforementioned research will be made, including a selection of illustrative interview excerpts, and interested readers are referred to the original sources for further information.

Stressors: some illustrative examples

Before presenting the leadership model, a few illustrations of stressors faced by military leaders in Afghanistan will be provided. The idea is to give a 'taste' of what these leaders have to deal with.

Stressors are often multiple in nature. Single or sometimes repeated confrontations with severely psychologically demanding episodes constitute one type (Elliot & Eisdorfer 1982). Another type of strain comprises accumulated stress, which tends to follow long-term service of a first-responder character (Marmar *et al.* 1999, Michel 2005). A third form is moral stress, which refers to painful reactions that might arise when an individual is conscious of the morally appropriate action that a situation requires but cannot carry it out due to formal laws and regulations or institutional obstacles; for example, lack of time, lack of leader support and power relations. Alternatively, this type of strain can occur when one acts according to one's conscience but against organizational regulations and norms (Jameton 1984).

Sample episodes reported by Larsson and Hyllengren (2013, p. 28) include the following. Group Commanders reported: 'Managed to discover and catch an individual who had placed an IED [Improvised Explosive Device]', 'Was shot at from 100 meters. Civilians in between. Could not shoot back', and – more generally – stressors derived from morally difficult situations dealing with killing or wounding enemies (Nilsson *et al.* 2012). Continuing with Platoon and Company Commanders (Larsson & Hyllengren 2013, p. 28), one said: 'Riot when a mosque was closed/moved' and another: 'Accident with a severely wounded soldier who should be evacuated via helicopter immediately. The evacuation was led poorly because of unclear routines and lack of experience.' Other examples, reported by Fors Brandebo and Larsson (2012) and Nilsson *et al.* (2012), include use of force; balancing one's own and others' security, sending out subordinates in to high-risk areas (high probability for IEDs and attacks) without sufficient equipment and dealing with one's own and subordinates' grief in the case of death. Finally, a couple of examples provided by Strategic-Level Commanders (Larsson & Hyllengren 2013, p. 28): 'Slow reaction and lack of support from the UN and the national political level' and 'A decision based on insufficient information to send troops to X where the risk of casualties was high.' Additional illustrations are stress in relation to being ultimately responsible for the safety of the unit not being able to provide sufficient equipment for a sufficient number of soldiers for the assignment and dealing with the media, subordinates and relatives in case of death (Fors Brandebo & Larsson 2012).

A theoretical model

The theoretical framework is presented in Figure 7.1.

The leadership model implies that a number of individual and contextual characteristics interact and shape a military commander's appraisal or sense-making of a given situation. Applied to what is taking place, this meaning

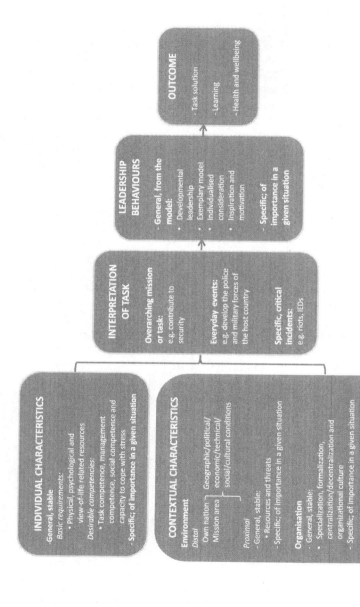

Figure 7.1 Theoretical model of leadership (modified from Larsson *et al.* 2012a).

in turn generates a number of leadership behaviours which, to a greater or lesser degree, affect the outcome. This concept of leadership therefore implies an acceptance of an interactional person-by-situation paradigm (Endler & Magnusson 1976). This is one of the most solid theoretical frameworks in psychology. Another conceptual anchor of the model is an emphasis on the classical device that the truth lies in the eye of the beholder. This means that the appraisal and interpretation are subjective to the military leader, rather than the objective reality that governs his or her reactions and behaviour.

In the following, key aspects of each box in the model are introduced. For space reasons, the presentations are brief. Interested readers are referred to the original sources for further details (mainly Larsson 2006, Larsson et al. 2003, Larsson & Eid 2012).

Individual characteristics

This box in the model consists of two broad areas: general and stable personal characteristics and aspects that are more specific and may be of great importance in a given situation, for instance the situation of a military commander. Two main classes of general and stable leader qualities are identified in the model: basic prerequisites and desirable competencies. Somewhat simplified, the basic prerequisites include individual characteristics such as physical fitness, intelligence, creativity, personality and view-of-life (Yukl 2002). The model includes four desirable competences. Task-related competence deals with the leader's ability to have the necessary knowledge and skills in relation to the task at hand (Hersey et al. 1969/2001, Jacobs & Jaques 1991). Two facets of management-related competence are included in the model: intra-organizational and extra-organizational. Examples of the first are knowing how to apply the formal rules, to structure, to prioritize and make decisions, to coordinate and so on. Examples of the latter are an ability to view one's own organization from the outside and to detect important events in the external world and understand their significance for one's own activity. Two facets of social competence are identified: flexibility and balance in social interactions. Finally, the capacity to cope with stress draws on the writings of Lazarus (1991, 1999) and here as well two facets are included: problem-focused coping and emotion-focused coping.

The basic requirements affect the development of the desirable competencies. The more favourable basic requirements a leader has, the greater the potential to develop the desirable competencies, and vice versa. The model also implies that a favourable combination of these two characteristics is a necessary condition for successful leadership. However, neither of them is sufficient in itself and one cannot make up for the other. Although important, they do not constitute any guarantee for successful leadership, because this is also affected by environmental conditions (discussed shortly). Generally speaking, the basic requirements are assumed to exhibit a higher degree of temporal and cross-contextual stability than the desirable competences. There is more room for adult learning and development within the latter area and a large body of literature exists on both areas.

The model component 'Specific; of importance in a given situation' is intended to capture specific individual traits, competences, skills and so on that can be of vital importance in a specific situation. An individual may for instance be physically weak; have a low intelligence level; a neurotic personality, be socially incompetent and so on, but may also possess a specific skill that can be crucial in a given situation. The case of irregular warfare has been found to put a particularly strong emphasis on leaders' self-awareness and cognitive ability in order to reduce the ambiguity connected with this kind of warfare. Strong leader character has also been found to increase the insecurity level among insurgents (Wyszynski 2005). Examples of specific individual characteristics found to be of particular importance to military officers at the strategic level are shown in Table 7.1.

Contextual characteristics

This box in the model consists of three major domains that constantly influence each other: the environment, the organization and the group. Each of these can be further subdivided as below.

The environment

The environmental domain includes two dimensions in the present analysis, one more distal and one more proximal. This broad division is intended be general (Hersey *et al.* 1969/2001). The distal or remote environment contains aspects such as geographical; political; economic; technical, social and cultural conditions in the mission area, as well as the similar aspects in the homeland. For instance, when it comes to constructs in the mission area, understanding cultural aspects and the local balance of power can be crucial. Reactions from family members back home, increased homeland media attention and goals and resources provided by the political level are additional distal sources of influence on military commanders.

The proximal environmental aspects can be further subdivided into conditions that are general and stable and those that are more situation-specific. The more general and stable aspects include a permanent threat of an enemy or aggressor; climate and infrastructural conditions; legal aspects, media contacts and so on (see Larsson & Hyllengren 2013 for a further discussion of general and stable environmental conditions).

When Sweden started its engagement in Afghanistan, leaders had to adjust to a new type of warfare as well to unfamiliar environments. In previous peacekeeping missions, Sweden has been a part between two clearly defined opponents fighting each other. In Afghanistan, Swedish officers and soldiers were faced with the fact that they were also looked upon as the enemy. Irregular warfare, including threats like IEDs, has placed new demands on

Table 7.1 Specific individual aspects of importance to military officers at the strategic level (Larsson *et al.* 2012a)

Aspect	Comments
Training and exercises	Swedish military officers at the strategic level have few preparatory exercise possibilities at this level.
Language skills	Fluent English is an absolute requirement for leaders at the strategic level to be able to handle the information received and to be accepted by and able to interact with higher-level officers (often American or British).
Culture competence	Knowledge of how the local society works is essential. More in-depth knowledge of how culture, customs, political leadership and clan or tribe structures work in the host country may also be needed.
NATO competence	Pre-mission knowledge of NATO procedures and chain-of-command regulations are a great asset.
Knowledge of the Swedish political system	Pre-mission knowledge of the homeland political system system is valuable. For instance, knowledge of the duties of the Ministry of Foreign Affairs and an Ambassador.
Knowledge of a 'comprehensive approach' and collaboration	Training should be conducted interactively with civilian components, including political aspects, so that strategic-level officers are trained to understand collaboration and the political overall mission purpose.
Recruitment skills	Military strategic leaders tend to find it desirable to recruit Commanders who are directly subordinate to themselves. Mixed age and gender balance is usually an advantage.

leaders compared to previous missions. A soldier in Afghanistan reported the following after an IED detonation in which no enemy was present:

> We went bloody ballistic, especially when you jump out of what's left of your car and you're looking for a target to deal with and it's a frustration in itself – you don't find one. So there's no avenue for this frustration and the first farmer we come across we sort out there and then, but he could have just as easily been shot because you're so enraged that someone is trying to do this to you.
> (Fors Brandebo & Larsson 2012, p. 10)

Regarding the environment, Sweden has been operating in quite a large area with mountain and desert terrains. Swedish soldiers have encountered extreme temperature variations and inadequate or often non-existent road systems. The environment has been considered as giving the enemy an unfair advantage (Fors Brandebo & Larsson 2012).

Context-specific, proximal environmental conditions are likely to be different across different operations. An example provided by the aforementioned sample of Swedish commanders on duty in Afghanistan is what they labelled 'the Afghan game'. This includes an inability to count on loyalty, because people can change sides overnight. It also implies that it is difficult to wash away longstanding and deeply-rooted local practices by trying to impose a Western legal system. An example from Afghanistan is that Sharia law dominates in many villages and that, as a Military Commander, one may receive invitations to visit beheadings. As such, these aspects –which can range from severely demanding to non-existing – make the operating environment vary in stability and predictability (see Lazarus' (1991, 1999) writings on situational factors influencing appraisal processes). To conclude, the prevailing environmental characteristics can, more generally, be regarded as an illustration of a situation in which a postmodern military organization is deployed to solve tasks in a pre-modern context.

The organization

Organizational aspects constitute another important contextual domain. According to the theoretical model, this domain is also made up of more general and stable aspects, as well as more specific ones that are of importance in a given situation. Regarding the latter, a couple of commander-related organizational aspects of importance in a given situation are presented in Table 7.2.

Regarding the general, stable aspects, four issues will be emphasized here, all of which also include a number of interrelated qualities.

First, specialization. This dimension includes three elements from classic organization theory: horizontal, vertical and spatial differentiation. Horizontal differentiation concerns the degree of similarity/dissimilarity between the assignments and the competence required of people at the same hierarchical level. A leader can, for example, feel that it is easier to lead a large group (large control span) in which the members all have similar tasks and levels of competence than a smaller group in which the members' tasks and competence profiles vary greatly. Vertical differentiation concerns the number of hierarchical levels in an organization. Finally, spatial differentiation describes the degree of geographical extent of the organization's tasks.

Second, the dimension of formalization concerns the degree to which the execution of tasks is governed by rules and regulations. One source of rules and regulations is intra-organizational. Typical examples are found in so-called 'high reliability' organizations such as air traffic control and nuclear power plants. The logic behind this is that some operations are so complicated and risky that their execution must be tightly controlled. The other source of formalism is extra-organizational. Examples here are laws and profession-based guidelines of best practice. A high amount of formal restrictions obviously reduces the space for tactics and local cultural variation.

Third, the dimension of centralization/decentralization focuses on power and control. This can vary from a position of highly-centralized power and control to a high degree of decentralization of the power to make decisions. An aspect observed several times in the Swedish task force in Afghanistan,

Table 7.2 Specific organizational aspects of importance to military officers at the strategic level (Larsson *et al.* 2012)

Aspect	Comments
Long working hours	The working outlet is frequently 16–20 hours a day for 6 months, with one or two leave periods. In addition, Officers are on constant standby when in the operation area.
Unit culture	It is important to have early nominations of subordinate Commanders and to have dialogues on values, methodology, approaches and goals. These guidelines will then affect all activities – from recruitment and training to proper conduct – during the actual mission.

which concerns the question of how to make a basically bureaucratic, hierarchical organization more adaptable to situational demands, is the occurrence of so-called 'boundary spanners'. This is about individuals who have a comparatively free role towards the environment. It could be described as 'act first and ask for sanctioning later.' It presumes that the management has a strong trust in these individuals. As links, they can act with a considerable amount of freedom and network with boundary spanners from other agencies. They can be described as part of 'the survival kit' of a bureaucratic organization in times of crisis and have been observed in civilian as well as military contexts (Alvinius *et al.* 2010).

A final aspect considered here is organizational culture. Three of Abrahamsson's and Andersen's (2005) organizational culture components will be mentioned here. They all have intra-organizational focus, rather than a more general cultural dimension emphasis such as *Gemainschaft vs Gesellschaft* (Tonnies 1887) or individualism vs collectivism (Hofstede 1991, Hofstede & Hofstede 2005). One component concerns routinized behaviour in the ways in which people interact in the form of rituals, ceremonies and verbal discourse. Shared norms in working groups constitute a second component. The third is the feeling or climate that characterizes interactions between the members of the organization, as well as those with their customers, clients and so on.

The group

Group characteristics constitute the third and final contextual characteristic affecting the leadership of Commanders. 'Group' refers here to the people who are closest to the Commander, such as the immediate subordinate Commanders and key staff members. General, stable group conditions include group composition and classic social psychological aspects such as roles, norms and cohesion. Roles and norms are assumed to vary from clear and accepted to diffuse and unaccepted. Cohesion can vary from strong to weak. Thus, the group characteristics can range from a situation with clear

Table 7.3 Specific group aspects of importance to military officers at the strategic level (Larsson *et al.* 2012a)

Aspect	Comments
Diverse role expectations	Strategic staff members from non-Scandinavian countries tend to put much more emphasis on the Commander role than is usually the case in Sweden. Commanders need to be aware of this and to show a high degree of flexibility.
Civilian advisors	Civilian advisors must be given time during staff meetings to present their views. Commanders need to create forums for this and to support them.

and accepted norms and roles and strong group cohesion to unclear and unaccepted norms and roles and weak group cohesion. Social psychological processes such as communication and conflict resolution are also included.

Some situation-specific group characteristics are presented in Table 7.3.

Interpretation of the task

The rationale behind the interpretation box in the model is the classic psychological device that the truth is in the eye of the beholder. This means that the basis of a Commander's decisions and actions will not be the objective external reality; instead, his or her appraisal will form an inner representation of a subjective reality. When the person–environment relationship is combined with the subjective process of appraisal, the personal significance of that relationship comes to the fore. Lazarus (1999) labels this the relational meaning of a given person–environment encounter. He continues:

> Appraisals are commonly based on many subtle cues in the environment, what has been learned from previous experience, and a host of personality variables, such as goals, situational intentions, and personal resources and liabilities. All of this provides a basis for a decision about how to respond.
>
> (Lazarus (1999) p. 81)

Because all encounters with the environment are continually changing and generating feedback about the psychological situation, appraisals are also continually changing. An individual may, for example, interpret the message of a high-level manager as threatening, but change his/her appraisal and feel optimistic when the message has been explained in detail by the immediate supervisor.

Trust is a critical factor when leaders and subordinates interpret a given situation (Larsson & Eid 2012). In a Swedish–Norwegian study of trust in military leaders (with most illustrations coming from service in Afghanistan), two broad domains were identified that contribute to trust if positive and to lack thereof if negative. One was labelled 'individual-related characteristics' and includes personal attributes and experience and competence; the other was labelled 'communication- and relationship-related characteristics' and encompasses aspects such as showing consideration and inspiration and using effective communication. Compared to data from other mission areas, leaders' competence in battle was more emphasized in the Afghanistan case (Fors Brandebo *et al.* 2013).

Generally speaking, a high degree of trust is functional in military units. However, sometimes too much trust can be dysfunctional, leading to individuals taking unnecessary risks. Regular units often have high levels of trust even before deployment, and, since leaders in this context are dependent on trust from their subordinates, they might interpret this as utterly favourable (Sweeney 2010). Given the validity of this line of reasoning, it becomes important for leaders of these kinds of units to pay attention to the potentially dark sides of trust (Fors Brandebo & Larsson 2012); the phenomenon shows similarities to group-think (Janis 1972).

The 'interpretation of task' part of the model (Figure 7.1) has three foci, mirrored from the perspective of a Mission Commander: the superior interpretation of the overarching mission or task, the interpretation of the everyday events and the interpretation of specific critical incidents (such as riots, IED attacks and the like).

First, regarding the superior interpretation of the overarching mission or task, the ultimate goal is to contribute to sufficient security in order to generate a political solution. The latter can only be done by the people of the host country. Part of the duties of the Commander is to facilitate the process of handing over the responsibility to the host country's authorities.

Second, from a leadership perspective, the following issues have been highlighted by Swedish mission commanders when it comes to sense making of everyday events: getting information out to the local population (which can be difficult when the infrastructure is not functioning or non-existent); developing the police and military forces of the host country, developing milestones and reconciliation points in order to follow up the development and winning the people's support (since it is difficult to defeat the insurgents completely, the people's support for them must be reversed)

Third, interpretation of specific critical incidents. Military leaders' appraisal of critical events and their coping efforts have been the subject of a large number of studies (see Kolditz & Brazil 2005). An illustration from a recent study of morally stressful encounters faced by Swedish officers in Afghanistan (Nilsson *et al.* 2015) showed that accumulated appraisals of daily stressful events rendered more negative long-term emotional reactions than the most morally extreme situation an Officer had experienced. This can possibly be understood in the light of cumulative stress and repeated everyday hassles following taxing everyday events. This would be in line with the aforementioned writings of Lazarus and colleagues (DeLongis et al. 1982, Lazarus 1984). A practical implication that this points to is the importance of having a well-functioning everyday work organization, in terms of the availability of resources and regulations, as well as a high-quality formal support system (Nilsson et al. in press).

Leadership behaviours

Leadership behaviours are also divided into two parts in the theoretical framework: general and situation-specific. The general leadership behaviours can be understood against the backdrop of the developmental leadership model (Larsson et al. 2003). Being an exemplary model is the first requirement: being yourself; showing courage; being true to your values, practicing what you preach and so on. Showing individualized consideration is the second part of general leadership behaviours. It is important to utilize every opportunity to talk to your officers and soldiers, while also being able to listen. A third general aspect is providing inspiration and motivation: daring to trust others, to delegate and to know that you are not always entirely in control: this is a necessary risk. Directly subordinate Commanders must be allowed to take responsibility for solving their tasks. Trust is a way to lead. Follow-up controls are perceived very differently by subordinates if they feel that they are trusted compared to if they expect you only to search for their mistakes. Perhaps even more important than exhibiting these favourable leadership behaviours is to refrain from destructive ones such as arrogance, being false and ego-oriented, being a coward and being unclear and unorganized (Larsson et al. 2012).

The conceptualization of general leadership behaviours is heavily influenced by the writings on transformational leadership and the full range of leadership models (Avolio 1999, Bass 1998). However, some alterations were made from the original American model (Larsson et al. 2003, for details). One example is the concept of charisma, which is central in transformational leadership model. In the Swedish model it has been replaced by inspiration, because in a Scandinavian leadership culture charisma appears to evoke negative associations of elitism.

Four situation-specific leadership demands made of Commanders will be discussed here: handling a number of acts of balance, cooperation/collaboration, emotional management and soft, hard and smart power.

Acts of balance

A number of acts of balance have been noted in leadership research. An obvious one concerns the use of resources, which tends to be limited; it is a leadership task to make the best of it. Another act of balance was noted in a study of an unexpected riot in Kosovo in 2004 (Larsson et al. 2007). Here, events unfolded so quickly that there was no possibility for the chain of command to function. Lower-level leaders such as Platoon and Group Commanders had to take charge. They reported a need to strike a balance between freedom of action and structure. Freedom meant acting according to one's own judgement and structure meant to 'go by the book'. Similar findings have been reported in civilian crisis management situations (Alvinius *et al.* 2010). A third example of acts of balance has been reported by Fors Brandebo and Larsson (2012), who studied leadership from the lowest to the highest level in connection with IED attacks in Afghanistan and found that the key leadership element could be summarized as 'recapture control'. This includes control of self, of the unit and of the task. Within each of these three aspects, several acts of balance were identified; for example:

A means of recapturing control of self is emotional control, for example venting frustration without letting it lead to a dysfunctional desire for revenge, or allowing oneself to grieve despite a fear of losing authority. A Swedish officer expressed it like this (Fors Brandebo & Larsson 2012, p. 12):

> But then when this happened, there was this real frustration and anger towards someone you can't identify. It could've been anyone. And after a number of these incidents, you know, obviously you, if I say so myself, that you kind of stop trusting the locals. And sometimes of course this wasn't fair. We sort of bottled it up, yes, like, 'yep I'm shaking hands with you today but were you the one who was out last night burying mines? Or, were you the one shooting at us with RPG or something else?
>
> I don't know if it would have been a good thing to fully show my emotions at the scene down there; I was probably a bit afraid of not being able to control my grief properly if I let it surface and take hold.
> (A troop leader, Fors Brandebo & Larsson 2012, p. 13)

Cognitive control involves balanced appraisal/sense-making of the event with balanced decision-making. In the case of the IED attack, military leadership could mean having the confidence to make less-informed decisions when needed without acting incautiously. Gaining control of one's own forces involves expressive and instrumental control in terms of a balanced focus on emotional and functional recovery and a balanced personal presence or absence in the afflicted group. Finally, recapturing control of the task means taking control over the mission. Examples include balancing risk-taking with safety concerns, handling superiors and the media. What follows is an illustration from a high-level officer:

> If you break off because something has just happened, then it might be right to stop what you're doing possibly. [...] Is the camp going to be attacked now? Yes, then I have to break off and find out what's happening. But by the next day you're already back out working more actively.

> It depends on how long you interrupt what you're doing for it to feel like that. Because I think that just when the incident happens that's when you can't say, 'well, we're going to carry on like nothing's happened.' It has to be OK to say, 'What's the situation now?'
>
> (Fors Brandebo & Larsson 2012, p. 18)

Summarizing the findings on acts of balance, effective leadership in extreme situations requires balancing emotional, cognitive, and physical perspectives. Failing to do this may lead to unfavourable consequences for the leader as well as their subordinates in terms of lack of trust, decreased motivation, frustration and anger that might get out of hand (Alvinius 2013, Fors Brandebo & Larsson 2012, Hannah et al. 2009).

Collaboration

Another cluster of situation-specific leadership behaviours deals with a multitude of collaboration processes. Some of the most common are illustrated in Figure 7.2.

Some key collaboration aspects related to the various actors mentioned in Figure 7.2 are presented in Table 7.4.

The core of collaboration in multinational military missions appears to be confidence-building. Three underlying processes have been identified with respect to this: cultural smoothness, structural smoothness and smoothness in risky situations (Alvinius et al. 2014).

Cultural smoothness means an ability to handle cultural codes, manners and customs, rituals and so on in order to avoid conflicts or tensions. It includes knowledge and skills related to more general cultural codes, a wide spectrum of social strategies and symbolic actions, language and more specific aspects such as the handling of local hospitality, meal culture and hygiene habits. As a Liaison Officer states:

> But as well, you could see those who had a knack of adjusting to this, you know, joining in and cheek-kissing right, left and centre and so on. If you find that difficult, maybe you shouldn't be working as a liaison officer if you can't take it; you must be able to loosen up, you must be able to, you know, when in Rome, do as the Romans, so to speak.
>
> (Alvinius et al. 2014, p. 230)

Structural smoothness means an ability to understand and handle structures of power, status, hierarchy and so on. Examples include an awareness and ability to display authority through age and formal rank, through clothing, appearance and equipment, by exhibiting task-related competence and by strategic selection of interpreters. A higher-ranking Officer states:

> If they cancel meetings, it's not right to accept it with a smile and say; 'well ok we'll see you next week, if you're busy now.' You might have to

Figure 7.2 Examples of collaborating actors (Larsson *et al.* 2012a).

play up your rank perhaps, appear to be a little offended, slam your fists on the table or say, this is not acceptable to me – it's completely unacceptable that you won't meet with ISAF.

(Alvinius *et al.* 2014, p. 233)

And finally, smoothness in risky situations implies an ability to appraise the significance of various external demands, which may prompt emotions such as fear, anger, frustration or shame in all collaborative actors. This kind of smoothness requires an ability to manage one's own emotions and remain in control. Critical skills include sensitivity for determining whether the atmosphere of a collaborative situation may become threatening. The talent for having a calming effect on the collaborator and the ability to extricate oneself from dangerous situations are other indicators of this kind of smoothness. An example from a Liaison Officer (Alvinius *et al.* 2014, p. 235) 'He was upset because we closed this restaurant due to the increase in drugs. But I often thought it worked, I had quite a calming effect on people I went in and talked to.' All three kinds of smoothness were frequently observed among Swedish officers in Afghanistan (Alvinius *et al.* 2014).

Table 7.4 Collaboration actors and key leadership behaviours for military officers at the strategic level (Larsson *et al.* 2012a)

Actor	Comments
Swedish Armed Forces	Swedish military personnel are known for their dedication and their good attitude towards others. A key task for strategic officers is to work on this continually.
Swedish civilian actors	The value of having civil representations and an Ambassador in the host country is high when putting pressure on the authorities in the host country. An open attitude towards different civilian cultural patterns is recommended.
Public opinion and family at home	Be prepared for negative media comments. Do as much as possible in advance to build up confidence in your family members and have information channels in place, as a pre-emptive measure.
The host nation's military forces and police	Be prepared to collaborate with local forces of lower quality, with a lot of members whose education levels vary and where corruption is common.
Interpreters & NGOs	Be prepared to interact with the local population with the help of interpreters. Realize that you cannot fully understand what goes on between the interpreter and the locals.
Media in the host nation	Learn to build up relationships with the local media characterized by trust. Try to use the local media to get information out.
Opponents/insurgents	Talking about collaboration in connection with the insurgents may sound strange and one should never underestimate their military skills. In this context, collaboration could mean trying to create opportunities for them to make a living doing something other than fighting.
Allied forces from other nations	Cooperation with other nations is demanding as many cultural thresholds must be crossed. A good command of English is essential.

Emotional management

One area of particular interest regarding emotion management is emotional contagion. This basic idea of this concept is that a leader, due to his/her heightened position of power and status in relation to his/her subordinates, has an ability to influence his/her subordinates through his/her own emotions and feelings. Emotion and behaviour contagion is defined as 'the tendency to catch and feel emotions and/or behaviours which are similar to and associated with others' (Kemper 2011, p. 163). This is usually an automatic response from the subordinates, which can often be seen through overt behaviours such as mimicking of facial expressions.

Research has demonstrated that leader emotional displays influence emotions through mood contagion (Bono & Ilies 2006). Bass and Avolio (1994) found that positive emotions have been suggested to inspire and motivate employees. It is also a way to show what is and is not allowed, which influences the behaviour of the group. This was reported from an officer in Afghanistan when discussing the routine created by his group leader:

> We had a routine to sit together and go through what has happened, which made it natural to be able to discuss things when something really did happen. It created a feeling that it was okay to do so and to discuss emotional subjects. It can inspire subordinates to 'go the extra mile' and exhibit high levels of organizational commitment. Naturally, if positive emotions can be spread to others so can negative emotions, such as fear.
> (Nilsson *et al.* in press)

Soft, hard and smart power

Nye (2008) suggests that seduction is more powerful than coercion when it comes to acquiring what is desired from other individuals. He also proposes that soft power, which entails making others desire the same outcomes as you, is a tool of seduction. Soft power is an indirect approach to obtain the visions and goals that individual covet. One way to use this power indirectly is by changing the emotional environment to a more favourable milieu. Additionally, soft power can also be used by creating myths or other agreeable stories about the leader's visions and/or goals. Napoleon is believed to have created stories concerning his greatness, which is a way of using soft power.

Soft power can entail a leader's attractive personality, his/her moral values or the values and visions that he/she aspires to convey. The leader would possess the ability to create goals and visions that others wish to achieve; this could rely on how attractive these goals were to the subordinates. Soft power is often considered to be a way of influencing and affecting subordinates to desire what is beneficial from the leader's point of view. Moreover, this type of power is seen as attractive and 'friendly' and can lead to subordinate participation, instead of merely obedience due to fear of losing one's employment. However, this is still a way of manipulating or influencing others and their goals (Nye 2008). Soft and hard powers are often combined to strengthen the leader's desired way of reaching a set goal. The ability to combine both is termed smart power (Nye 2008).

The line between using soft power with good intentions for the organization and less commendable, ego-driven motives can be thin. This means that the conscious use of soft power requires high levels of self-awareness and moral strength on the part of the leader. Frequent examples of use of emotional contagion and soft power were identified among Swedish officers in Afghanistan (Alvinius *et al.* 2014, Nilsson *et al.* 2012). It is possible that the ambiguous character of an irregular warfare context provides a more open environment for these kinds of influence mechanisms compared to a well-ordered, strictly bureaucratic setting. It is also possible that the freedom of emotional expression varies across hierarchical levels, implying that the so-called organizational feeling rules, or emotional regimes (Taylor & Ladkin 2009), offer greater possibilities at lower levels and more emotional mastery at higher levels.

Outcomes

The leadership model (Figure 7.1) predicts that a number of individual and contextual characteristics interact to shape a military leader's appraisal of a given situation. This interpretation in turn generates a number of leadership behaviours which, to a greater or lesser degree, affect the outcome (Larsson & Eid 2012). The outcome is probably the most difficult part in this series of predictions to validate. Obvious questions arise regarding for whom the outcome is effective, in what way, and when (short- and long-term).

As outcomes of organizational activities have multiple determinants, leadership being just one of them, one should not expect strong associations. Drawing on results from the coping and health area (Folkman 1985), it could be argued that proximal, short-term and limited aspects (for instance, number of mistakes or near misses during a given time period) will co-vary more strongly with the followers' will/intention and actual behaviour than distal, long-term, complex aspects (for instance, a successful end state at the macro level).

The 'Outcome' box of the leadership model (Figure 7.1) contains three aspects: functional task solution, learning for the future and health and wellbeing. Regarding the first of these, the typical response from former commanders concerns difficulties in defining and measuring what is meant by 'end state.' Examples of measurable partial goals include support from the host country population, amount of money spent (Swedish tax money), schools, healthcare and so on (quantity and quality).

With regard to learning aspects, one idea that was mentioned in the interview on Afghanistan experiences was that the Swedish Armed Forces should build up a pool of strategic officers from which to choose. For instance, three generals could split a longer mission time between themselves. Each one serves in the strategic operational headquarters during a shorter period of time, but then returns after a short while as a well-known commander.

Concluding with the health and wellbeing aspect, the aforementioned study on moral dilemmas and moral stress (Larsson *et al.* under review) showed that negative long-term emotional reactions co-varied with low scores on the personality dimension 'emotional stability'. Given this observed importance of individual psychological factors on negative outcome reactions, a practical organizational conclusion is that these potential vulnerability factors should be thoroughly screened during the selection process.

Conclusions

A summary of the key challenges and leadership lessons identified in our studies of Swedish troops in Afghanistan follows. If we begin this final section by relating our findings at large to the characteristics of postmodern Armed Forces as described by Moskos *et al.* (2000, see Chapter 1), the outcome could be summarized as: 'true description, but Sweden has been there for a while.' Thus, the Afghanistan mission included more fuzzy borders between the civil and the military spheres, the branches of military service, participants from different nations and so on. The mission could also be described as consisting of irregular war contexts rather than large-scale regular operations. In the Swedish case, however, this has also been true in previous missions; the ones in former Yugoslavia in particular. It should be noted, though, that the number of actual combat episodes was considerably higher in Afghanistan.

Looking at the challenges from a narrower leadership perspective, it should be observed that much of the daily leadership at company level and below remains fairly conventional. In the Swedish case, with its plug-in role in the mission at large, the multinational aspects mentioned by Moskos *et al.* (2000) were mostly relevant at the Force Commander level and for officers serving in higher staffs.

Possibly the most valuable lessons learned is that the broad array of empirical findings could be related to a *theoretical model of leadership* in a meaningful way. Drawing on the classical device that there is nothing as practical as a good theory, this means that the model presented can function as a road map for future missions: to guide selection; training; organizational design, evaluations and the like.

A lesson regarding challenges is the multiple characters of stressors in missions like the one in Afghanistan. Accumulated stress over long periods of time combined with acute, extremely stressful episodes has been a typical component of warzones throughout history. An additional issue – certainly not new, but more frequent in Afghanistan – was moral dilemmas. This is to be expected in this kind of mission, and officers and soldiers should prepare for it.

Selection of individuals with the required psychological make-up and competences is an organizational evergreen. In mission areas characterized by irregular warfare, particular emphasis should be placed on cultural competence and adaptability to rapidly-changing demands on leadership behaviours.

One of the most important tasks for a military leader to be able to perform is the ability to share visions and goals with his/her subordinates. In order to do this, the leader must be able to overcome the physical barrier of not being in direct contact with many subordinates that he/she should inspire vision in, motivate and give orders. This chapter has been particularly interested in leadership styles that have been linked to emotional leadership, and the latter's connections with the military leadership and motivating subordinates. Many of the tasks of military leaders often require them to be emotional managers – of both their own emotions and those of others – in order to successfully perform their tasks. This is especially true in emotionally charged environments, such as those encountered in Afghanistan.

Leaders can use their power and status alone to achieve their goals but they often only succeed with achieving a submissive response when doing so. In order to gain subordinates' trust and active participation, a smooth way of using their power is necessary. These different power techniques can be used to gain personal and organizational goals, with *smart power* being the most influential. Ultimately, the military leader should look to find ways to increase organizational commitment from their subordinates while also respecting their wills and autonomy within the organization.

Finally, we would like to broaden the perspective and point to some consequences for military leadership at large. Since 2003, the Swedish Armed Forces have used 'developmental leadership' (Larsson *et al.* 2003) as its official leadership model. In terms of competencies and performance, there is significant evidence that the Swedish military leadership has stood up well in Afghanistan. This can be seen as a validation of its leadership model. However, it should be noted that three areas need to be more deeply addressed in the model: emotion management, cultural management and English-language skills. The first aspect – emotional management – requires a particularly important change to the prevailing leadership doctrine, the latter of which could be described as clinically free from emotions. But, as one of our informants pointed out: 'That's not the way the world is.' Special attention should also be paid in the future to severe stress reactions – including, but not exclusively, post-traumatic stress disorder (PTSD). A recent literature review on mission-related stress in military veterans, ordered by the Swedish Parliament (Michel 2014), clearly pointed to leadership as one of the most important factors when it comes to prevention of and recovery from stress-related problems.

From a research perspective the collected leadership studies presented here could be seen as a case study, making generalizations to other nations and types of conflict difficult. Nevertheless, we believe that many of the findings also have relevance to other smaller nations that have 'plug-in' roles similar to those that Sweden has had.

References

Abrahamsson, B. & Andersen, J.A. (2005) *Organisation:Att beskriva och forsta organisationer* [*Organization: To describe and understand organisations*] 4th edition. Malmo: Liber.

Alvinius, A. (2013) *Bridging boundaries in the borderland of bureaucracies: Individual impact on organizational adaptation to demanding situations in civil and military contexts* Ph.D. dissertation. Karlstad: Karlstad University, Faculty of Arts and Social Science.

Alvinius, A., E. Danielsson & G. Larsson (2010) 'Structure versus freedom: Leadership during the rescue operation following the 2004 tsunami' *International Journal of Emergency Management* Vol. 7, No. 3–4, pp. 304–22.

Alvinius, A., C. Kylin, B. Starrin & G. Larsson (2014) 'Emotional smoothness and confidence building: Boundary spanners in a civil–military collaboration context' *International Journal of Work Organisation and Emotion* Vol. 6, No. 3, pp. 223–39.

Asnani, V., U.D. Paney & R.K. Tripathi (2003) 'Stress and job satisfaction among security personnel operating in counterinsurgency areas' *Journal of the Indian Academy of Applied Psychology* Vol. 29, No. 1–2, pp. 45–52.
Avolio, B. (1999) *Full leadership development: Building the vital forces in organizations.* Thousand Oaks, CA: SAGE.
Bass, B.M. (1998) *Transformational leadership: Industry, military, and educational Impact.* London: Lawrence Erlbaum Associated.
Bass, B.M. & B.J. Avolio (Eds) (1994) *Improving organizational effectiveness through transformational leadership.* Thousand Oaks, CA: SAGE.
Bono J.E & R. Ilies (2006) 'Charisma, positive emotions and mood contagion' *The Leadership Quarterly* Vol. 17, No. 4, pp. 317–34.
DeLongis, A., J.C Coyne, G. Dakof, S. Folkman & R.S. Lazarus (1982) 'Relationship of daily hassles, uplifts, and major life events to health status' *Health Psychology* Vol. 1, No. 2, pp. 119–36.
Elliot G.R. & C. Eisdorfer (1982) *Stress and human health.* New York: Springer.
Endler, N.S. & D. Magnusson (1976) 'Toward an interactional psychology of personality' *Psychol Bull* Vol. 83, No. 5, pp. 956–79.
Erbes C.R., T. Kyle, C. Leskala & J. Leskala (2009) 'Treatment presentation and adherence of Iraq/Afghanistan era veterans in outpatient care for post-traumatic stress disorder' *Psychological Services* Vol. 6, No. 3, pp. 175–83.
Folkman, S. (1985) 'The relationship between coping and health: Where should we look?' Paper presented at American Psychological Association Meeting, Los Angeles, CA.
Fors Brandebo, M. & G. Larsson (2012) 'Influence of IED attacks on leadership: Dealing with the invisible enemy' *Res Militaris* Vol. 2, No. 3, pp. 1–26.
Fors Brandebo M., M., Sjoberg, G.Larsson, J. Eid & O. Kjellevold Olsen (2013). 'Trust in a military context: What contributes to trust in superior and subordinate leaders?' *Journal of Trust Research* Vol. 3, No. 2, pp. 125–45.
Friedman, M.J. (2006) 'Post-traumatic stress disorder among military returnees from Afghanistan and Iraq' *The American Journal of Psychiatry* Vol. 163, No. 4, pp. 586–93.
Hannah, S.T., M. Uhl-Bien, B. J. Avolio & F. L. Cavaretta (2009) 'A framework for examining leadership in extreme contexts' *The Leadership Quarterly* Vol. 20, No. 6, pp. 897–919.
Hersey, P., K.H. Blanchard & D.E Johnson. (1969/2001) *Management of organizational behavior: Leading human resources*, 8th edition. London: Prentice-Hall International.
Hofstede, G. (1991) *Cultures and organizations.* Maidenhead, NY: McGraw-Hill.
Hofstede, G. & G.J. Hofstede (2005) *Cultures and organizations: Software of the mind.* New York: McGraw-Hill.
Hoge C.W., C.A Castro, S.C. Messer, D. McGurk, D.I. Cotting & R.L. Koffman (2004) 'Combat duty in Iraq and Afghanistan: Mental health problems and barriers to care' *The New England Journal of Medicine* Vol. 351, No. 1, pp. 13–22.
Jacobs, T.O. & E. Jaques (1991) 'Executive leadership' In Gal, R. & A.D. Manglesdorff (Eds) *Handbook of military psychology.* New Work: Wiley, pp. 431–7.
Jameton, A. (1984) *Nursing practice: The ethical issues.* Englewood Cliffs, NJ: Prentice-Hall.
Janis, I. L. (1972) *Victims of groupthink.* Boston, MA: Houghton-Mifflin.
Kemper, T.D. (2011) *Status, power and ritual Interaction: A relational reading of Durkheim, Goffman and Collins.* Burlington, VT: Ashgate Publishing Ltd.
Kolditz, T.A. & D.M. Brazil (2005) 'Authentic leadership in *extremis* settings: A concept for extraordinary leaders in exceptional situations' In Gardner W. L., B.J. Avolio &

F.O. Walumbwa (Eds) *Authentic leadership theory and practice: Origins, effects and development*. Amsterdam: Elsevier JAI, pp. 345–56.

Larsson, G. (2006) "The developmental leadership questionnaire (DLQ): Some psychometric properties' *Scandinalvian Journal of Psychology* Vol. 47, No. 4, pp. 253–62.

Larsson, G. & J. Eid (2012) 'An idea paper on leadership theory integration' *Management Research Review* Vol. 35, No. 3–4, pp. 177–91.

Larsson, G. & P. Hyllengren (2013) 'Contextual influences on leadership in emergency type organisations: Theoretical modelling and empirical tests' *International Journal of Organizational Analysis* Vol. 21, No. 1, pp. 19–37.

Larsson, G., L. Carlstedt, J. Andersson, L. Andersson, A. Johnasson, E. Johansson, P.-O. Michel & I. Robertson (2003) 'A comprehensive system for leader evaluation and development' *Leadership & Organizational Development Journal* Vol. 24, No. 1, pp. 16–25.

Larsson, G., T. Haerem, M. Sjoberg, A. Alvinius & B. Bakken (2007) 'Indirect leadership under severe stress: A qualitative inquiry into the 2004 Kosovo riots' *International Journal of Organizational Analysis* Vol. 15, No. 1, pp. 23–34.

Larsson, G., M. Fors Brandebo, S. Nilsson (2012) 'Destrudo-L: Development of a short scale designed to measure destructive leadership behaviours in military context' *Leadership & Organizational Development Journal* Vol. 33, No. 4, pp. 383–400.

Larsson, G., S. Nilsson, P. Hyllengren, A. Ohlsson, G. Waaler & K. Kallenberg (under review) *Stress reactions following moral dilemmas among first responder professionals*. Submitted for publication.

Lazarus, R.S. (1984) 'Puzzles in the study of daily hassles' *Behavioral Medicine* Vol. 7, pp. 375–89.

Lazarus, R.S. (1991) *Emotion and adaption*. New York: Oxford University Press.

Lazarus, R.S. (1999) *Stress and emotion: A new synthesis*. London: Free Association Books.

Marmar, C.E., D.S. Weiss, T.J. Metzler, K.L. Delucci, S. Best & K.A. Wentworth (1999) 'Longitudinal course and predictors of continuing distress following critical incident exposure in emergency service personnel' *Journal of Nervous Mental Disease* Vol. 187, No. 1, p. 15.

Michel, P.-O. (2005) *The Swedish soldier and general mental health following service in peacekeeping operations*. Uppsala, Sweden: Acta Universitatis Upsaliensis.

Michel, P.-O. (2014) *Insatsrelaterad stress hos militara veteraner* [Mission-related stress in military veterans]. (Rapport Serie F:41). Forsvarshogskolan, Institutionen for sakerhet, strategi och ledarskap, Ledarskapscentrum.

Moskos, C., J.A. Williams & D.R. Segal (2000) 'Armed forces after the cold war' in Moskos C., J.A. Williams & D.R. Segal (Eds) *The postmodern military: Armed Forces after the Cold War*. New York: Oxford University Press, pp 1–13.

Nilsson, S., E. Jonsson, M. Fors Brandebo & G. Larsson (2012) 'Military professionalism of the Swedish Armed Forces in the 21st century' in Stouffer J. & D. Lindsay (Eds) *Threats to military professionalism: International perspectives*. Kingston, Canada: Canadian Defence Academy Press, pp. 169–94.

Nilsson, S., P. Hyllengren, A. Ohlsson, K. Kallenberg, G. Waaler & G. Larsson (2015) 'Leadership and moral stress: Individual reaction patterns among first responders in acute situations that involve moral stressors' *Journal of Trauma & Treatment* Vol. 4, pp. 261–71.

Nye, J.S. (2008) *The powers to lead*. New York: Oxford University Press, Inc.

Sweeney, P.J. (2010) 'Do soldiers reevaluate trust in their leaders prior to combat operations?' *Military Psychology* Vol. 22, No. 1, suppl 1, pp. 70–88.

Taylor, S.S. & D. Ladkin (2009) 'Understanding art-based methods in managerial development' *Academy of Management Learning & Education* Vol. 8, No. 1, pp. 55–69.

Tonnies, C. (1887) *Gemeinschaft und Gesellschaft.* Leipzig: Fues's Verlag.

Wyszynski, J.L. (2005) *Adaptability: Components of the adaptive competency for US Army direct and organizational level leaders.* Fort Leavenworth, Kansas.

Yukl, G. (2002) *Leadership in organizations* 5th edition. Saddle River, NJ: Prentice Hall.

8 Introducing gender perspectives in operations
Afghanistan as a catalyst[1]

Robert Egnell

Introduction

The military interventions conducted since 9/11 have witnessed plenty of tactical and operational-level adaptations to tackle the challenges faced in the complex operational theatres in Iraq and Afghanistan. One of the more contested adaptations has been the introduction of gender perspectives in operations and the increasing roles of women. Specific gender-related functions such as Gender Field Advisors, Gender Focal Points, Female Engagement Teams and Cultural Support Teams have been created, and gendered analysis and planning have to some extent been introduced into staff processes and operations.

The Swedish Armed Forces (SAF) have been among the forerunners in implementing a gender perspective in military organizations and operations. Despite considerable resistance from parts of the organization, during the last decade the Swedish military has gone through an impressive process of change, which started with highly limited and isolated gender-related projects and today involves an institutionalised gender organisation that has worked to mainstream a gender perspective, conduct training and establish specific gender-related functions such as Gender Field Advisors and Gender Focal Points. The Gender Field Advisors have been deployed with Swedish and international units in conflicts around the world during this process, and have thereby gained important experience and continued to refine the Swedish approach to gender implementation in military operations. The latest development has been the establishment of the Nordic Centre for Gender in Military Operations, a NATO-appointed Centre of Excellence (COE) that aims to function as a platform for continued implementation of a gender perspective in Sweden and abroad (Egnell 2014).

This chapter aims to increase our understanding about the nature of these organizational adaptations and processes of change. It asks two questions:

1. What influence has the Swedish engagement in Afghanistan had for the implementation of a gender perspective in the Swedish Armed Forces during the past decade?

2. What consequences and lessons can be identified from these implementation processes – in terms of both the specific gender studies debate and broader organizational change processes in the security sector?

The chapter seeks to answer these questions by initially describing the broader background to the change processes and subsequently studying the more specific nature of the change process in the Swedish Armed Forces during operations in Afghanistan. The main argument is that the relatively impressive change process can be explained by a combination of normative imperatives, tactical adaptation and an unusually well-managed organizational change process. The mission in Afghanistan proved to be an essential catalyst for these processes. However, given the importance of Afghanistan and counterinsurgency thinking during expeditionary operations, the question is: what will happen now that the Swedish Armed Forces have withdrawn from Afghanistan and are completely shifting focus from international operations to national defence?

The early years of the change process

In general terms, the Swedish societal context can be described as one of strong societal support for women's rights and gender sensitivity. However, the first formal impetus for introducing gender perspectives in military operations was external and consisted of the international process of writing and passing the landmark United Nations Security Council Resolution 1325 on women, peace and security (Interview with Charlotte Isaksson 4 April 2011).

In general terms, UNSCR 1325 not only addresses the unique and disproportionate impact that armed conflict has on women but also recognises the undervalued and underutilised contributions that women make to conflict prevention and resolution, peacekeeping and peacebuilding. The resolution moves beyond the traditional protection of women as victims or non-combatants to stress the importance of women's full and equal participation as active agents in peace and security organizations (UNSC 2000).

A closer look at UNSCR 1325 reveals that it is intended to be a strategic framework for conducting more effective and sustainable peace negotiations, peacekeeping missions and conflict resolution interventions by the international community. It encompasses a range of complex issues, including judicial and legal reform, as part of state building; security sector reform; formal and informal peace negotiations; peacekeeping, political participation and protection from and responses to sexual violence in armed conflict. UNSCR 1325 and four subsequent resolutions under the umbrella of the women, peace and security agenda (UNSCR 1820, 1888, 1889 and 1960) lay out actions to be taken by governments, the United Nations and other international and national actors. There are four main pillars:

Participation: The participation and inclusion of women (including civil society actors) in the decision-making and execution of activities related to peacemaking, post-conflict reconstruction and the prevention of conflict;

Protection: The protection of women and girls in armed conflict (including in refugee and displacement situations through peacekeeping and policing, constitutional, electoral and legal processes and social and economic recovery) and the training of military and civilian personnel (including peacekeepers) in the protection of women (including zero tolerance of sexual exploitation and abuse of local populations);

Prevention: Prevention of conflict-related sexual violence and effective reporting of violations and protection of victims; and

Gender Mainstreaming: The systematic implementation of a gender perspective in peacekeeping and peacebuilding (as per UNSCR 1325) by all Member States, especially in the context of peace missions led by the UN (Egnell *et al.* 2014, p. 21).

It is important to emphazise that implementing a gender perspective through these four pillars entails not only providing instruction for external development and security strategies – issues of output in other countries and organizations – but also internal efforts inside governments and organizations. This chapter therefore distinguishes between the implementation of a gender perspective *internally* (efforts inside the Swedish Armed Forces) and *externally* (with regard to their participation in international operations).

Since UNSCR 1325 was passed the Swedish Armed Forces have reported on the organization's work to combat discrimination, including discrimination related to gender or sexual orientation. In early 2003, the third attachment (regarding personnel issues) of the Swedish Armed Forces' report for 2002 stated that, as part of its equality work, the Armed Forces had been directed by the Ministry of Defence to arrange a national knowledge-building and competence surveying seminar with regard to UNSCR 1325/2000. This was the start of the Swedish Armed Forces' work to implement the UN resolution in its work, and, during 2002, task group 1325/2000 was established in order to contribute to this development (Swedish Armed Forces 2003, p. 28).

The 2004 Government Appropriation Directive required the Armed Forces to report on their continuing work for increased awareness concerning UN resolution 1325 (2000) (Swedish Government 2004). The following year, the same requirement was repeated, and the Government added that education should continue to be developed 'so that personnel [who will participate in international crisis management] will have a sound understanding of how they should act according to [UNSCR 1325] in the area of operations' (Swedish Government 2005).

In the end, the formal paper trail for the implementation of UNSCR 1325 in the Swedish Armed Forces is something of a facade. The Government was neither entirely clear about the tasks entailed by UNSCR 1325 implementation nor very supportive of the processes that the Armed Forces initiated. Most of the work that was conducted was therefore the result of the actions of various change agents who devised their own activities and solutions and who thereby dragged both the political leadership and the Armed Forces along with them.

The first serious change process was that of 'Genderforce' – an interagency project on gender involving a number of key government agencies, but also civil society groups like *Kvinna till Kvinna* [Woman to Woman] (Swedish Armed Forces 2007). The project was limited in scope but two important developments took hold: the Gender Field Advisor concept and training course and the Gender Coach Program. Despite positive evaluations and a request to continue Genderforce, it was allowed to be discontinued on 31 December 2007, largely due to the fact that the partner agencies declined to finance the project (Interview with Isaksson 9 May 2011). However, the Swedish Armed Forces continued their work and, most importantly, the recommendation from Genderforce to establish a full-time position for implementing a gender perspective was acted upon.

Increased momentum in Afghanistan

Towards the end of the Genderforce project, the Swedish Armed Forces took over the British Provincial Reconstruction Team (PRT) in Mazar-e-Sharif in Northern Afghanistan. A Swedish contingent was at the same time deployed with the European Union military operation in support of the United Nations Organization Mission in the Democratic Republic of the Congo (MONUC) during the election process (Operation EUFOR RD Congo) in the Eastern DRC. The Swedish Armed Forces were in other words facing serious challenges in the field of operations – something that, intuitively for a military organization, could signal a moment to disregard gender and women altogether to focus on the 'more serious' (or kinetic) issues. The opposite was true, however.

In 2006–07, the security situations in Afghanistan and Iraq were deteriorating dramatically, signalling a failure of the international community to understand the nature of the problems and how best to deal with them. The strategic buzzword of the day became 'counterinsurgency' – a concept that emphasized winning the hearts and minds of the local population, the importance of civil–military cooperation and cultural understanding. The US Army/Marine Corps Counterinsurgency Field Manual (FM 3-24) describes the first historical principle of such operations as: 'Legitimacy is the main objective' and 'to foster development of effective governance by a legitimate government' (US Army & USMC 2006, p. 37). Lessons from both Iraq and Afghanistan clearly highlighted a need to engage better with the local population – including women.

Garfield argues that defeating the political subversion of insurgencies requires making a difference in the lives of the local population as early as possible. This involved efforts to ensure fair treatment; the creation of jobs;

improvements in education and medical services; providing a bearable standard of living, basic personal security and some form of legitimate representative governance (Garfield 2006, p. 16).

Military presence and activity are vital both to establish the necessary level of security and for coercive purposes. However, military activity can only work in a support function to the civilian activities of political and economic reform (US Army & USMC 2006, p. 37). As an example, the commander of the International Security Assistance Force (ISAF) in Afghanistan accurately notes that the Afghan people will decide who wins. The Government of Afghanistan and ISAF are therefore involved in a struggle for the support of the local population (ISAF Headquarters 2009).

This was a serious diversion from more conventionally-focused military organizations like the US Army. For the Swedish Armed Forces, which have a peacekeeping tradition, these concepts seem rather natural – although the kinetic aspects of counterinsurgency operations (the clear hold build) proved to be more of a challenge. While counterinsurgency seemed intuitively commonsensical to the Swedish contingent, it still highlighted a gap in competence and capability in terms of approaching the Afghan population in general and women in particular. The response to this challenge was to deploy Gender Field Advisors to the PRT in Afghanistan – a concept tested in the DRC for the first time in 2006.

The Gender Field Advisors

Describing the work of the Gender Field Advisors in generic terms is difficult, as it has been a position that has constantly evolved over the years in Afghanistan. This process of change has been based on lessons learned and changed policies, as well as the personalities and preferences of the Gender Field Advisors and their commanding officers. Making the Gender Field Advisor role as effective as possible is an entirely new and untested process that has necessitated plenty of experimentation and innovation to overcome challenges and to improve what was already working. Each individual Gender Field Advisor has contributed to this process by introducing and testing new routines and instructions for themselves and their successors. Many of the challenges faced in early deployments have therefore been dealt with and sometimes solved.

Nonetheless, according to the Swedish Armed Forces, the Gender Field Advisor:

> is responsible for the implementation of UNSCR 1325/2000 and UNSCR 1820/2008, in order to mainstream gender issues at all levels of the military's work. The role of the GFA can vary depending on the size and type of the operation, the mandate, the operational area and reinforcing or deterring structures in the operational area. An introductory analysis of equality and gender relations in the prospective Area of

Responsibility (AOR) will provide a platform for all other work and measures. During the mission, the GFA supports the Commanding Officer in operational planning and is responsible for the overall implementation and mainstreaming of the gender efforts in the mission. Other tasks that the GFA is responsible for during his/her time abroad consist of:

- Being an asset from a security perspective (Force Protection through good relations with the citizens of the AOR)
- Providing a link to important civilian elements in the local community
- Directly supporting the commander in the planning, conduct and evaluation of operations, by implementing a Gender Perspective in the operational work
- Educating, monitoring and supporting the Gender Focal Points
- Presenting a gender analysis related to the operational work in the AOR.

(Swedish Armed Forces undated, p. 3)

Several interviewees have reported that the nature of the Gender Field Advisor function was very unclear, both to the Gender Field Advisors and to their commanders and colleagues (Interviews with GFA 17 June 2011b, 9 June 2011; Interview with CO 29 June 2011).

While supposedly generic, the Gender Field Advisor concept has largely been developed within the specific context of the Swedish contribution to the ISAF in Afghanistan. The Gender Field Advisor Standard Operating Procedures (SOPs) were originally based on the guidance documents from the European Union military operation in the Republic of Chad and in the Central African Republic (EUFOR Tchad/RCA) Gender Advisor, which in turn had been based on the guidance documents from the EUFOR RD Congo Gender Advisor, all developed by the Gender Advisor.

Gender Field Advisors have been appointed by the Commanding Officer in close cooperation with the Senior Gender Advisor at the Swedish Armed Forces HQ. They serve 6 months in Afghanistan and follow the same rotation as the Armed Forces in general – as opposed to Political and Development Advisors, who serve for 12 months and are appointed by the Swedish Ministry of Foreign Affairs and the Swedish International Development Agency. They have been recruited from both military and non-military positions and possess varying backgrounds and education. Only two have been civilians, and it has been a conscious decision to focus on recruiting military personnel in order to ensure sufficient organizational knowledge and understanding. Some interviewees have stated that they were recruited at a relatively late point in time and thus did not take part in all of the preparations that the rest of the unit did, including team-building activities (Anonymous Interview 17 June 2011).

The first Gender Advisors were deployed without much preparation or instructions, as a result of inadequate time being available for developing training modules or structures for preparing individuals for such tasks. However, there was always a contact person (most often the Senior Gender Advisor) at Swedish Armed Forces Headquarters to whom the Gender Advisors could continuously turn for advice and guidance during the mission.

Even in the early stages, a structure was put in place with mandatory pre-deployment training and preparations for the Gender Field Advisors. This has included:

1. Attending the Gender Field Advisor course (now at the Nordic Centre for Gender in Military Operations)
2. Participating as a Gender Advisor in an international staff exercise, such as the Combined Joint Staff Exercise, Viking or Illuminated Summer
3. Undergoing a one-day qualitative psychological evaluation, equivalent to the evaluation for aspiring colonels, and
4. Receiving a pre-mission brief by the Senior Gender Advisor at the Directorate of Operations.

Over time, a Gender Annex to the Operation Plan for the Swedish ISAF PRT has also been developed and revised. The original version was less specific and gave significant freedom to the Gender Field Advisors themselves to prioritize and structure their work. This was a hard task to perform if the unit was not 'culturally ready' for some aspects of implementing a gender perspective. As an example, during these early stages, different Gender Field Advisors would prioritise the various tasks – such as supporting staff work or coordinating with external actors – differently. Over time, a standardized prioritisation of the tasks was created. For example, taking an active part in the planning process was deemed to be one of the most important tasks, while coordinating with external actors, such as non-governmental organizations (NGOs), was one of the least important.

The Commander's use of the Gender Field Advisors is an important aspect. Through the Gender Field Advisor's participation in the Command Group, the Gender Field Advisor has direct access to the Commanding Officer (Interview with CO 28 June 2011). Active support from the Commanding Officers has been crucial for the Gender Field Advisors to complete their tasks successfully, although such support has varied substantially. Some Commanding Officers have expressed public support and priority for the implementation of a gender perspective, but have in practice showed little interest in it (Interviews with GFA 9 June 2011, with GFA 17 June, 2011b and with GFA 29 June 2011). According to a former Gender Advisor, while her Commanding Officer would make decisions that she suggested, as Gender Advisor she would also be made responsible for ensuring that they were implemented (Interview with Axmacher 2008). One Commanding Officer had previously participated in the Genderforce project and thereby had knowledge of what implementing a gender perspective entails and what the role of a Gender Field Advisor is (Interview with GFA 13 June 2011). Such previous knowledge resulted in greater support for the work of the Gender Field Advisors.

The deployment of Swedish Gender Advisors – first to the DRC and later in greater numbers to Afghanistan – clearly began in an unstructured and unprepared manner, but has continuously evolved and improved over time thanks to persistence, learning and leadership. It should also be noted that it was a very conscious decision by the Senior Gender Advisor to start deploying Gender Advisors before the organization was ready and before all the necessary structures, instructions, concepts and training were developed. By learning from practice rather than theoretically perfecting the function at home, the progress in implementing a gender perspective is deemed to have gone much faster – something that is obvious in the advantage that Sweden holds compared to most other nations. Waiting for the bureaucratic processes to develop before acting would have taken much longer, especially within an organizational culture involving so much resistance. The deployment of Gender Advisors can thereby be viewed as a long organizational learning and development process. The organization improves with each set of lessons learned. Given the many external factors that shape the circumstances and possibilities for a Gender Advisor to succeed in his/her work, the organization highlights that, when things do not go as planned, the individual Gender Advisors cannot be held responsible for the lack of implementation of a gender perspective (Interview with GFA 13 June 2011).

Consolidation: institutionalisation and norm diffusion

From the early years of project-based work on gender issues, the section above illustrated an increasing influx of gender directives in the formal documents from within the organization as well as from the political leadership, as well as a growing pool of people with some level of expertise in these areas thanks to courses, seminars, gender coaches or deployment as gender advisors. The final phase to date has involved the consolidation and institutionalisation of these achievements – a process described below and taking place partly as a consequence of operations in Afghanistan (Egnell *et al.* 2014).

The Nordic Centre for Gender in Military Operations

The Nordic Centre for Gender in Military Operations (NCGM) merits particular attention, as it provides the first example of a truly institutionalised gender organisation within the military – the bricks and mortar of the achievements to date. Efforts towards establishing the Centre commenced in the summer of 2008, when the idea for a centre was first proposed by the Norwegian and Swedish Armed Forces. The idea at this early stage was for the Centre to:

> assist in developing concepts and mandates for gender-sensitive operations, facilitate/conduct training and education of key personnel,

compile lessons learned and carry out evaluations of gender-sensitive operations. Furthermore, it is meant as a watchdog for 1325 in the respective defence forces. Implementation is set for 2011 and estimated to involve 8–10 persons (from a mix of nations) to be located in one of the Nordic countries.

(NORDSUP, 2008, p. 22)

Previously, the Nordic countries had co-established a mixed MOT team in Afghanistan following the all-female MOT Juliet. However, the project of a Nordic mixed MOT team was quickly abandoned. The need for raising awareness and competence with respect to implementing a gender perspective in military operations was nonetheless clearly identified, and the idea of establishing the Nordic Centre was aired. Following a period of much activity – during which the Swedish Senior GA, inter alia, did much preparatory work – a Nordic Defence Cooperation (NORDEFCO) report formally recommended the establishment of a common centre for gender in military operations (Axmacher, interviewed 2012). The importance of gathering lessons learned and institutionalising training of gender advisors for Afghanistan was a key component in the creation of the Centre, which was finally inaugurated on 24 January 2012.

The Centre is located, together with the Swedish International unit (SWEDINT), just outside of Stockholm. The staff includes instructors, analysts and persons responsible for cooperation and development. As already noted, the Centre has the potential to play a key role in supporting further efforts to strengthen the Armed Forces' implementation of a gender perspective. The Centre is also well-positioned to play an important role in supporting similar implementation developments in other countries. While the main focus will be the Nordic countries' military organizations, the target audience also includes other NATO, EU and UN countries (Swedish Armed Forces 2011b). In that spirit, on 22 February 2013, the Swedish Armed Forces signed a Memorandum of Understanding with Headquarters, Supreme Allied Command Transformation and Supreme Headquarters Allied Powers Europe that formalized Sweden's Nordic Centre for Gender in Military Operations (NCGM) as the lead for gender education and training by designating it as the Department Head (DH) for all NATO-led curricula concerning gender. The Centre is thereby in a unique position to capture and disseminate the lessons of the Swedish experience, as well as the experiences of NATO partners, to the militaries of other countries.

The Gender Focal Points

A single Gender Field Advisor would have a difficult time influencing the conduct of operations; a more institutionalised mainstreaming of a gender perspective was needed. One solution was to appoint Gender Focal Points within the specific units. According to the Swedish Armed Forces information folders, having Gender Focal Points appointed within the respective units:

> is a well-tried method for integrating a gender perspective into the different branches and units. Gender Focal Points are appointed by their superiors and allocate approximately 5 per cent of their working time to the task of implementing gender measures in the field.
> (Swedish Armed Forces undated, p. 3)

The Focal Point is also expected to assist the Commander in implementing procedures dealing with gender issues; inform and train troops on gender issues in operations; receive reports from witnesses on gender-related problems, collect lessons learned regarding gender issues related to operational work and stay in regular contact with the Gender Field Advisor, to whom the Focal Point reports every two weeks or as soon as possible on matters of urgency (Swedish Armed Forces undated, p. 3).

Since around 2008, all rotations in Afghanistan have had designated Gender Focal Points in every platoon and section of the staff prior to deployment. They have generally been described as important assets for Gender Advisors and Gender Field Advisors, although they have clearly been used to varying degrees (Swedish Armed Forces undated, p. 3). In general, the Gender Focal Point's usefulness to the Gender Advisor or Gender Field Advisor has probably been the result not only of the Gender Focal Point's personal motivation but also, more importantly, of his or her Commander's commitment to implementing a gender perspective (Interview with GFA 16 November 2011).

Mixed and Female Engagement Teams

In addition to Gender Field Advisors and Gender Focal Points, other organizational innovations have been employed to improve the implementation of a gender perspective. Notably, the Swedish Armed Forces have experimented with various Female and Mixed Engagement Teams (FETs and METs), as well as Military/Mobile Observation Teams (MOTs) that have been dedicated to working on this issue (Egnell *et al.* 2014).

First, in 2006, before a Gender Field Advisor was deployed to the Swedish PRT, an all-female team – 'MOT Juliet' – was already established. This was an experiment with an all-female MOT that consisted of only three female officers (there were no more) and therefore lacked the capabilities of a normal MOT, which normally includes six people. None of the female officers had any previous operational experience and their task was poorly defined. The only direction given was to act as a 'tentacle' among the local female population. They were also supposed to build networks, support local women and provide security. While the officers reported positive experiences overall in MOT Juliet, they also stated that they faced obstacles such as a lack of transportation, support and understanding from other mission members (Burenius 2009, Ivarsson & Edmark 2007). While MOT Juliet was in many ways a good idea, it lacked a number of fundamental prerequisites for success (Interview with Susanne Axmacher 8 February 2012). Consisting as it did of only three people, MOT Juliet needed support from extra soldiers for force protection. Since the other units were reluctant to give up their own resources, this often limited MOT Juliet's mobility outside the camp. Nonetheless, the three women who took part in MOT Juliet reported that it was an interesting time and that they had also achieved some small successes – not least a feeling that they had become role models for local women simply by being there, driving the vehicles and participating in meetings (Swedish National Defence College undated). The challenges of MOT Juliet ultimately led to a lessons learned process, which concluded that the Swedish Armed Forces should use mixed teams in a prepared and structured way rather than employing all-female teams. Therefore, MOT Juliet was not succeeded by any similar all-female teams in subsequent rotations.

A second attempt was a Nordic cooperation project. The Swedish Armed Forces were tasked with establishing a MOT 1325, which was to be a Nordic multinational team with gender focus. The 2009 Organization Mission stated that the team would be established in 2009 (Swedish Armed Forces 2009, p. 6). For unknown reasons this was not realized, and instead of the Nordic MOT 1325 the Swedish contingent commander established a Swedish 'MOT Y'. The leader of MOT Y was a male captain, recruited because he was highly respected by colleagues and thought to have the proper disposition for understanding the importance of implementing a gender perspective. He was allowed to recruit his own team members, but his second-in-command was required to be a woman, and both sexes had to be equally represented within the MOT. They were given supplemental education and training in addition to the regular training package given to all MOTs. Although the Senior Gender Advisor had initially opposed the establishment of MOT Y as a substitute for MOT 1325, it was reportedly a successful initiative (Interview with CO 29 June 2011).

The challenges faced when attempting to set up Mixed Engagement Teams are one of the more blatant examples of the organization's resistance to gender-related work. The directive to create such teams was an assignment to all Swedish units in Afghanistan from the Chief of Joint Operations. However, some officers in leading positions resisted this notion and refused to recruit enough women to establish effective METs. In one instance, it took additional pressure in the form of a personal meeting with the Chief of Joint Operations to move matters forward. A number of women were eventually recruited, but with very short notice before the unit's departure to Afghanistan. This is turn made their integration into the units difficult (Interview with Axmacher 25 October 2012).

Examples exist that provide evidence of increased operational effectiveness from using METs. In one case, the Swedish Armed Forces conducted patrols in Southwestern parts of their area of operations, where ISAF had not operated previously. The Swedes needed to inform the local population of their mission. Because they had chosen to conduct the patrol with a MET, they were able to communicate with all elements of the local community, including the women (Interview with CO 9 November 2011a). The impact of this is impossible to fully assess, but there are clearly potential benefits from such 'complete social engagement'.

In another case, female members of MET received information about a Taliban Commander unlawfully collecting taxes in the area when they visited a school that men were not allowed to access. Thanks to this information, the male members of the team, working with the Afghan National Police, were able to arrest the Taliban Commander, thereby also freeing the area of the unwanted taxation (DCAF 2011, p. 8).

Several interviewees stated that mixed teams were able to communicate with a broader array of people, which thereby increased operational effectiveness. The reason for this is that heterogeneous units, by counteracting group-think, result in more perspectives being considered; this in turn creates an organizational culture better suited to the different forms of complex peace operations and counterinsurgency. For example, according to a former Commanding Officer, men and women look for different things when searching houses, thereby contributing to a broader intelligence picture (Engelbrektson 2007, p. 22). Furthermore, it helped to moderate an overly masculine tone of communication within the unit. One Gender Field Advisor stated that all-male patrols were met with more hostility and aggression than mixed teams in the area of operations (Isaksson 2006, p. 5). The general MOT structure (not just the gender-focused MOTs) was eventually abandoned because of the worsening security situation; having small units in soft-skin vehicles patrolling far from the home base was simply too dangerous.

The capability to establish mixed teams, including METs, has been circumscribed by the shortage of female soldiers and officers. Initiatives have been taken to increase the number of women within the Swedish mission in Afghanistan. The Chief of Joint Operations authored a directive stating that the proportion of women in MOTs and provincial offices (POs) was to increase noticeably from late 2007 on. Despite this, little progress has been made, and in late 2011 approximately fifty women could be found among the roughly 500 members of the unit – that is, only approximately 10 per cent (Interview with GFA 11 November 2011).

Apart from female soldiers and officers, an asset considered critical to successful work with local women is the availability and use of female interpreters by the Swedish Armed Forces in carrying out their mandate. Because of the lack of female military interpreters, the Swedish Armed Forces have been dependent on hiring local women as interpreters. In general this has been challenging, because Afghan culture often precludes women from working outside of the home. As a result, the Swedish Armed Forces have been forced to seek the permission of close male family members of the potential female employee. Furthermore, local female interpreters have been constrained in their work because they are usually not allowed to travel during the night; in some cases, chaperones have been used to allow female interpreters to participate in operations.

Mentoring of Afghan National Security Forces

An increasingly important part of the Swedish work in Afghanistan became the mentoring of the Afghan National Security Forces (ANSF). This can be divided into the Swedish Armed Forces' Operational Mentor Liaison Teams (OMLTs), which have focused on the Afghan National Army, and mentoring of the Afghan National Police by civilian police advisors. The latter have been active in mentoring Afghan female police officers and have cooperated in this with the Gender Field Advisor (Radestad 2011, p. 4).

The OMLTs work closely in partnership with the Afghan National Army units that they mentor, including participation in specific operations that may last several days. Former Gender Field Advisors stated that, to their knowledge, Swedish OMLTs do not mentor on the implementation of a gender perspective (Interviews with GFA 11 November 2011, 16 November 2011). One recent Gender Field Advisor reported that he advised his Commanding Officer in operational planning to ensure that both ISAF and the Afghan National Security Forces included a gender perspective when conducting common search operations (Radestad 2011, p. 3). The Swedish Armed Forces have so far refrained from using any women as military mentors, reportedly out of concern that the Afghan National Army counterparts would perceive this as culturally insensitive (despite the fact that the Afghan National Army includes women). Other countries, including the United States, do have female military mentors working with Afghan units (Interview with GFA 11 November 2011).

As operations in the last years of operations in Afghanistan increasingly focused on training and mentoring, plans for providing more training on Resolution 1325 and the practical implications for the work of ANSF were developed. Additionally, women were being recruited to the OMLTs. Furthermore, one interviewee stated that the Afghan National Security Forces often demonstrate a well-developed, albeit tacit, gender perspective. For example, they use female members during operations to search women (Interview with GFA 9 June 2011). More recently, the Swedish contingent in Afghanistan has also conducted a number of training days with female Afghan police officers with the purpose of increasing their operational competence. This training has focused on three competences: searching suspects and vehicles, providing combat first aid and using a firearm. The Swedish unit also supports the gender function of the Afghan National Police by attending planning meetings with the higher leadership and by stressing the need for women in operations.

Discussion

By studying the Swedish case of gender integration it becomes clear that two primary sets of external factors have driven the process towards integrating a gender perspective in the Swedish Armed Forces. The first are directives from the Swedish Government, which in turn were motivated by the adoption of UNSCR 1325 in 2000. Sweden was the second country (behind Denmark) to adopt a National Action Plan (NAP) for the implementation of UNSCR 1325 by various parts of the Government, including the Armed Forces (Gumru & Fritz 2009). This happened in 2006, and in 2009 an updated action plan for the period 2009–12 was adopted. In 2015, a third iteration will be presented – most likely the first in the world. This first driver is thus political and normative in nature: the Armed Forces reacted to a changed normative environment prompted by political decisions by the UN and the Swedish Government.

The second important set of drivers emerged as the implementation of political decisions progressed. The Swedish Armed Forces realised that integrating a gender perspective in international operations could contribute to enhancing military effectiveness. This is reflected, in part, by the new Military Strategic Doctrine of 2011, and is discussed therein under the heading 'Gender: an example of effects-based thinking' (Swedish Armed Forces 2011b). In essence, operational lessons during the last two decades – whether we call them stability operations, peacekeeping, state building or counterinsurgency operations – point to the importance of understanding women's roles in society and collecting intelligence from all parts of society, as well as the ability to engage or interrogate women and operate with cultural sensitivity. When pursuing the strategic aims of operations – regardless whether these are defined as victory, protection of civilians or stabilization – being able to apply a gendered analysis or operational approach and bring female perspectives and capabilities to bear is therefore of great importance to achieving the desired effects. The combination of these political/normative factors and the tactical lessons from the field – especially in Afghanistan – created an unusually good environment for organizational change.

It should nonetheless be noted that these 'external factors' do not fully explain the Swedish frontrunner role when it comes to these issues. Most countries have had identical external imperatives for change but have secured very little adaptation or organizational change. The fact that Sweden is a relatively gender-equal society clearly plays a small role. However, those general values were not present within the organizational culture during the change process, and we therefore have to complement the analysis of the change process with equally internal factors.

First, a very small number of key actors – or agents of change – effectively managed the change process. It is difficult to overstate the importance to this process of Charlotte Isaksson, who was the architect of the entire process until she left for a similar position with NATO. In the Swedish military, she created and then held the position of the first Swedish Armed Forces Senior Gender Advisor and built an entire organization of gender experts and advisors around her. However, the large impact of this single actor would not have been possible without the support from a number of surrounding people – not least since she, as a civilian, lacked the authority that accompanies being an officer within an organization structured around formal hierarchies.

Second, the analysis in this chapter ascertains that the change agents within the Swedish Armed Forces made a strategic decision to approach the implementation of a gender perspective in the organization as an issue of operational effectiveness – as opposed to one of 'merely' gender equality, women's rights or human resources. The basis of this decision was the reasonable assumption that the introduction and implementation of a gender perspective was likely to face strong resistance within the male-dominated organizational culture of the Swedish Armed Forces. This limited tactic never reflected the more ambitious aims of the implementation process as envisaged by the key agents of change, or the more ambitious agenda entailed in Resolution 1325. However, the decision-makers hoped that this limited 'inside' approach would be a useful way of gaining entry to the organization and building a platform from which to pursue a more ambitious long-term agenda.

Third, the relative success of the Swedish experience in developing a framework for implementing a gender perspective can also be partly explained by how the process was managed through the work of the Senior Gender Advisor, and by the receptiveness of the Chiefs of Joint Operations who served during this period of change. A key decision was to strategically place the Senior Gender Advisor directly under the Chief of Joint Operations in order to maximize the credibility and centrality of the Senior Gender Advisor position. This was in contrast with other countries, which have tended to organize the units responsible for implementing a gender perspective within their policy planning processes or Human Resources departments, thereby effectively sidelining Gender Advisors and diminishing the importance of implementing a gender perspective as crucial to the core tasks of the organization.

In contrast, and as mentioned previously, the benefit of the Swedish structure is that it considered a gender perspective to be an issue of operational effectiveness rather than 'just' a politically-laden human resources issue of women's rights and participation. The core task of military organizations is to fight and win the nation's wars, or to apply organized violence or the threat of such violence in pursuit of the national leadership's political aims. This is what these organizations are structured, trained and equipped to do, which means that arguments about equal women's rights and gender balancing simply do not generate interest. In other words, a gender perspective focused on operational effectiveness is seen as more relevant within the military organization. The strategic placement of the Gender Advisor and the focus on operational effectiveness not only amplified the implementation of a gender perspective in the Swedish Armed Forces as a core issue of output in terms of operations, but also sent a strong signal to the organization regarding the importance of a gender perspective in the conduct of military affairs. When presenting a gender perspective as an issue of operational effectiveness, it not only addressed the core task of the organization, but also uses language with which military commanders are more comfortable and familiar (Egnell et al. 2014).

In sum, the external and internal factors helped to create a 'perfect storm' for change in the Swedish case. Ranking the importance of the different factors or disaggregating them for testing purposes is very difficult. It is nevertheless clear that the strategic approach to focus on gender as an important factor for operational effectiveness would not have gained much traction unless supported by actual lessons from the field of operations supporting this notion. The importance of Afghanistan as a catalyst therefore cannot be overstated. Officers and soldiers saw first-hand the need for women and gendered approaches in the field of operations. This meant that the change process was pursued through a double grip of political and normative imperatives from above, and tactical lessons and understanding from below. Afghanistan was also of great importance as a testing ground for new approaches and tools. Gendered approaches in operations; Field Advisors; Focal Points; Standard Operating Procedures, order templates and female and mixed teams could all be introduced, developed and tested within the context of a real and sustained operation, which certainly speeded up the process of change. The fact that it was an operation within which counterinsurgency approaches were applied – emphasizing cultural understanding and support to the local population – only increased the importance of gender perspectives. Afghanistan therefore became the perfect catalyst and testing ground for developing these perspectives.

Back to the future: dismantle, retain or expand?

The realization that the operations in Afghanistan have been instrumental in promoting and developing a gender perspective within the Swedish Armed Forces raises interesting questions about the future. The Swedish military has more or less withdrawn from Afghanistan and, with increasing rumblings from Russia, the focus of the Swedish Armed Forces is switching from an almost complete focus on international operations to territorial defence and the Baltic region. There is a risk that the relatively fragile change process will therefore be undone. The argument can be made that, while a gender perspective has a place in peacekeeping- and counterinsurgency-type operations, the same cannot be said for conventional military operations. The risk of this argument gaining foothold is increased by the fact that it correlates with the general organizational culture of all military organizations: a preference for interstate conventional warfare. As the Armed Forces reorganize for national defence under the constraints of limited defence budgets, there is a distinct risk that the Nordic Centre for Gender in Military Operations (NCGM), the active focus on Gender Advisors and Focal Points and the ongoing process of cultural adaptations will be lost, with the assertion that there are more important priorities.

There is plenty of logic in such arguments, but given the clues of the type of warfare we are likely to expect in the contemporary era, it may still be a big mistake. Even wars involving the great powers have been of the 'hybrid' type (including both conventional and unconventional aspects) – not least the conflict in Eastern Ukraine, which shows the complexity of operations and the prevalence of irregular forces and propaganda. Understanding the local context, winning the support of the population and achieving legitimacy in the eyes of the local and global communities are still of great relevance, which means that gender perspectives are still of great utility. The gender aspects of the organization are quite limited and relatively cheap, while the rewards may in some cases be large. Throwing the progress made onto the dust piles of history may therefore prove to be a big mistake. The Swedish Armed Forces have plenty of experience when it comes to dismantling organizational competence – and the costs of trying to retrieve that competence – from the downsizing of the force after the Cold War. It would be a shame to make the same mistake again.

It should also be noted that, despite the successes, the work to implement Resolution 1325 still faces considerable resistance from within the military establishment. Still, there is plenty of room for a continued implementation of a gender perspective. Should the Armed Forces choose to expand this work over the coming years, it is important that they not only aim to take new and bold steps, but also seek some form of consolidation by continuously wearing down the resistance. Not least, the argument must be made that this is not just an important aspect of expeditionary international operations, but also one of national defence and regional stability.

Steps to continue the work to include a broader understanding of gender issues – and to attribute increased importance and status to them – must also include reaching more layers of the organization; for example, through gender mainstreaming training, officer education and field exercises. This will also require increased resources, political backing and command authority within the organization. Such changes will also risk creating increased resistance, as they inevitably challenge existing power structures, standard operating procedures and cultural preferences. Finding a balance between consolidation and further change is going to be imperative and will require plenty of *fingerspitzengefühl*.

Specifically, a next step in the process to integrate a gender perspective further into the Swedish Armed Forces should be to include a concrete agenda for ending sexual violence in war, as part of broader mandate of Protection of Civilians. This is actually a step that should have been included in the initial implementation package, since it addresses the military effectiveness in fulfilling political mandates and the aims of contemporary international operations. Nonetheless, while sexual violence and civilian protection are increasingly emphasized in UNSC directives for operations, military organizations have been slow in adopting training, methods and doctrine to execute these mandates effectively. This trend can be partially explained by the fact that these challenges have traditionally been beyond the scope of a conventional security agenda, which focuses on resolving international conflicts or state-level challenges to international order and stability.

There are also a number of elements of the Swedish Armed Forces Headquarters' approach to implementing a gender perspective that require increased attention in the coming years. First, the role, nature and resources of the Senior Gender Advisor must be reconsidered. The current robust list of tasks is not commensurate with the limited resources of this 'office'. The work of the Senior Gender Advisor includes ensuring that the entire organization, including the units in the field, performs its tasks in accordance with UNSCR 1325. It also includes drafting all background materials and sections of orders, as well as providing advice to different staff functions. Placing the responsibility for integrating a gender perspective on an advisory function is untenable in the long run; either this responsibility and accountability must be transferred to those with formal command authority, or the Senior Gender Advisor should be given command authority equal to an appropriate rank – thereby being able to issue orders and control resources. To be responsible for the cultural and structural changes of the Armed Forces is a tall order for a single individual, who has also thus far lacked the brass on the shoulders and the credibility and authority that this brass bestows in an inherently hierarchical organization. All sound strategies have to balance the ends with the ways and means. Given the ambitious aims of the integration of a gender perspective in the Swedish Armed Forces, resources for implementing this perspective must be increased – otherwise, all the policies and strategies for the implementation of such a perspective risk being reduced to mere window dressing.

Second, the switch to a more ambitious strategy that explores the transformational potential of a gender perspective should also take into consideration the key positions within the Headquarters, in which a gender perspective is essential and where Gender Advisors would be, if not necessary, of great assistance. The staffs for strategic and operational analysis and planning of operations are central levels for a gender perspective, both as an added-value tool and as a vehicle of more far-reaching transformation. In this way, a gender perspective could not only influence the tactical conduct of operations in the field but also the Armed Forces' analyses of conflict situations and international security (through support for a gender perspective within military intelligence) and the future development of the Swedish Armed Forces (through support within the command and production staffs). Again, this does not mean that the aim of increasing military effectiveness through implementation of a gender perspective should be abandoned; in fact, quite the contrary.

Third, the Swedish Armed Forces need to increase their efforts to recruit more women, with a focus on international operations and particular emphasis on combat roles. The primary rationale for increasing the number of women should continue to be operational effectiveness and the implementation of a gender perspective in the area of operations. Interviewees have noted that a larger proportion of women in the unit would make it easier to implement a gender perspective (Interview with GFA 17 June 2011). This would create not only an organizational culture more receptive to a gender perspective, but also units with more flexibility in the field, by making it possible to communicate and interact with women in the area of operations and thereby acquire a broader intelligence picture. Given the difficulty of recruiting and retaining soldiers and officers, the question is whether the Swedish Armed Forces can afford *not* to succeed in the continued work of making the organization more gender balanced and palatable for a broader recruitment base – not least women. If the organization remains steeped in a traditional masculine-dominated culture, the possibility of recruiting the necessary talent may indeed decrease – along with its legitimacy within society.

Fourth, while this chapter certainly seeks to avoid a one-size-fits-all approach, it is clear that the work of Gender Field Advisors could be streamlined into fewer activities and that a number of externally-focused activities should be abandoned. Avoiding the repetition of past mistakes in the recruitment and training processes of future Gender Field Advisors also requires the use of lessons learned. However, it should also be noted that – with respect to situations in which a gender perspective has been important – the collection of lessons learned from members of the mission *other* than Gender Field Advisors is almost as important. In the end, it is the soldiers in the field – who conduct daily operations among the population – who can report back on the usefulness of a gender perspective. Furthermore, systematic collection of data regarding a gender perspective from the field, including sex-disaggregated data, is important for the evaluation of the effects of operations. Information regarding sexual and gender-based violence and human trafficking should be included in such data. Close cooperation with different NGOs could also potentially be beneficial within this field.

Beyond the military headquarters, there is plenty of unfinished business in other branches of the Swedish Armed Forces. The establishment in early 2012 of the Nordic Centre for Gender in Military Operations within the Swedish Armed Forces may, with time, compensate for the previous reliance on a single person and limited staff. However, a risk of creating a dedicated Centre for Gender in Military Operations is that gender-related work may become isolated therein and the rest of the organization might use the Centre's existence as an excuse to de-emphasize the implementation of a gender perspective. As an example, a pre-deployment training unit continues to shirk the responsibility of providing gender integration training by continuously relying on temporarily utilised gender experts. This allows them to avoid building any competence of their own and to actively resist the integration of a gender perspective into their work. To avoid such behaviour, it is important that gender issues be mainstreamed throughout the organization, and that the Centre be employed as a resource for achieving more far-reaching aims. Gender Advisors and Gender Focal Points should therefore be spread throughout the organization to impact upon schools and training facilities at all levels, thereby normalising a gender perspective in all military activities: an important development, and one already in motion.

Finally, beyond the standing units, the work of gender mainstreaming must involve the schools and training centres of the Armed Forces. It is here that new generations of soldiers and officers are socialised into the military culture, and where the competence and perspective of senior officers can be updated and broadened. It is of utmost importance that a gender perspective is included in all of their courses and exercises. By mainstreaming a gender perspective within the schools and training centres, the potential arises for real and long-term cultural change, as well as attrition of organizational resistance. Again, the introduction of Gender Field Advisors and Gender Focal Points in these institutions should be a high priority – higher than deploying them to the standing units.

Note

1 This chapter draws from and builds on a book by Robert Egnell with Petter Hojem and Hannes Berts (2014), *Gender, military effectiveness, and organizational change: The Swedish model*. London: Palgrave MacMillan.

References

Burenius, L. (2009) *Kvinnor i internationella insatser? En undersökning om hur kvinnligt deltagande kan påverka internationella insatser* [Women in international operations? An investigation of the effects of female participation in international operations]. Stockholm: Swedish National Defence College.

DCAF (2011) '*Gender and Defence Transformation: Transforming national structures, sustaining international operations*'. Geneva: DCAF

Egnell, R. with P. Hojem & H. Berts (2014) *Gender, military effectiveness, and organizational change: The Swedish model*. London: Palgrave MacMillan.

Engelbrektson, K. (2007) 'Resolution 1325 increases efficiency' in Nyqvist, A. (Ed) *Good and bad examples: Lessons learned from working with United Nations Resolution 1325 in international missions*. Stockholm: Genderforce, Swedish Armed Forces.

Garfield, A. (2006) *Succeeding in Phase IV: British perspectives on the US effort to stabilize and reconstruct Iraq*. Philadelphia: Foreign Policy Research Institute.

Gumru F.B. & J.M. Fritz (2009) 'Women, peace and security: An analysis of the National Action Plans developed in response to UN Security Council Resolution 1325' *Societies Without Borders* Vol. 4, pp. 209–25.

ISAF Headquarters (2009) *ISAF Commander's Counter-Insurgency Guidance*. Available online at www.nato.int/isaf/docu/official_texts/counterinsurgency_guidance.pdf (accessed 18 September 2009).

Isaksson, Charlotte (2006) 'Final Report on gender work inside EUFOR RD Congo', Swedish Armed Forces internal report, 15 December.

Ivarsson, Sophia & Lina Edmark (2007) *Utlandsstyrkans internationella insatser ur ett genusperspektiv. Hinder och möjligheter för implementering av FN resolution 1325 [A gender perspective on the operations of the international units]*. Stockholm: Swedish National Defence College.
NORDSUP (2008) 'NORDSUP progress report,' 16 June, 22.
Radestad, Urban (2011) 'GFA roll i operativ verksamhet – två exempel från Afghanistanstyrkan 2011' [GFA's role in operations – Two examples from the force in Afghanistan], Swedish Armed Forces internal report, 2011.
Swedish Armed Forces (2003) 'Försvarsmaktens årsredovisning 2002, Bilaga 3: Personalberättelse' [Swedish Armed Forces yearly report 2002, Appendix 3: Personnel]. Stockholm: Swedish Armed Forces.
Swedish Armed Forces (2007) 'Sammanfattning, slutredovisning och rekommendationer avseende projektet Genderforce', [Conclusion, final report, and recommendations regarding project genderforce], internal Swedish Armed Forces report, 19 November.
Swedish Armed Forces (2009) 'Verksamhetsuppdrag för 2009 och (prel) 2010 samt inriktning av verksamheten 2011' [Taskspecification for 2009 and (preliminary) 2010 including direction of the activity in the year 2011]. Stockholm: Swedish Armed Forces.
Swedish Armed Forces (2010) 'Verksamhetsuppdrag för 2010 och (prel) 2011 samt inriktning av verksamheten 2012' [Task specification for 2010 and (preliminary) 2011 including direction of the activity in the year 2012]. Stockholm: Swedish Armed Forces.
Swedish Armed Forces (2011a) 'Available jobs', 10 October 2011.
Swedish Armed Forces (2011b) 'Militärstrategisk doktrin (MSD12)' [Military Strategic Doctrine]. Stockholm: Swedish Armed Forces.
Swedish Armed Forces (undated) *Gender & operational effect. The Gender Field Advisor function in the Swedish Armed Forces*. Unpublished briefing. Stockholm: Försvarsmakten.
Swedish Government (2004) 'Regleringsbrev för budgetåret 2004 avseende Försvarsmakten' [Appropriation direction]. Stockholm: Swedish Government.
Swedish Government (2005) 'Regleringsbrev för budgetåret 2005 avseende Försvarsmakten' [Approapriation direction]. Stockholm: Swedish Government.
Swedish National Defence College (undated) 'Intervju med kvinnliga officerare i MOT Juliette' Available online at www.fhs.se/sv/forskning/forskningsprojekt/pagaende-projekt/ledarskap-under-pafrestande-forhallanden/1325/utlandsstyrkan/pagaende-missioner/afghanistan/intervju-med-kvinnliga-officerare-i-mot-juliette/ (accessed 24 May 2012).
United Nations Security Council (UNSC) (2000) 'Resolution 1325', S/RES/1325.
US Army & USMC (2006) *Counterinsurgency field manual*. Chicago: University of Chicago Press.

Interviews

Interviews with Susanne Axmacher 8 February 2012 and 25 October 2012.
Interviews with Charlotte Isaksson 4 April 2011, 9 May 2011 and 24 August 2015.
Interview with CO 28 June 2011.
Interview with CO 29 June 2011.

Interview with CO 9 November 2011a.
Interview with CO 9 November 2011b.
Interview with GFA 17 June 2011a.
Interview with GFA 17 June 2011b.
Interview with GFA 9 June 2011.
Interview with GFA 13 June 2011.
Interview with GFA 17 June 2011.
Interview with GFA 29 June 2011.
Interview with GFA 11 November 2011.
Interview with GFA 16 November 2011.

9 A veteran at last

The Afghan experience and Swedish veterans policy

Ralph Sundberg

Introduction

In 2014, Sweden celebrated 200 years of peace. This is a truly remarkable feat for a formerly great European power whose influence rested partly on its military prowess. Taking this long period of absence of war into consideration, it might appear as no great puzzle that the business of caring for veterans of war has not taken centre-stage within the Swedish Armed Forces (SAF) or Swedish politics overall. For those who have no veterans of war, other areas of policy may naturally take precedence. Despite its fortuitous 200 years of peace Sweden has, however, been no stranger to the killing fields of the world, owing to its comparatively major commitment to peace support activities. This lengthy engagement in – primarily – United Nations (UN) peacekeeping and observer forces began in the Gaza Strip in 1956 and has included naval missions to Somalia and Lebanon, blue berets in many of the states of former Yugoslavia, Special Forces deployed to the Democratic Republic of Congo and finally the contingents sent to Afghanistan in support of NATO's International Security Assistance Force (ISAF). Coupled with a significant portion of Gross Domestic Product (GDP) being earmarked for foreign aid, this intense engagement in peace-support operations prompted former Foreign Minister Carl Bildt to dub his country a 'humanitarian superpower' (Government of Sweden 2013). Since the 1950s, Sweden has deployed some 60,000–100,000 soldiers to peacekeeping and peace-support operations around the globe (Swedish Armed Forces 2014, Swedish Official Inquiry 2014). The true number of men and women who have been deployed is as yet unknown (although the Swedish Armed Forces' official figure is 85,000), since no complete statistical data are available. To an extent, this is a reflection of the fact that Swedish policies and organizational structures concerned with veterans' affairs have – until recently – been lacking in a comparative perspective.[1]

While organizational structures and policies to cater to the rights and wellbeing of homecoming soldiers have, of course, existed since the start of the Swedish engagement in peace support operations, it was not until the passing of a parliamentary bill in 2010 (made into law in 2011) that changes materialized that were significant enough to bring Sweden up to par with (for instance) its neighbours Norway and Denmark in terms of veterans' affairs. This bill and the changes that it brought were the consequence of a series of Official Inquiries of the Swedish Government (SOUs), the first of which was commissioned by the centre-right Government in 2007. It was thus commissioned shortly after Sweden had stepped up its engagement in northern Afghanistan, assuming control of Provincial Reconstruction Team Mazar-e-Sharif (PRT MeS) from the British (in 2006), and less than 2 years after Sweden's first combat fatalities during the ISAF commitment.[2] In terms of timing, it thus appears that Sweden's increasing embroilment in NATO's operation in Afghanistan – as well as the new realities that this entailed in terms of casualties – may be key to understanding why these veterans' reforms came about and why they took the form they did.

A rivalling interpretation is available however, which focuses instead on Sweden's wide-ranging reforms of its security and defence policies. Government decisions in 1995, 1999 and 2004 staked out a new path for Sweden's security strategy and subsequently for the SAF (see chapters 1 and 3 in this volume for more in-depth descriptions). Over the years that followed, conscription was abolished (or, more precisely, made dormant) and the Armed Forces converted itself from a conscript army focused on territorial defence to a modern all-volunteer force with its operational edge geared towards international military deployments (finally enshrined in the Government's 2009 defence bill). An overt consequence of this 'new' direction is that engagement in international missions has become a cornerstone of the SAF's raison d'être. The veteran reforms can thus also be viewed as a natural consequence of this parallel process of modernization and 'internationalization' of the Armed Forces, as a quantitative increase in deployments necessarily entails an increase in the number of veterans.

This chapter investigates the factors that lay behind the creation of the wide-ranging reforms of 2010 in order to understand the impact of the Afghan experience on Swedish policies for veterans. After delineating Sweden's policies and structures before and after the 2010 reforms, the roots of these alterations are traced inductively through an analysis of interviews with the key players and policy makers who initiated, drove and influenced the contents and direction of the reform process. It is argued that evidence derived from those involved in the reform process itself points towards the engagement in Afghanistan being only one of several factors that converged at a crucial stage for security and defence policy to spawn the identified reforms. The Afghan factor was, however, an important driver of the reforms, and its effects were both direct and indirect.

Veterans of peace support operations: new, or the same as before?

Much has been written on the post-Cold War growth in the importance for Western militaries of so-called 'operations other than war'. The main argument put forth has been that these types of operations have become – and will continue to be – the defining sphere of operations in the future, and that this entails challenges for military organizations that differ from earlier ones (see, for instance, Britt & Adler 2003, Dandeker & Gow 1999, Easton *et al.* 2010; see also Chapter 1 in this volume). Identified problems and challenges span the identity conflict between constabulary (or 'peacekeeping') values and traditional military values (Moskos 1975, Franke 1999, 2003), soldiers' possible dislike of peacekeeping vis-à-vis warfighting (Avant & Lebovic 2000, Miller 1997) and the new types of stressors encountered in peace-support operations of various kinds (Brounéus 2014, Schok *et al.* 2008). From the perspective of veterans' affairs, these new missions and the challenges that they bring present both positive and negative new influences. Peace-support operations are in general less bloody affairs than are regular armed conflicts, decreasing the individual's risk of death, injury and exposure to traumatic events. Consequently, not only can we expect fewer and less severe physical casualties, but also lower levels of Post-Traumatic Stress Disorder (PTSD) and other mental health disorders. On the negative side, a complicated picture of new types of stressors – such as role conflicts, extensive boredom and frustrations induced by hopelessness and humiliation – has emerged to challenge our perceptions of what experiences a veteran returns home with. As such, the vivid image of the broken Vietnam veteran needs to be somewhat reformulated to have relevance when portraying this 'new' type of veteran. This in no way means that soldiers in peace-support operations do not face potentially traumatic and debilitating stressors and exposure, but instead that the checklist of important factors for wellbeing looks somewhat different. In addition to exposure to actual combat, research has identified such diverse salient factors as uncertainty of mission content and ambiguity in terms of what actions are permissible (Adler *et al.* 2003); controlling one's aggression as a neutral party (Litz 1996); being witness to horrific acts without being able to help, being humiliated and being disliked by the local populace, whom one is supposedly there to help (Weisaeth 2003, see also Chapter 7 in this volume).

How does one actively and effectively counter these 'multiple ill-defined unexplained symptoms' (Weisaeth 2003, p. 207)? Veterans' affairs more broadly should not only concern how we support returning soldiers, but also how we prepare soldiers for their missions and how we treat them during such deployments. As such, a holistic view of veterans policies concerns not only possible medical care after returning home but also applying the correct forms of vetting, training and psychosocial support during deployment, just as it should not only concern post facto medical treatment but also how we try to make sure that medical treatment is not necessary. In line with this perspective, Sareen and colleagues (2010) found that, among peacekeepers, psychological health problems were not only predicted by exposure to traumatic events but also by predeployment personality traits, the number of deployments undergone and post-deployment stressors. In the same study, Sareen and colleagues (2010) also found that the meaningfulness of the mission, post-deployment social support and a positive perception of homecoming buffered negative effects. Other research has also highlighted the importance of moderating and buffering stress during deployments, pointing to how strong group cohesion and camaraderie, good leadership and strong family bonds have a positive effect on morale, wellbeing and retention rates (Michel 2014, Moldjord *et al.* 2003). Thus, good policies for veterans' affairs adopt a holistic view of wellbeing, which expands well beyond the idea of treating the wounded and distressed and providing economic benefits or restitution after homecoming.

Sweden and its veterans before 2010

It would be difficult to argue convincingly that Sweden had no need for the reforms of 2010. Although Swedish soldiers saw little combat in the time period between the deployment to the Democratic Republic of Congo[3] (1960–64) and their increased engagement in ISAF, studies conducted on the Swedish battalions stationed in Bosnia during and after the first Yugoslav civil war have demonstrated exposure to a high number of combat stressors, as well as stressors related to both military deployments in general and those more common in peace-support operations. Fatalities and casualties in the United Nations Protection Forces (UNPROFOR) and the Implementation Force (IFOR) were low overall, but a full 17 per cent of soldiers serving in the Balkans had been fired upon and 27 per cent had been under shelling almost daily (Johansson 2001). Among Swedish UNPROFOR staff, 16 per cent also stated that they had 'often' or 'occasionally' witnessed death. These stressors coexist with the common frustrations of peacekeeping deployments, such as humiliation and feelings of powerlessness, which are well known to take physical, psychological and emotional tolls (Weisaeth 2003). Larsson *et al.* (2000) found that 35 per cent of Swedish soldiers deployed to the UN peacekeeping mission in the former Yugoslavia had experienced some type of traumatic event during the mission. Finally, psychosocial support stressors – such as separation from family, friends and loved ones – occur also during peace-support operations and are known to have significant effects on morale and psychological wellbeing (Michel 2014). This is not to say that the policies and structures that were in place before 2010 did not engage with these issues at all (because they did) but rather that, with Sweden's overt ambitions to reform its Armed Forces in the direction of increasing participation in international missions, reforms were necessary to further raise the quality and cost-effectiveness of veterans' affairs and associated matters, as well as to handle an increasing number of veteran-classified soldiers.

Despite the many and sometimes hazardous deployments endured by Swedish veterans, the little research that exists on their physical and psychological health points towards comparatively positive conclusions in terms of health and wellbeing. Although few completely reliable figures are available, post-deployment PTSD rates, symptoms of anxiety and depression and alcohol abuse among veterans of the Afghan campaign were, between 6 and 18 months after returning home, well within the boundaries of rates among the Swedish general population. Those who had experienced heightened combat exposure were, however, worse off (Liljegren 2012). One should also keep in mind that pre-deployment rates of psychological problems within the soldier population were significantly lower than among Swedes in general, pointing towards the existence of stressors on mission as well as the importance of a sound vetting process that can select well-suited individuals for service. Population-based studies making use of public records also show that, when compared to the overall population, Swedish veterans (deployed between 1990 and 2011) had lower risks of suicide and lower risks of using psychotropic drugs than the average Swede (Pethrus 2013, Pethrus et al. 2014). Nevertheless, psychosocial and physical health problems as a consequence of international service did of course occured within the ranks of Swedish soldiers.

Although Sweden did not have an overarching and tightly coordinated policy concerning the veterans of its Armed Forces before the 2010 reforms, some actors, organizations and policies in this overall area of course existed. Laws, regulations and agreements with union representatives of soldiers and officers were all in place and regulated the responsibilities of the Armed Forces vis-à-vis returning soldiers. The Swedish Government's Official Inquiries on veteran policies, as well as significant critiques levelled by the officer's union and non-profit organizations involved in veterans' affairs, have focused on several issues that they identify as shortcomings (Swedish Official Inquiry 2007, 2008).[4] The most important of these critiques (as identified by those individuals and organizations that were heavily involved in drafting the reforms) concerned:

(1) the lack of a holistic approach towards veterans' affairs in terms of organizational structures;
(2) that the SAF were committed only to short-term follow-ups of returning soldiers;
(3) a separation of the pre-, during and post-deployment phases in terms of the individual soldiers' wellbeing; and
(4) a lack of recognition of both the merits and the sacrifice involved in serving in overseas deployments.

The overall goal of the reforms was formulated as giving recognition to, and strengthening the social security of, Swedish soldiers deployed to peace-support operations (Swedish Official Inquiry 2014).

Point 1 above concerns the fact that Sweden – in comparison with other countries, Nordic and otherwise – lacked some form of organizational structure in which a single department or office was the unifying actor for strategic, policy and practical work for veterans' affairs. A range of different actors were instead responsible for specific parts of, for instance, possible rehabilitation of psychiatric or other casualties. Additionally, this important work was carried out on more or less an ad-hoc basis. All of the not-for-profit organizations interviewed – as well as representatives of the Armed Forces – agreed on this point and tended to highlight it as the most important factor that needed reform. Allan Widman, the Liberal Party MP who led all of the consecutive Government inquiries, commented: 'We didn't have a lot of veteran policy' and further specified that the overall policy area was fragmented and 'too confined' (Widman 2014).

The second point has mainly been linked to the fact that, in terms of medical follow-ups of returned soldiers, the SAF was only responsible for 5 years and only as a subsidiary. This meant that any other employer that a soldier might have after a completed international deployment was held responsible for the soldier's possible rehabilitation (which mainly affected those on mission-specific contracts). A related critique was the bureaucratic jungle that injured soldiers had to navigate in terms of insurances and where to get help: something deemed difficult to handle without the assistance that was terminated after a maximum of 5 years. In terms of consequences for the individual soldier, organizations concerned with veteran support (such as *Fredsbaskrarna* (the Peace Berets)) strongly stressed that this was especially problematic concerning 'the invisible wounds' (mental health problems) (Wiktorsson 2014) and that this lack of long-term responsibility often sparked much resentment against the Armed Forces among soldiers.

Point 3 concerned a failure to see the chain of 'recruitment–training–deployment–return–follow-up' through a holistic lens. This critique was related to point 1, in that differing parts of the Armed Forces were responsible for these different phases. A remark made by SAF Major General Lindstrom during a seminar on veterans' policies in 2008 was identified by some interviewees as an example of this lack of a much-needed holistic perspective. When discussing the situation of deployed soldiers and their dependents back home, Lindstrom allegedly stated the following about the SAF: 'We employ the soldier, not the entire family' (quoted in Arvidsson 2008). He was thus denying the important role that the safety and stability of the family plays in the wellbeing and operational effectiveness of the deployed soldier. Another much-cited example in the interviews concerns the importance of the recruitment process and its professionalism in relation to soldiers' wellbeing while deployed, as not only the soldiers but also their home front status must be vetted.

The final point reflects the broad mandate given to the investigators that compiled the Government's Official Inquiries. An overall concern was identified (and shared by the veterans associations especially) that participation in overseas military missions was not rewarded in terms of merit or respect. This concern ranged from a lack of appreciation from the public and the political establishment of services rendered to the services' effects on promotions within the SAF itself (see also Alvesson & Ydén 2008). This point thus relates directly to both how the SAF chose to reward deployment and what status should be given to those who are on the frontlines of Sweden's new security policies. A general sentiment identified in the interviews and shared by the SAF (here in the form of Colonel Anders Stach, Head of the Veterans Division) was that 'there was a denial of their service, vis-à-vis internationally deployed staff, and that is not acceptable under any circumstances' (Stach 2014), and that, 'In reality, it wasn't even admitted that Sweden had veterans before the government inquiries began' (Wranker 2014). Recognition was viewed as especially important in terms of the respect awarded by Government and Parliament, as 'The state – the Government of Sweden – makes decisions on deploying personnel who risk life and health to implement security and humanitarian principles. If you expose individuals to risk and danger you must take responsibility for those decisions' (Stach 2014).

In addition to these four points, several others were raised in the many hundreds of pages of the Government's inquiries and during the interviews with the key players and organizations involved in the process, but not all can be given equal attention. However, of general importance is a number of more symbolic suggestions presented, which either overtly or covertly suggest reforms to 'unify' the military as an institution. One such suggestion was to eradicate the use of the terms and structures that refer to the 'International Expeditionary Force' [*Utlandsstyrkan*], so as to demonstrate clearly that the previous separation between territorial defence and overseas deployment is now non-existent. This suggests that, in addition to seeking to create improvements for the soldiers, the reforms were also geared towards aligning the policies surrounding all aspects of veterans' affairs with the foreign policy direction of Sweden.

The reforms of 2010

The main attempt to resolve the issues identified by the Government's inquiries came in the form of new legislation. The bulk of reforms were enshrined in a bill introduced (and accepted) in Parliament in 2010 (Government Bill 2010) and subsequently made into law on 1 January 2011. The bill contained several alterations to the laws that governed soldiers sent on overseas missions and the affairs of veterans, but also a number of proposals for reforms that the Government wished the SAF to enact but could not order it to pursue. Such reforms included the Government's pronounced wish that the SAF set up a veterans administration to coordinate all veterans' affairs, as well as issues regarding employer–employee relationships, by which it was left to the unions to negotiate agreements with the SAF.[5] The outcome of the reforms was, nevertheless, relatively far-reaching.

The problems identified earlier in the fourpoint list were all addressed either partially or fully. The lack of a holistic perspective on, and a strategic approach towards, veterans' affairs was met with the creation of a special Veterans Division [*Veteranavdelningen*], based at the SAF's HQ and tasked with advising the Armed Forces, coordinating of all veterans' issues, being the point of contact for all veteran soldiers and supporting research within this sphere. This division is also tasked with taking the lead in engaging the whole of society (not just the Swedish Armed Forces) in veterans' affairs. In terms of responsibilities for the veteran soldiers' health and wellbeing, the subsidiarity principle was partly abolished, as was the time horizon (5 years) of the Armed Forces' responsibilities for support of and medical care for returned soldiers.[6] Veterans thus became the subjects of specific laws that cater to their special needs and increase their social security. Relating to the health and wellbeing of soldiers and the wish for an integrated perspective on the deployment cycle (point 3), new guidelines required the posting of more than 20 psychologists and psychiatrists at the battalion level (for most battalions), as well as the appointment of specific coordinators of veterans' affairs at all battalions. A stronger emphasis was also to be placed on the situation of relatives and dependents throughout the entirety of the deployment cycle. An important change concerning this point was a stronger formalization of ties with not-for-profit veterans' associations and the possibility of the Armed Forces providing funding for such organizations. Agreements were made in 2013 to support four such organizations. Finally, in terms of recognition and merit, an official Veterans Day celebration was instituted (on 29 May each year) and a veterans monument erected in Stockholm. New medals to reward deployed soldiers were also part of this package for increased recognition. However, the task of raising awareness in the overall labour market of the general merit of international deployments is still ongoing. Overall, though, the majority of goals staked out in 2010 must be said to have been reached (Swedish Official Inquiry 2013, 2014).

Consequently, the reforms should be viewed as having raised the profile of veterans' affairs within the Armed Forces, strengthened the social and medical security and rights of veteran soldiers and funnelled a significant amount of new resources towards the issue of psychological, psychosocial and physical support functions before, during and after deployments. Such resources can now be supplied by both the Armed Forces themselves and several not-for-profit veterans' organizations. Surveys carried out on approximately 1,200 veterans indicate that satisfaction with the implementation and functioning of policies related to veterans' affairs was significantly higher among those soldiers who had participated in international deployments after 2008, and who have thus (to an extent) been exposed to at least some of the reforms mentioned (Wester *et al.* 2013). Practically all of the key players and organizations interviewed for this chapter also agreed that implementation had gone well overall and that the larger issues identified in the Government's inquiries had indeed been dealt with (to differing degrees). However, all interviewees – as well as the last Government report – identify future challenges, as well as areas in which reforms are still necessary. Among these are, for example, the need to raise awareness among the general public of even the existence of the concept of veterans' affairs;[7] to raise awareness on the labour market of the merit of having participated in international deployments, to widen the concept of 'veteran' also to include deployed police personnel (among others) and possibly to create a Department and/or Centre for Veterans' Affairs to coordinate between governmental entities on both the local and national levels.

The Afghan or the 'international' factor?

In a matter of a few years, Swedish veterans' policy thus made a swift transition from 'non-existent' (in the words of several of the key players) to more or less on par with that of its neighbours Finland, Denmark and Norway. These reforms thus represent a sudden sea change for a state and a military organization that had long been engaged in devoting thousands of soldiers to peace operations annually. Pressing questions consequently include why the issue of veterans' policies had previously been almost ignored as well as why these specific reforms occurred at this specific point in time. While a full investigation into this puzzle could likely fill an entire volume of its own, I attempt to elucidate and analyze relationships and links between turning points and factors of importance identified by the key actors and individuals that were involved in drafting, vetting and implementing the 2010 reforms. To identify these individuals and actors I relied on a snowballing technique, asking each respondent to name further individuals that he/she thought possessed the insights necessary for understanding and mapping the reform process. This technique resulted in interviews with some 10 individuals, representing the Armed Forces itself, the parliamentary level and the most important Swedish veteran and veterans' dependents' organizations. A full list of interviewees and their place in the process is available at the end of this chapter.

'A well-paid vacation': the absence of veterans' affairs

Turning first to the question of why Swedish veterans' policies 'did not exist' before the reform process began in 2007, the interviewees presented a relatively coherent image of institutional/organizational, cultural and historical factors, which together produced the comparative Swedish disinterest in these issues.

In terms of institutional/organizational factors, several of the key players interviewed point to the SAF's organizational structure as a factor that effectively downgraded or obscured the issue of veterans' affairs. This factor is most visible in the Government inquiries through how steps are taken to eradicate the concept of the 'International Expeditionary Force' (Swedish Official Inquiry 2007, 2008, 2014). To the interviewees, the issue revolves around the fact that before the defence and security policy reforms of 1999–2005 (but even more so before the missions to Yugoslavia in the early 1990s) – which oriented Sweden away from territorial defence and more clearly towards international missions – the Armed Forces could be viewed as consisting of two overlapping but somewhat separate government agencies. One such agency was (from this perspective) oriented toward territorial defence (sometimes labelled the 'War Department') and the second toward international deployments (sometimes labelled the 'Peace Department', or the 'UN Department'). This organizational structure created an institution within which territorial defence was the 'real' job and UN missions were demoted to a lower status (see Angstrom 2010 for a depiction and for an analysis of the causes of this divide). Widman, the primary investigator of the Government's inquiries on veterans' affairs, identified this state of affairs as having serious repercussions for the individual soldier:

> This separation of the Armed Forces and the International Expeditionary Force that existed presented an image of us having two different agencies, or two different actors. And that what happened in the International Expeditionary Force wasn't really the responsibility of the Armed Forces [...] and there were even people who actually believed that these were two separate entities.
>
> (Widman 2014)

Concurrent with the veterans' affairs reforms, and as has been mentioned previously, Sweden's focus on territorial defence decreased in favour of a more international orientation throughout the 2000s. Consequently, this 'separation of entities' was abolished both manifestly and in the abstract, as: 'The national and international became one through the creation of standing regiments [...] now when we deploy internationally we do not build a detachment from several regiments, but pinch off a corner from a standing regiment' (Stach 2014). As such, it would appear that the reorientation towards international missions both increased the merit of serving abroad and demolished an existing separation of the 'two types' of soldiers.

A second institutional issue relates to the personnel reforms of the 2000s, as well as concerns about how international missions were staffed. Before the reforms that made international service compulsory for all employees within the SAF if requested, many of Sweden's UN missions were staffed by civilian volunteers who had undergone conscript training and signed a contract that enlisted them only for the deployment at hand. As such, the detachments were immediately disbanded and the soldiers returned to their previous employments after homecoming from a mission deployment. Several interviewees identify this as a factor that diluted the sense of responsibility for these ex-soldiers within the SAF and/or decreased the visibility and knowledge of the issue of veterans within the organization.

These institutional/organizational factors are strongly linked to the aforementioned lingering cultural issues, such as the idea that territorial defence was the 'real job' and international deployment something very different. This was an issue identified by several interviewees. To an extent this culture can be seen as related to the issue of military doctrine, in which territorial defence was the primary issue. There appears, however, to have also existed a notion of international service as 'well-paid vacations' (Korstrom 2014); a remnant of such calm and low-intensity Swedish missions as those to the Gaza Strip (starting in 1956) and Cyprus (starting in 1964). This again served to decrease the merits of international deployment, as well as to obscure the heavy toll that such deployments can take on the individual. As international deployments were also staffed on a voluntary basis (both volunteer civilians and professional soldiers all choose to go freely), signing up for international deployment was frowned upon to a certain extent, as it entailed 'abandoning' one's job in the territorial defences (see also Viktorin 2008 on the SAF's then-prevalent view on spending resources on international deployments). Not only did such a culture mean that veterans of foreign missions could be viewed as 'work abstainers' (Wranker 2014, Lofvendahl 2014), but it also appeared to affect how international missions were valued internally within the SAF. Presenting a somewhat dissenting view, but with the same type of consequences, former Minister of Defence Odenberg stated that:

> I don't think it was really a downgrading of international deployment, because I think it was often viewed as at least somewhat important. But every regimental commander was his own closest ally, for the simple reason that you prioritize your own tasks. [...] But one has to ask what this meant for the merit rating of having conducted international missions. Sometimes it feels like sitting at a desk at HQ has been more highly valued than having been posted abroad and commanded actual units in the field.
>
> (Odenberg 2014)

A second cultural aspect identified by some has been a previous lack of focus on so-called 'soft' values within the Armed Forces: a relative unawareness of the importance of emotional and social issues to the soldier's functioning. This lack of 'soft' values is perhaps best exemplified in the previously-cited quote from Lindstrom: that 'We employ the soldier, not the entire family' (quoted in Arvidsson 2008). Along these lines, a certain 'traditional' culture would seem to have been dominant within the SAF as well as among many soldiers (and also, to be fair, within the unions):

> The SAF's commitment to the soldier's dependents was highly limited; they viewed it as just deploying an employee, after which it was his or her responsibility to deal with all other issues. [...] This was a value-based issue, on both the union side and the employer side we had people who had worked in an environment with a tradition where a man alone takes care of his family; which might be an especially strong tendency in the military.
>
> (Lofvendahl 2014)

In sum, cultural factors within the SAF such as the ones delineated upon above would appear to have meant that the topic of international deployments – and subsequently veterans' affairs and related matters – did not gain prominence within organizational structures or culture. As a consequence, they appear to rarely have been discussed in-depth before the mid-2000s.

Turning to the last factor that appears to have contributed to the relative absence of veterans' policies entails turning to Swedish history; more specifically, the 200 years of peace celebrated in 2014. Some of the interviewees claimed that this state of affairs – fortuitous though it may be – served to create both a certain naiveté in Swedish society overall regarding what military deployments may entail and blindness on the political and military levels concerning a lack of medical and psychosocial capabilities. Put differently, neighbouring countries that are highly similar in most socioeconomic and cultural respects (such as Norway and Denmark) already had certain veterans' policies in place, as well as a cultural awareness of and respect for war veterans due to their historical experiences of war. Consequently, as such types of awareness have been lacking, so have initiatives to remedy or even identify a problematic situation.

Viewed together, the preceding paragraphs present a complicated network of factors at different levels of analysis, which do not clearly identify one single 'scapegoat' factor that can be held responsible. Although critique was levelled by several of the interviewees toward the inertia of the SAFs bureaucratic structures in relation to veterans' affairs, one needs to be aware that the organization was never in breach of any Government or Parliament rules or laws regulating its work.[8] Although the culture within the SAF also appears to be a salient factor in explaining why no reforms were forthcoming from the inside, one wonders why no such suggestions were instead offered from citizens or from the political level. Relevant factors here appear to be a lack of awareness on the political level of what international missions can entail in terms of casualties (of both the physical and psychological kind) and a lack of public interest in veterans' issues, the latter presumably due to the comparatively low levels of fatalities experienced during Swedish international deployments, as well as Sweden's peaceful history. Consequently, if one wishes to disperse blame, this will be no easy task.

'We sent them there': factors for action

If the factors listed and articulated in the previous section were key in understanding why Sweden's veterans' policies were subpar before the reform process, it is logical to assume that one or several of these factors were reversed or counteracted either before or during the initiation of the reform process. In what follows, I will attempt – via the voices of the key players involved – to track both why these reforms occurred at all and why they materialized at this specific point in time.

The introduction to this chapter specified that two prime suspects for the reforms were available: first, the effect of Sweden's participation in the NATO mission to Afghanistan, and second, Sweden's overall reorientation towards international deployments more generally. Of course, these two factors are interlinked in some respects, as participation in the ISAF mission can be viewed as a consequence of changes in security and defence doctrines.

Nevertheless, it is possible to study their effects separately via a study of the key actors' thoughts and actions.

When open-endedly asking the key actors about why the reforms took the form they did and why they occurred at this specific point in time, three dominant themes became apparent:

(1) the Swedish participation in Afghanistan and the consequences it both produced and promised to produce,
(2) the shift towards internationally-oriented Armed Forces and what this entailed in terms of personnel reforms, and
(3) having finally reached a critical mass of attention to, and awareness of, the urgency for change.

A range of related factors were also mentioned and are noted below, where deemed relevant.

Starting with the question of the Afghan experience, this was mentioned as important by all interviewees but was not always the first point to which they drew attention; neither was it always named as the primary cause of the events that unfolded. At the political level, primary investigator Widman (who almost single-handedly raised the issue of veterans' policies in the Swedish Parliament) commented that:

> The Afghan mission played a big role. I had started making a ruckus before this, but that we initiated an investigation and subsequently made new laws and got the issue on the table was tightly related to Afghanistan. And not least that [Minister of Defence] Odenberg understood that this was going to become an issue [...] Afghanistan represented something new, and serious words were beginning to be spoken, and it made politicians more receptive to these issues.
>
> (Widman 2014)

Comments on this direct effect of the involvement in Afghanistan were plentiful and mainly revolved around the possibility of taking casualties:

> Our participation in Afghanistan, in a high-intensity conflict area, is of course important. Operating in high-intensity areas where armed combat and its consequences are a reality, that has an effect [...] and it is obvious that if our personnel might come home in coffins, this yields a strong impact that affects the entire process. You can draw a parallel to Denmark, where developments accelerated rapidly, due to their huge losses in Afghanistan.
>
> (Stach 2014)

On this point, it was clearly identified by the interviewees that a realization dawned within the SAF (and among all others involved) that, in terms of preparedness for fatalities, physical and psychological casualties, injury and support for dependents, the existing structures simply would not do. Odenberg (the former Minister of Defence) agreed with this perspective, viewing the Afghan deployment as one of the most important catalysing factors, but also added that the planning for Sweden's lead role in the Nordic Battle Group (NBG) (set up in 2008) and the possibilities that this unit would be deployed to combat missions also shone a light on the shortcomings in veterans' policies (Roosberg & Weibull 2014 also identified preparations for the lead role in the NBG as a driver for change within the SAF). Again, however, this entails paying attention to a lack of structures for dealing with possible casualties.

Seen from another, related perspective, the mission to Afghanistan was the culmination of a series of increasingly belligerent, dangerous and difficult international missions that Sweden chose to engage in. In this view, the realization of the necessities of sound veterans' policies has grown cumulatively over the years and the 'well-paid vacation' mirage has slowly been demolished as the realities of missions to Former Yugoslavia, Liberia and the DRC have begun to sink in among individual soldiers, politicians and the SAF itself:

> The missions have changed. We have a completely new operational environment, more violent after the end of the Cold War [...] and this entailed that we took casualties, slowly but surely, in true combat. So, [we saw] changes in the tasks, making them more difficult and with new RoE:s. So at last people realized 'oh, this is dangerous'.[9]
>
> (Korstrom 2014)

Such a perspective also identifies Afghanistan as a salient factor for change, but views it more as a powerful driver or 'the straw that broke the camel's back': 'I see the Afghanistan mission as the catalyst of this process [...] it was an important factor and the fuel that made it impossible to ignore these issues [veterans' policies]' (Wranker 2014). The insights that appear to have been caused by the looming dangers of Afghanistan can be linked to the cultural and historical issues identified in the preceding section. There, it was noted that, for a long time, the relatively calm missions frequented by the SAFs soldiers had given rise to a certain notion of international missions as low-risk enterprises for the individual. Sweden's shift in focus towards the highly violent conflict in Afghanistan appears to have counteracted any such notions or preconceptions, opening up a sense of urgency in terms of resolving the lingering veterans' issues.

The second prominent theme in the interviews, which was spontaneously mentioned almost as often as the deployment to Afghanistan, concerns the personnel reforms that culminated with a Government Bill in 2009 (Government Bill 2009). Again, this bill entailed that conscription was made dormant and that the entirety of the SAF would be staffed on a voluntary basis by employed personnel. Concurrently, deploying to international missions became compulsory if so ordered by the SAF. There was wide agreement among the interviewees that this radical change in policy transformed the SAF's perspective on its responsibilities vis-à-vis its deployed soldiers:

> I believe that the personnel reforms had an effect on both the SAF and the political level, when they realized that there would be consequences and that their responsibilities would increase when it was no longer voluntary to deploy on international missions. So, related to this, the insight appeared that responsibility had to be taken for those forced to deploy.
> (Lofvendahl 2014)

Representatives of the SAF itself agreed with this perspective: 'Our shift to making conscription dormant and relying on an all-volunteer force with standing units was of course one part of this [of why the reforms occurred when they did]' (Stach 2014). A transformation into an all-volunteer force also makes it important for a military organization to be able to recruit personnel, as well as to uphold strong retention rates so as to retain good 'bang for the buck'. Some interviewees subsequently maintained that a sound veterans' policy would also be important in these respects:

> Abolishment of conscription was one part of this [the initiation of reforms]. This made the SAF into a different kind of employer than it was before; this raised the issue also in the public eye. And it means they had to start thinking about recruitment – how to enhance recruitment – and how to retain personnel [...] that we have to take responsibility is now visible. And that's also related to retention of personnel.
> (Karlsson 2014)

As such, it seems that the personnel reforms that the SAF was going (and has gone) through should be considered a second salient factor that brought on the reforms. However, tracing this factor further back in a possible causal chain means identifying the larger shift in Swedish defence doctrines, away from territorial defence, as a more ultimate cause (see Chapter 3). Irrespective of where one locates a possible causal process variable, this factor for change can be directly related to the institutional and cultural factors identified earlier, in that it made international deployment a possibility and a responsibility of all personnel. No longer would a large bulk of deployed soldiers simply disperse and be removed from the SAF's view; rather, many would remain within the organization even after the mission was completed. This factor can thus be seen as counteracting the interpretation of the SAF as having two distinct tasks (the national and the international), as well as making the consequences of international service the concern of all staff.

Both of these factors identified as important to the reform process can be related to the third factor: that a critical mass of attention and awareness at the military, political and societal levels was reached around 2006–08. The notion that Sweden was engaging in more dangerous, difficult and different missions than before can, for instance, be viewed as a cumulative process of awareness-building that began with the taxing missions to Bosnia (as suggested by Korstrom 2014, Wiktorsson 2014).[10] The interviewees from not-for-profit organizations in particular suggested that a range of events occurred within close temporal proximity and thus resulted in a critical mass of attention. Such events included the presentation of surveys and new research on the situation for dependents of deployed personnel; increasing amounts of combat exposure for the Swedish contingents deployed with ISAF, the founding of new civil society organizations within the veterans' sphere and a refocusing of already-existing organizations towards these issues. The not-for-profit actors – such as the Peace Berets, dependents' organizations and the Officer's Union – thus identified an element of chance in getting veterans' affairs on the table:

> The media suddenly started to write about it [veterans], and TV shows and documentaries about life in Afghanistan were produced. All of a sudden the issue appeared [...] In some way, all of the actors involved managed to get the issue up for discussion at the same time.
> (Lofvendahl 2014)

The Peace Berets – another of the consultative bodies to the Government Inquiry that would follow – stated that:

> We were also a little lucky [...] By chance we had just started planning our vision when the Government's official investigation by Allan Widman began, so we could show it to him immediately: 'This is what we want'. Pure luck in a way.
> (Wranker 2014)

It would also appear that an important factor in raising awareness and drawing attention was the interest that Swedish media began to take in the dealings of the SAF in Afghanistan and at home. Although the Swedish deployment to Afghanistan did, of course, not go unnoticed before 2006, the topic grew in prominence beginning that year.[11] This is not the place to discuss the logic of the media and attempt to trace the roots of this change reliably, but it did occur parallel to the not-for-profit organizations starting to reach out more actively with their agenda. Also worth mentioning is the fact that practically all of the interviewees point to the concerted efforts of the not-for-profit organization as crucial to how the reform process was shaped and completed.

The third factor identified by interviewees as a salient cause of there being no true veterans' policies being in place is the historical one. It was here argued that Sweden's 200 years of consecutive peace had relegated veterans' affairs and similar issues to a place of non-existence in the public and political consciousness. The critical mass of sudden attention identified in the earlier paragraphs appears to have broken this spell of naiveté and placed the issue of veterans' affairs on the agenda at an expedient moment during which larger processes of change were occurring within the SAF. As a result, a realization of the possible costs of international deployment could grow among all segments of society, providing further impetus for change. However, one should consider the extent to which it would have been possible to reach this critical mass of attention and awareness had it not been for the highly publicized losses that Sweden experienced in Afghanistan in 2005[2] and later. Consequently, this factor of awareness cannot be considered as a stand-alone variable, as the Afghan experience affected it directly.

Overall, it is not possible to claim any monocausality regarding the 'why' and 'how' of the veterans' affairs reforms. Instead, the factors identified interacted to produce a situation in which reforms were seen as necessary by practically all parties involved. Colonel Stach – Head of the Veterans Division – summarized this perspective succinctly:

> The shift to an all-volunteer force and having experienced high-intensity exposure, in combination with having a few actors who have actively pushed the issue forward outside of the SAF and an increase in research and our knowledge: these are the fundaments of the progress we have made.
>
> (Stach 2014)

Concluding discussion

Returning now to the overarching questions that drive both this entire volume and this chapter: what has the analysis presented here revealed in terms of the effect of the Afghan experience on Swedish veterans policies? Can we speak of an 'Afghan effect', or did the reforms materialize from a process that would have been inevitable due to changes in Sweden's overall security and defence policies? The answer is probably both. Additionally, few of the factors for change identified here can be viewed in isolation from the others.

The Swedish engagement in Afghanistan and the casualties that it both produced and promised to produce were identified by the key actors as important factors for veterans' reforms to come about and to take the shape that they did. But the overall personnel reforms that resulted from the transformation into an all-volunteer force were deemed to be as – or almost as – important. These two factors were in themselves interlinked, as well as related to Sweden's paradigmatic shift away from territorial defence and towards international engagements. Thus, if one wishes to identify anything close to an ultimate cause, this overall reorientation should be viewed as such a possible factor; one which produced a cascade effect that rippled through organizational, political and societal structures. Through such a perspective, the veterans' reforms ultimately stem from Sweden's moves towards becoming a military organization of the postmodern type and the professionalization that this entailed (Moskos *et al.* 2000).

The current state of affairs would thus likely have materialized sooner or later irrespective of participation in the ISAF mission: personnel reforms would likely still have occurred, veterans organizations would have continued to grow as a consequence of other missions and awareness of Sweden's further engagement in peace-support operations (and their costs) would have spread. The harsh realities of the engagement in Afghanistan should nevertheless be classified as having been of such magnitude as to deserve a special place in any narrative of the evolution of Swedish veterans' policy. If not the initiating factor, it should be viewed as the fuel that stoked the fire and that managed to simultaneously align the range of factors identified in this chapter – whether by chance or not. One is here reminded of the quote from Mattelaer, which appeared on the first pages of this volume: 'In military terms, the Afghan campaign has served as a critical wake-up call for European militaries, many of which had not seen genuine combat action since the Korean War' (Mattelaer 2011, p. 132). In the Swedish case, the Afghan campaign served as a 'wake-up call' for not only the military establishment but also a set of crucial actors: veterans' and dependents' organizations, the unions, at least parts of the political echelon and the media. While attention to the issue of veterans' affairs should be classified as growing even before the 2006 intensification of Sweden's commitments to ISAF (specifically, the takeover of PRT MeS), the Afghan factor served to elevate the issue, bind together actors, organizations and interests and thus create a critical mass that might otherwise have materialized much further down the road.

The Swedish case illustrates an interesting outcome for the broader field of organizational and societal change in the field of military studies. As was made visible earlier, institutional/organizational, cultural and historical factors had served to prevent any in-depth discussions of or action in the field of veterans' policy. The SAF's organization and culture were only slowly changing in this respect, as was the public's historical narrative of Sweden as being uninvolved in military expeditions. The shock of the Afghan experience can, however, be viewed as being of such magnitude that it was able to induce a substantial impetus for change. This change reverberated through identities, culture and organizational spheres known to otherwise be substantially inert. This clearly illustrates the power of the Afghan experience. Thus, even if the shift in terms of Sweden's veterans' policy needs to be viewed as a multicausal outcome, it is likewise correct to agree with King's view that 'Europe's entry into Afghanistan is likely to be decisive in the transformation of Europe's Armed Forces' (King 2011, p. 27) far beyond the strategic and operational contexts.

Notes

1 In what follows, I will make use of a definition of 'veteran' that encompasses any soldier who has participated in at least one overseas peace-support operation or similar mission. From the perspective of the Swedish Armed Forces anyone who has been employed by this organization is part of the broader term of 'veteran', but I rely here on a narrower and more common definition. Also of note – perhaps

especially in relation to the chapter's title – is the fact that, before the initiation of the reforms discussed in this chapter, the SAF lacked a definition of who was or was not a veteran.
2. Two soldiers, First Lieutenants Jesper Lindblom and Tomas Bergqvist, were killed by an IED attack on their vehicle in November 2005.
3. See Kettner (1972) for a study of the individual-level effects of this deployment on Swedish soldiers.
4. The veteran policies of the Swedish Armed Forces – as well as the implementation of the 2010 reforms – were vetted in a series of Government's Official Inquiries (SOUs, in Swedish bureaucratic language) between 2007 and 2014.
5. This latter state of affairs is a consequence of the Swedish model of delegating many labour issues to the parties of the labour market. In this case, this was done mainly to the Officer's Union and the SAF.
6. More precisely, under the new regulations these responsibilities are not linked to a timeframe but are somewhat reduced after a period of 5 years.
7. In a nationally representative sample of Swedish citizens studied in 2012, 60 per cent of respondents had 'no opinion' on whether or not Sweden provided enough support to veterans, implying that the bulk of the public remain uninformed on the issue (Ydén & Berndtsson 2013).
8. Most interviewees also stated that, once the reform process was initiated, the SAF was both effective and forthcoming in resolving the identified issues.
9. RoE:s means Rules of Engagement.
10. Bengt Wiktorsson is a retired officer and current Chairman of Sweden's Veterans Association Peace Berets (*Sveriges Veteranförbund Fredsbaskrarna*).
11. As an illustration, a keyword search in the Swedish press archive (*Mediearkivet*) using the phrase 'veterans' policy/ies' (*veteranpolitik*) yielded 0 hits before 2006 and 127 hits from 2006 and later.

List of interviewees

Jonsson-Assander, Maria: Swedish Armed Forces' employee. Was involved in the first drafting of the SAF's dependents' policies and served as an expert on the Government's Official Inquiries on veterans' policies. Interviewed on 12 December 2014.

Karlsson, Cesilia: Founder and Head of InvidZonen. InvidZonen was founded in 2007, is a non-profit organization for supporting veterans and their families and acted as a consultative body for the 2007–14 Official Inquiries of the Swedish Government. Interviewed on 19 November 2014.

Korstrom, Per-Erik ('Pekka'): Retired Officer and former Chairman of Sweden's Veterans Association Peace Berets (*Sveriges Veteranforbund Fredsbaskrarna*). Interviewed on 5 November 2014.

Lofvendahl, Peter: Retired Officer and Director of Officersforbundet, the Swedish Officer's Union. Officersforbundet is a labour union that organizes both officers and contracted soldiers and that acted as a consultative body for the 2007–14 Official Inquiries of the Swedish Government. Interviewed on 26 November 2014.

Odenberg, Mikael: Chairman of *Svenska Kraftnat* and former Minister for Defence in 2006–2007. Odenberg was Minister for Defence when the first SOU on veterans' affairs was commissioned. Interviewed on 24 November 2014.

Philipsson, Andreas: Director and Dependents' Support Coordinator at Soldathemsforbundet: the Swedish Soldiers' Homes Association. The association provides support for veterans and dependents in several locations in Sweden (attached to garrisons), and acted as a consultative body for the 2007–14 Official Inquiries of the Swedish Government. Philipson was also an expert in the Government's Official Inquiries on veterans' policies. Interviewed on 24 November 2014.

Stach, Anders: Colonel and Head of the Swedish Armed Forces' Veterans Division. Interviewed on 5 November 2014.

Widman, Allan: Swedish Liberal Party (*Folkpartiet*) Minister of Parliament and Chairman of the Parliamentary Defence Committee. Chairman (and primary investigator) of all of the Official Inquiries of the Swedish Government (SOUs) on veterans affairs. Interviewed on 6 November 2014.

Wiktorsson, Bengt: Retired Officer and current Chairman of Sweden's Veterans Association Peace Berets (*Sveriges Veteranforbund Fredsbaskrarna*). The Peace Berets were founded in 1983, are a non-profit organization for supporting veterans and acted as a consultative body for the 2007–14 Official Inquiries of the Swedish Government. Interviewed on 5 November 2014.

Wranker, Bo: Retired Officer and former Chairman of Sweden's Veterans Association Peace Berets (*Sveriges Veteranforbund Fredsbaskrarna*). Wranker was also an expert in the Government's Official Inquiries on veterans' policies. Interviewed on 29 November 2014.

References

Adler, A.B., B.T. Litz & P.T. Bartone (2003) 'The nature of peacekeeping stressors' in Britt T.W. & A.B. Adler (Eds) *The psychology of the peacekeeper*. Westport, CT: Praeger, pp. 149–67.

Alvesson, M. & K. Ydén (2008) 'Karriarstyrda officerare skapar inkompetent forsvar' [Career driven officers creates an incompetent defence] *Dagens Nyheter* 11 June.

Angstrom, J. (2010) 'Forsvarsmaktens internationella insatser: I den svenska sakerheten eller identitetens tjanst?' in Engelbrekt, K. & J. Angstrom (Eds) *Svensk sakerhetspolitik i Europa och varlden* [Swedish security policy in Europe and the world]. Stockholm: Norstedts Juridik, pp. 169–202.

Arvidsson, C. (2008) 'Vi gor det mojligt'[We make it possible] *Svenska Dagbladet* 30 June.

Avant, D. & J. Lebovic (2000) 'US military attitudes toward post-Cold War missions' *Armed Forces & Society* Vol. 27, No. 1, pp. 37–56.

Britt, T. W. & A.B. Adler (Eds) (2003) *The psychology of the peacekeeper: Lessons from the field*. Westport, CT: Praeger.

Brounéus, K. (2014) 'On return from peacekeeping: A review of current research on psychological wellbeing in military personnel returning from operational deployment' *Journal of Military and Veterans' Health*, Vol. 22, No. 1, pp. 25–30.

Dandeker, C. & J. Gow (1999) 'Military culture and strategic peacekeeping' *Small Wars and Insurgencies* Vol. 10, No. 2, pp. 58–79.

Easton, M., M. Den Boer, J. Janssens, R. Moelker & T. Vander Beken (2010) *Blurring military and police roles*. The Hague: Eleven International Publishing.

Franke, V. (1999) *Preparing for peace: Military identity, value orientations, and professional military education*. Westport, CT: Praeger.

Franke, V. (2003) 'The social identity of peacekeeping' in Britt T.W. & A.B. Adler (Eds) *The psychology of the peacekeeper*. Westport, Connecticut: Praeger, pp. 31–51.

Government Bill (2009) *Regeringens proposition 2008/09:140 Ett anvandbart forsvar* [A useful defence], 19 March.
Government Bill (2010) *Regeringens proposition 2009/10:160 Modern personalforsorjning for ett anvandbart forsvar: vissa fragor om Forsvarsmaktens personal* [*Modern personnel supply for a useful defence: some issues about the SAFs personnel*], 18 March.
Government of Sweden (2013) *Regeringens deklaration vid 2013 ars utrikespolitiska debatt i riksdagen* Available online at www.regeringen.se/contentasse ts/3f435e49030a4954a799aa5d8e044c9a/regeringens-deklaration-vid-2013-ars-utrikespolitiska-debatt-i-riksdagen-onsdagen-den-13-februari-2013 (accessed 17 August 2015).
Johansson, E. (2001) *The UNknown soldier: A portrait of the Swedish peacekeeper at the threshold of the 21st Century*. Karlstad: Karlstad University Studies.
Kettner, B. (1972) 'Combat strain and subsequent mental health: A follow-up study of Swedish soldiers serving in the UN forces 1961–62' *Acta Psychiatry Scandinavian Supplement* Vol. 230, pp. 1–112.
King, A. (2011) *The transformation of Europe's Armed Forces: From the Rhine to Afghanistan*. New York: Cambridge University Press.
Larsson, G., P.-O. Michel & T. Lundin (2000) 'Systematic assessment of mental health following various types of posttrauma support' *Military Psychology* Vol. 12, No. 2, pp. 121–35.
Liljegren, M. (2012) Presentation at the Swedish Armed Forces veterans' research seminar. Stockholm: Swedish Armed Forces 12–13 April.
Litz, B.T. (1996) 'The psychological demands of peacekeeping for military personnel' *PTSD Clinical Quarterly* Vol. 6, pp. 1–8.
Mattelaer, A. (2011) 'How Afghanistan has strengthened Nato' *Survival: Global Politics and Strategy* Vol. 53, No. 6, pp. 127–40.
Michel, P-O. (2014) Insatsrelaterad stress hos militara veteraner: En vetenskaplig litteraturoversikt [Mission-related stress in military veterans: A literature review] Appendix 6 in Swedish Official Inquiry (2014) *Svensk veteranpolitik Ett ansvar for hela samhallet* [*Swedish veterans' policy A responsibility for the whole society*] Vol. 27. Stockholm: Statens Offentliga Utredningar.
Miller, L. L. (1997) 'Do soldiers hate peacekeeping? The case of preventive diplomacy operations in Macedonia' *Armed Forces & Society* Vol. 23, No. 3, pp. 415–50.
Moldjord, C., L.K. Fossum & A. Holen (2003) 'Coping with peacekeeping stress' in Britt T.W. & A. B. Adler (Eds) *The psychology of the peacekeeper: A multinational perspective*. Westport, CT: Praeger, pp. 169–84.
Moskos, C. (1975) 'UN peacekeepers: The constabulary ethic and military professionalism.' *Armed Forces & Society* Vol. 1, No. 4, pp. 388–401.
Moskos, C., J.A. Williams & D.R. Segal (2000) 'Armed forces after the Cold War' in Moskos, C., J.A. Williams & D.R. Segal (Eds) *The postmodern military: Armed Forces after the Cold War*. New York: Oxford University Press, pp.1–13.
Pethrus, C.-M. (2013) *Militar utlandstjanst och sjalvmord: En svensk populationsbaserad registerstudie* [International military service and suicide: A population-based Swedish study] Master's thesis. Uppsala: Uppsala University.
Pethrus, C.-M., K. Johansson, K. Neovius & M. Neovius (2014) *Militar utlandstjanst och uthamtning av antidepressiva lakemedel: En populationsbaserad registerstudie* [International military service and prescription of anti-depression

medication: A populationbased registers' study] Stockholm: Swedish Armed Forces.
Roosberg, H. & A. Weibull (2014) *Forsvarsmakten efter ISAF: Lardomar och paverkan pa militarstrategisk niva* [The Swedish Armed Forces after ISAF: Lessons and effects at the military–strategic level]. Stockholm: FOI.
Sareen, J., M.B. Stein, S.L. Belik, M. Zamorski & G.J. Asmundson (2010) 'Is peacekeeping peaceful? A systematic review' *Canadian Journal of Psychiatry* Vol. 55, No. 7, pp. 464–72.
Schok, M.L., R.J. Kleber, M. Elands & J.M.P. Weerts (2008) 'Meaning as a mission: A review of empirical studies on appraisals of war and peacekeeping experiences' *Clinical Psychology Review* Vol. 28, pp. 257–365.
Swedish Armed Forces (2014) Sa tar vi hand om vara veteraner [This is how we take care of our veterans]. Available online at http://blogg.forsvarsmakten.se/kommentar/2014/03/06/sa-tar-vi-hand-om-vara-veteraner/ (accessed 17 August 2015).
Swedish Official Inquiry (2007) *En svensk veteranpolitik, del 1 Ansvaret for personalen fore, under och efter internationella militara insatser* [*A Swedish Veterans' Policy, part 1: Responsibility for the personnel before, during and after international military missions*] Vol. 77, Statens Offentliga Utredningar.
Swedish Official Inquiry (2008) *En svensk veteranpolitik, del 2 Ansvaret for personalen fore, under och efter internationella militara insatser* [*A Swedish Veterans' Policy, part 2: Responsibility for the personnel before, during and after international military missions*] Vol. 91, Statens Offentliga Utredningar.
Swedish Official Inquiry (2013) *Den svenska veteranpolitiken Statligt bidrag till frivillga organisationer som stodjer veteransoldater och anhoriga* [*The Swedish veterans' policy: State contributions to voluntary organizations supporting veterans and their families*] Vol. 8, Statens Offentliga Utredningar.
Swedish Official Inquiry (2014) *Svensk veteranpolitik Ett ansvar for hela samhallet* [*The Swedish veterans' policy: A responsibility for the whole of society*] Vol. 27, Statens Offentliga Utredningar.
Viktorin, M. (2008) *Excercising peace: Conflict preventionism, neoliberalism, and the new military*. Stockholm: National Defence College.
Weisaeth, L. (2003) 'The psychological challenge of peacekeeping operations' in Britt, T.W. & A.B. Adler (Eds), *The psychology of the peacekeeper*. Westport, CT: Praeger, pp. 207–22.
Wester, M., L. Molin & H. Askenlov (2013) *Utvardering av veteranpolitiken* [*Evaluation of the veterans' policy*] (Vol. Memo 4894). Stockholm: FOI.
Ydén, K. & J. Berndtsson (2013) 'Efter Afghanistan? Forsvaret, kriget och svenskarna' [After Afghanistan? The Armed Forces, the war and the Swedes] in Weibull, L., H. Oscarsson & A. Bergstrom (Eds) *Vagskal* [At crossroads]. Goteborg: SOM-institutet, pp. 617–29.

10 Conclusions

Arita Holmberg and Jan Hallenberg

Ten years of Swedish presence in Afghanistan

The aim of this book is to capture the influence of international engagement for the transformation processes in the security and defence fields. The focus has been upon Sweden and its more than 10 years of involvement in Afghanistan. Through the careful mapping of different dimensions of the fields, the chapters in the volume asked what influence, if any, could be seen in policy, strategy, organization and practices. Overall, these focal points were also seen as gateways through which to detect expressions of a changing Swedish identity in international security affairs. The chapters began to problematize the consequences of the international engagement in Afghanistan. In this concluding chapter, the results are summarized and the different pieces of this puzzle are arranged and related to the transformation processes in the security and defence fields.

Taken together, the book contributes to a comprehensive picture of international engagement. The chapters stretch from the political and strategic level and how the international mission was rationalized to the issue of the legitimation of the use of force in relation to international law; from the experiences gained at the tactical level to military technological adaptations; from leadership experiences at the individual level and the national efforts to gender-mainstreaming operations to the development of a veteran policy. Together, these chapters dive into several all-European (if not transatlantic) transformation processes: most importantly the deepening integration of security and defence policy, the changing norms and practices regarding the use of force and the professionalization of the military.

The chapters show that Sweden has gone through major changes with respect to policy, strategy, organization and practice in the last decades. We have looked more closely at the role that participation in an international military operation has played for these transformation processes, and whether the Swedish self-image can be said to have changed. All of the chapters indicate that the Afghanistan mission was very important in the contexts that the authors have studied. It gained a level of attention in Swedish society that was comparable to the first couple of missions to Bosnia in the early 1990s.

Conclusions 183

Like the Balkan experience, the Afghanistan operation evolved over time. A key finding is that the Afghanistan mission took place in times of transformation and contributed to these processes with fuel and input, rather than driving them in the first place. Below we discuss how participation in the military mission in Afghanistan relates first to the changing Swedish identity in international security affairs and subsequently its relation to policy, strategy, organization and practices. Finally, we consider the relationship between this international engagement and the main transformation processes in the field. We also ask what comes after Afghanistan: will the transformation processes continue without the input provided by major international engagement?

Swedish identity change: accepting the use of the military as an instrument?

The 1990s and the 2000s have in many ways constituted formative moments in time, which have shaped the Swedish self-image in international security affairs. First of all, becoming part of the European security community led Swedish politicians to consider what was expected of Sweden in a new context. Participation in more challenging international operations was one major area in which Sweden took a much more active role during the 1990s than previously. Following the terrorist attacks upon the United States in 2001, the hesitance that had formerly existed concerning cooperation in some aspects of international security operations with the United States largely vanished.

Angstrom and Noreen describe how the Afghanistan mission dragged Sweden into an international engagement on an unprecedented scale, largely due to the wish to collaborate closely with NATO. In rationalizing this decision, a catch-all discourse was pursued, which managed to attract the broad political consensus that has traditionally been necessary in Sweden when it comes to decisions regarding the use of the military as an instrument. Despite what appears to have been a very firm conviction to participate in international security affairs in a new, much more active manner, Angstrom and Noreen find that the division between the national and the international in Swedish strategic culture withstands fundamental change; at least, it appears to have difficulties being implemented at the organizational level.

Ambiguity and the presence of different motivations behind states' participation in ISAF has been noted previously in the literature (Osinga & Russel 2014, p. 301). This does not, however, necessarily diminish the effects of these practices upon the actor. As noted by Osterdahl, in 2015, Sweden participated in a US-led coalition and decided to send a small number of troops to Iraq without a UN mandate. Such an action would have been unthinkable in the 1990s. Without a doubt, the Afghanistan mission – together with other aspects of active cooperation with NATO in the form of partnerships, for example – gradually led Sweden to assume a position in the transatlantic security community (not as a member of, but as a partner to, NATO), which required various actions, including the use of force. In this process, the self-image of Sweden as an actor in international security affairs has changed.

Due to its rather 'safe' field positions in the coalition framework, however, the post-Afghanistan debate in Sweden has been rather absent. Still, it must be noted that for the Swedish polity the concept of 'war' is a difficult term, in spite of the country's history of violent statecraft. Osterdahl shows that, in connection to Afghanistan, this was a debate that flourished in a way that was not as apparent following the interventions in the 1990s. By the start of the new millennium, the shift in Swedish policy with regard to the international use of force had become evident and thus also increasingly a source of debate. The slowly decreasing public support for international military engagement, discussed by Angstrom and Noreen, is an important indicator of this.

Security and defence policy transformation: from neutrality to solidarity

The three major transformation processes noted above – the deepening integration of security and defence policy, the changing norms and practices regarding the use of force and the professionalization of the military – have all made an imprint on Swedish security and defence policy. For Sweden, European integration in security and defence policy constituted a significant break with the past. Sweden had remained neutral following the Second World War, and at the same time pursued both an activist foreign policy and a 'go-it-alone' defence policy. Foreign, security and defence policy remained quite separate and the use of force was strictly confined to territorial defence. With the fall of the Soviet Union, Sweden chose to abandon neutrality, joined the EU and started cooperating more closely with NATO.

The conflicts in the Balkans and the perceived need on the part of Sweden to show actor capability in the context of the European security community made the country start to practice the use of force internationally. Its regained self-esteem in the security and defence fields also nourished cooperation with NATO and the US. The fact that membership of the EU made the notion of 'neutrality' superfluous also meant that the political leadership in Sweden was now much more open to cooperating with NATO. This was a cooperation that had also existed during the Cold War, but in a much more secret form. Now, that secrecy was largely abandoned. The Afghanistan mission did not, however, drive these policy changes – although it could be argued that it dominated the security and defence discourse in Sweden during the 2000s and was essential in the process leading to the realization of the defence reform in 2009. The depth, length and changing character of participation in ISAF led to demands for a Swedish position on many issues, some of which led to the identification of the need for policy change.

The book's chapters also show that the changing norms and practices regarding the use of force drove policy change in the Swedish security and defence fields in different ways. The Afghanistan mission was equally important in reinforcing the pressure for these changes. Examples can be found in the area of international law, in which increased participation in more demanding international engagement raised questions regarding how Swedish soldiers were to act in different situations. The realization of the dangers associated with the ISAF endeavour was also crucial in deciding on a Swedish veterans' policy. In addition, the Afghanistan mission came to symbolize much of Sweden's work in the area of UNSCR 1325, and the implementation of gender mainstreaming in both the development and security domain gained much attention. A more relaxed attitude towards the international use of force gradually developed, as analyzed by Osterdahl in Chapter 4. The traditional Swedish insistence on a UN mandate as a source of legitimacy largely remained, but it became more open to discussion.

The professionalization of the military is a trend that has been ongoing in the West for a couple of decades. The Swedish military developed in a similar fashion as most European Armed Forces (albeit perhaps somewhat more slowly); a process that climaxed with the abandoning of conscription in 2010. Participation in ISAF required an immense effort from the Swedish Armed Forces and new challenges were encountered over time. The seriousness of the mission appears to have gradually been understood in both political and military quarters, although there was resistance among the military, as discussed later. Angstrom and Noreen claim in Chapter 3 that the policies pursued during the 2000s contributed to making strategy appear ambiguous in relation to the transformation processes and international engagement taking place. The professionalization of the military is the most recent of these policy processes, and it remains to be seen how it will be developed given the decreased focus upon international engagement in Swedish security and defence policy following the presence in Afghanistan.

Strategy: a fashionable term with no content?

Since the end of the Cold War, the problems associated with formulating strategy have been discussed in the literature. A broadened security concept and new forms of threats made the traditional thinking regarding strategy somewhat obsolete. Angstrom and Noreen claim that Swedish strategic elites were inexperienced in pursuing strategy and more or less made it up as time went on. This 'was not the absence of strategy, but rather overlapping non-synchronized processes, ad-hoc, pluralist and unintentional. It was not absence of strategy, but a multitude of tacit strategies' (Angstrom & Noreen, Chapter 3). The result was an unintended ambiguity regarding the strategic ends, organization of forces and methods of the Swedish Armed Forces. As they put it: 'While the broader political ends and strategies of the Afghan intervention were formulated in New York, Washington, Kabul and Brussels, the Swedish Government in Stockholm still had to decide its contribution' (Angstrom & Noreen, Chapter 3).

This picture is confirmed by Johnsson, who claims that the major force transformation process that was pursued during the 2000s did not really reach the Afghanistan theatre of operations. Strategy need not, however, be formulated on a top-down basis. It can also evolve in a bottom-up process. According to Johnsson, the military units that were central to the ISAF task were temporary, tactical adaptations, which in most cases did not leave any major imprint upon the Swedish Armed Forces. This result is similar to the conclusions drawn in the edited volume by Farrell *et al.* (2014), discussed in Chapter 2. Bottom-up transformation, they noticed, did not reach above the tactical level in most participating countries. However, Johnsson argues that:

> This is not to say that no experience at the tactical level has led to more overarching and long-term change. Particular functional experiences, such as the use of the Tactical Air Control Parties or the very real battlefield work conducted by Mobile Medical Teams, have probably generated important insight into the training and equipping of their counterparts in the Swedish force structure. The extensive experiences of the Improvised Explosive Device Disposal teams have continually fed the training and equipping of the mine-clearing teams of the Swedish Armed Forces: a development that has also benefitted the force in Afghanistan. Last but obviously not least, a significant number of the Armed Forces' future leaders have experienced their career-defining moments in Afghanistan.
> (Johnsson, Chapter 5)

Another observation made by Johnsson in relation to the Swedish tactical adaptation could be related to the concept of 'second-order adaptation' also put forward by Farell (2014). This type of adaptation refers to countries 'inheriting' lessons from other participating states; in Sweden's case, Britain.

What is a perhaps more unexpected indirect conclusion from both Angstrom and Noreen's and Johnsson's chapters is that the strategic level was rather absent overall. The lack of a prominent role for strategy is interesting. Johnsson argues that there is a gap between the strategic level of capability development and the 'requirements in the field' (Johnsson, Chapter 5). The question is what this gap consists of and whether it is subject to change. The strategic level seems to have been caught in between the political and the operational/tactical levels, which received the most attention. This could be related to the relative immaturity of the situation. Swedish security policy was just beginning to change, which made international operations very political instances of policy, and the military was caught in managing the situation in the field, which led it to focus on the tactical level. Still, the strategic level has been sought after – particularly by the military. Another obstacle could be the Swedish strategic culture, highlighted by Angstrom and Noreen, which treats the international use of force as something on the margins and as not so important for the Swedish Armed Forces. Results from other research on the Swedish military participation in Afghanistan (Johnsson, forthcoming 2016) also indicate that the Swedish Governments in office during the military operations in Afghanistan seemed to be unwilling, or perhaps unable, to go from uttering various vacuous phrases about the importance of building democracy and the right of children to go to school to formulating political as well as military strategies that were explicitly geared towards reaching those goals.

However, one issue that could perhaps be termed 'top-down' and that *did* reach (something of) a breakthrough in Afghanistan was the implementation of UNSCR 1325. With the focus upon a comprehensive approach, a window of opportunity emerged to bring in the issue of women, peace and security. At the political level, this fitted well with the Swedish self-perception of a 'do-gooder' and a country in which equality between the sexes was really practiced in all walks of life. Implementing gender measures became a strong, normative, political rationalisation for international action (among many): something that is very clear in the Parliament decisions regarding participation in Afghanistan. However, as shown by Egnell, the measure was justified with the efficiency argument at the military level.

The 'absence' of strategy at the domestic level concerning international engagement could, however, have a 'natural' explanation in that smaller NATO states and partner states have some difficulty in foreseeing events, more or less by necessity, as a consequence of being lower in the political and military hierarchy. From this position, action is more about *re*action towards a multilateral strategy and domestic strategic thinking becomes secondary to more immediate political and operational needs.

The military organization in vogue: reluctant professionals

For Moskos (2000), international operations are a defining feature of the postmodern military. The international use of force gave the military a new purpose when the territorial threat diminished and the character of these missions used to be one part of the legitimation for the professionalization of the Armed Forces in countries that relied on conscription. It is clear also in the case studied in this volume that the role of the military as an instrument of policy was enhanced after the end of the Cold War. Participating in international missions fulfilled a political purpose and helped build the picture of Sweden as an active and responsible member of the EU and a partner with NATO. The Afghanistan mission in many ways constituted the peak of this development.

However, most chapters show that the military organization was reluctant to embrace the new tasks and manage the implications that followed from these. Internationalization presented the Swedish Armed Forces with a huge opportunity that the organization was at first hesitant to embrace (Eriksson 2006). The question remains what role the politicians played in this state of affairs. Their unwillingness to shape clear political and military strategy for Swedish actions in Afghanistan gave the military opportunities to shape its own actions while simultaneously making it more difficult for the Swedish military to pursue consistent actions on its own in the absence of higher-order political strategies.

Egnell shows how the issue of implementing a gender perspective hit the military organization from both the international (UN) and the national (government) level. In spite of resistance, the Swedish Armed Forces (reluctantly) found ways to implement UNSCR 1325 in international military operations. This required flexibility and organizational change and the Afghanistan mission constituted an appreciated frame against which to pursue this work. Since it was set in the international framework, however, Egnell expresses concerns regarding the issue's survival in the national context.

The strongest case for the argument that the Swedish military failed to take the opportunity that the intervention in Afghanistan offered is perhaps the conclusion reached by Sundberg, which shows that the Swedish Armed Forces themselves were the main reason why a Swedish veterans' policy was not developed until in 2010. Until the mid-2000s, international tasks were still managed in a separate department of the authority and a culture persisted that attributed low value to this work compared to the territorial defence tasks. Neither did this culture appreciate the 'soft' values that are clearly associated with managing veterans, notes Sundberg. Chapter 7 by Larsson et al. also points to emotional issues as one of the largest leadership challenges for the Swedish Armed Forces during and after international missions. These challenges are likely to have been even higher in the pre-Westphalian environment that Afghanistan constituted.

However, the military organization appears to have begun to loosen up at the end of the first decade of the twenty-first century. Sundberg concludes that the Afghanistan mission was important for the adoption of a veterans' policy because it highlighted the different, more dangerous character of the international missions, which were part of the changing security policy. There are thus two factors interacting here.

> In the Swedish case, the Afghan campaign served as a 'wake-up call' for not only the military establishment but also a set of crucial actors: veterans' and dependents' organizations, the unions, at least parts of the political echelon and the media. While attention to the issue of veterans' affairs should be classified as growing even before the 2006 intensification of Sweden's commitments to ISAF (specifically, the takeover of PRT MeS), the Afghan factor served to elevate the issue, bind together actors, organizations and interests and thus create a critical mass that might otherwise have materialized much further down the road.
>
> (Sundberg, Chapter 9)

At this time, however, the external threat perception started to evolve again in Sweden (after 20 years of beauty sleep) and the military organization was responding to this. Thus, the divided strategic culture (Angstrom 2015, Angstrom & Noreen Chapter 3) that was slowly beginning to merge was back again in very short order. It remains to be seen whether the professionalization of the Swedish Armed Forces (the last of the three transformation processes identified earlier on) will continue at the organizational level without the input provided by a major international mission such as ISAF. In the context of the near abroad, the strategic culture and the inability to transfer organizational learning from the international dimension to the national (which is also international, but in the near abroad) may come to inhibit further development. It is likely that both politicians and the military have difficulties in managing military action in the near abroad, something further discussed later.

Practices that matter: becoming a part of the community by undertaking international operations

In the beginning of this book, the question of identity and practice is discussed. Pouliot (2010) argues that it is important to consider not only the state's self-perceptions (as expressed in various declarations) but also that what states actually *do* is important for determining who and what they are.

Several chapters in this book rely on interviews as primary sources. Sundberg's words, summarizing his impression gained after interviewing many respondents on veteran' issues, may serve as an introduction:

> The shock of the Afghan experience can, however, be viewed as being of such magnitude that it was able to induce a substantial impetus for change. This change reverberated through identities, culture and organizational spheres known to otherwise be substantially inert. This clearly illustrates the power of the Afghan experience. Thus, even if the shift in terms of Sweden's veterans' policy needs to be viewed as a multicausal outcome, it is likewise correct to agree with King's view that 'Europe's entry into Afghanistan is likely to be decisive in the transformation of Europe's Armed Forces' (King 2011, p. 27) far beyond the strategic and operational contexts.
>
> (Sundberg Chapter 9)

Similarly, the chapter by Larsson *et al.* shows that with Afghanistan there was no longer room to deny the severity of the psychological situation in which soldiers in the field found themselves. Johnsson notes in his chapter regarding the tactical aspects of the Afghanistan mission that it was characterized by a tougher stance than had been the case in previous international missions; something expressed in, for instance, the recruiting of personnel to the operation. These realizations, across the spectrum of actors and institutions constituting the security and defence fields in Sweden, contributed to making the practices associated with the international use of force become 'normal' in Swedish practice. The boundaries and character of the practices were changing and expanding.

As Osterdahl shows, participation in ISAF raised new issues for consideration in relation to the laws in war. Osterdahl argues that the operation was indisputably legitimate and legal in international legal terms but that it also presented new issues for the Swedish political and legal context due to the mission's scope, intensity and duration. Several official inquiries concerning international cooperation, international operations, training in an international context and international law have been conducted, and though the conclusions of some of them are yet to be decided upon and implemented they clearly show a pattern in which previous restraints on the Swedish international use of force are loosened.

Practical needs in the mission area also challenged traditional ways of doing things within both the political and the military realms. As noted by Sivertun, the defence material acquisition process proved to be too rigid to be able to capture the requirements in the field. This has also been noted in previous literature concerning other countries. Furthermore, both Johnsson and Egnell point to organizational learning at the tactical level. The experiences may not have been transferred higher up in the hierarchy, but at least people on the ground were able to solve their tasks through innovation and the organization was able to respond sufficiently at the time. These practices and experiences are likely to have left a substantial imprint on these individuals. Since the mission in Afghanistan lasted over 10 years, a not insignificant number of people were involved in these experiences. Politicians have also adapted their decisions, opening up for more flexibility for instance in supplying reinforcements. In this case, a situation in Kosovo in 2004 was the trigger.

Several of the issues debated during the Afghanistan mission highlight the increasing cooperation with NATO that comes with this type of international practice. It could be argued that, with participation in the ISAF mission, cooperation with NATO finally became accepted in the Swedish security and defence policy context. As Osterdahl puts it:

> As to the institutional context in which Sweden contributes to international military missions, the ISAF experience is illustrative of an important development since the end of the Cold War: the ever-closer cooperation with NATO. This may be one of the most important politico–legal legacies of the Swedish experience in Afghanistan and also marks a radical departure from its former stance in security and defence policy. The close relationship to NATO arguably influences both the readiness to use international force at all – Sweden is prone to contribute to NATO-led international military missions – and the attitude towards possible justifications of the international use of force. With the move toward NATO, in practice Sweden moves away from its earlier strict allegiance to the UN and its Charter in matters of international peace and security.
>
> (Osterdahl, Chapter 4)

Still, there is political anxiety in some quarters when the issue of Sweden's relationship to NATO is discussed, and the public debate has intensified in the 2010s. It should be remembered that, even if Sweden clearly has increased its cooperation with NATO during the last two decades, such cooperation must be distinguished from full membership. This ultimate step in cooperating with NATO has slowly begun to be formally discussed in Sweden even though several parties – including the largest one (the Social Democrats) – remain unwilling to undertake such a discussion. The conclusion must therefore be that, for the time being, Sweden is still quite far from formal membership of the transatlantic defence organization.

While the changes in practice regarding the use of force had their course and the security and defence fields adapted accordingly, there are also traces of growing scepticism. Johnsson notes a growing awareness of the difficulties in achieving results through the means available, which connects to the post-Afghanistan debate in Europe and may turn out to be of importance. This could well be one of the most significant common experiences of the 'interventionist era' – both among European politicians and military – that may shape European positions on the use of force for a long time. Indeed, a similar lesson could be said to have been learned by the greatest military power of the modern era – the United States – as a result primarily of its experiences in Iraq and in Afghanistan.

International engagement and transformation in the security and defence fields

The overarching conclusion concerning the role of an international operation such as the Afghanistan mission in the transformation processes of the security and defence fields is that it fuels and impacts on these processes rather than drives them in the first place. In this section, three main transformation processes are discussed: the changing norms regarding the international use of force, the internationalization of security and defence policies and the professionalization of the Armed Forces.

In the 2000s, the issue of whether to participate in and use force internationally matured; through participation in ISAF, Sweden can be said to have now fully manifested its new self-image as an active participant in the European security community. Thus it also signed up to the transformation of international norms regarding the use of force. Although the number of international operations may be declining – or rather, their character is changing – Sweden continues to participate, most notably in Mali and in Iraq. The current reorientation of the Swedish defence towards the near abroad is the product of a perceived external threat rather than a disbelief in the ability of the military instrument to achieve peace and security. Sweden does not seem to be particularly affected by the international critical debate concerning liberal interventionism, and the political support for future actions is likely to be stable. Most established political parties appear confident to come to the conclusion that there are cases in which it is legitimate to use force to respond to severe violations of human rights. The military, however, may be sceptical towards re-expanding this area of activity. As noted by Johnsson, many within the organization are quite satisfied with doing national defence. The Armed Forces may, however, be divided in their views on this; younger generations are known to value international engagement more than older ones (Holmberg 2015).

The international dimension of the security and defence fields was very strong during the 2000s, something that was confirmed by the defence decisions of 2004 and 2009. The internationalization of policy was, however, already anchored in the processes developed within the EU and NATO. What the Afghanistan mission did was feed into and contribute to a deepening of this process in various ways, often through efforts to manage the 'problems' encountered in practice regarding how to apply norms and regulations in relation to the use of force or how to manage civilian and military personnel. Numerous public investigations were conducted and the professionalization of the Swedish Armed Forces took several crucial steps during this period in the direction of 'postmodern Armed Forces' (Moskos 2000). The fact that the daily challenges of the ISAF mission were present at this time likely contributed to the policy changes made. The essence of the reorientation of the Swedish defence that was the product of the defence decision in 2009 also continues with the new situation following Russia's aggression towards Ukraine. The Armed Forces still need to interact internationally and be professional and available; as such, this transformation process is likely to continue even without the input of major international engagement.

There is one area in which internationalization together with the Afghanistan mission fed into Swedish policies, strategy (at least on paper) and organization in a remarkable way. In the mid-2000s, the 'comprehensive approach' was the buzzword in NATO and this concept illustrates the blurring of foreign, security and defence policy that existed at the time. In Sweden, the Afghanistan mission became a central feature of Government efforts in implementing the comprehensive approach. Within a couple of years Sweden had an Afghanistan strategy with a joint webpage that was to include all aspects of the involvement in the country: from development support to military engagement. During this time different authorities worked intensively with the aim of coordinating their activities in both Sweden and Afghanistan. Gender/1325 issues were one of the focal points of this work. Here we see very clearly, however, that the framing of the issue as a matter of operational effects in international operations may not fit the discourse of the current reorientation of the Swedish defence (Lindberg 2015). It seems that the strategic culture within the Swedish Armed Forces does not recognize that a civil–military interface will remain also in a conflict involving the near abroad. This suggests that without external pressure there are limits to the transformation of the Armed Forces and that the characteristics associated with the postmodern military can be resisted should the opportunity arise.

The third transformation process is the professionalization of the Armed Forces. This process appears to be the least mature of the three (in Sweden). Conscription was abandoned only in 2010 and many questions remain regarding professionalization. The reform has been questioned and there is also a discussion about reintroducing conscription at the political level.

The Afghanistan mission's relation to processes of professionalization in the Armed Forces could be said to have two faces: on the one hand, problems related to the harsh practices and experiences of warfighting during ISAF and how these are related to the military organization, and, on the other, the need for updated regulations that fit a professional military. It has been officially recognized in the bills adopted concerning many international missions that a positive side effect of participating is that the Swedish Armed Forces receive training and increase their warfighting capability (Angstrom 2015, Holmberg 2013). Still, as has been noted in the chapters by Johnsson, Larsson *et al.* and Sundberg, the military organization has hesitated to adopt the experiences gained from international missions. This ambivalence could have to do with Swedish strategic culture, which does not value the international use of force in the same way as defence of the territory. However, it could also be that the Swedish Armed Forces are reluctant to embrace their professionalization, since this requires changes and places new demands on the organization, which the older generation of officers in particular may experience as difficult.

It could be argued that participation in the Afghanistan mission contributed to merging these three processes of transformation in the Swedish security and defence fields. Thus to some extent it reduced ambiguity and at some point during the 2000s the processes were actually quite coherent. This is likely to have facilitated the shift of the Swedish identity in international security affairs.

After Afghanistan: back to the Cold War?

It has been argued here that participation in international missions such as ISAF in Afghanistan has reinforced Sweden's relationship to the transformation processes in the security and defence fields through various forms of pressure for change. In particular, it has led to a revised identity in international security affairs for Sweden. So what happens to these transformation processes when not only is ISAF phased out but also the European security community as a whole experiences a kind of tiredness regarding external military interventions – and at the same time, Russia poses what many members of the community perceive to be a threat?

As has been argued here, changing norms regarding the use of force and the internationalization of security and defence policy appear to remain stable in Swedish security and defence policy. However, the current security environment does not allow for as many expressions of the new Swedish self-image as during the last decades. The Swedish Armed Forces are to focus on the 'national' arena and international military activism is likely to return to a marginalized position. It is possible that the distinction between the areas of foreign, security and defence policy will return once more. It is already apparent in the Swedish discourse that has characterized the period after the parliamentary elections in 2014. The Social Democratic/Green Government speaks of a feminist foreign policy at the same time as the 2015 defence bill has changed the previous focus of crisis management into a renewed focus on the traditional defence of the nation: it is a prominent feature of the discourse of this bill compared to the previous two defence decisions. The referent object in the defence policy discourse is the state, although political rationalizations in case of a solidarity operation in the Baltics would most certainly be related to human security. Norms regarding the use of force have changed – but is there political and social legitimacy for the use of force in the near abroad? In our assessment, Sweden will not remain impassive in the face of atrocities towards the population in an EU or NATO country, but any action must link the solidarity policy to humanitarian norms justifying the use of force.

The new Swedish self-image is still young and has not been tested in the near abroad. Neither has it found its expression in the organization of the Swedish Armed Forces. This is because a transfer of the lessons from the international arena far away to the international arena close by does not seem to have materialized. Consequently, Sweden risks focusing its defence according to the old 'go-it-alone' policy rather than the new solidarity policy. This argument suggests that a gap remains between foreign and defence policy in Sweden as well as between the political and military levels. However, many of the changes made during the twenty-first century as a consequence of the requirements of international missions actually facilitate military tasks in the near abroad. As discussed by Osterdahl, a number of regulations have been or are soon to be changed that affect the use of military force.

References

Angstrom, J. (2015) 'Forsvarsmaktens internationella insatser: I den svenska sakerhetens eller identitetens tjanst?' [International missions: In the service of Swedish security or identity?] in Engelbrekt, K., A. Holmberg & J. Angstrom (Eds) *Svensk sakerhetspolitik i Europa och varlden* [Swedish security policy in Europe and the world] 2nd edition. Stockholm: Norstedts, pp. 233–64.

Eriksson, A. (2006) *Europeanization and governance in defence policy: The example of Sweden Stockholm Studies in Politics* 117. Stockholm: Department of Political Science, Stockholm University.

Farrell, T. (2014) 'Introduction: Military adaptation in war' in Farrell, T., F. Osinga & J.A. Russell (Eds) *Military adaptation in Afghanistan.* Stanford: Stanford University Press, pp. 1–23.

Holmberg, A. (2013) 'Swedish security strategy in the twenty-first century: What role for human security?' in M. Kaldor, M. Martin & N. Serra (Eds) *National, European and human security: From co-existence to convergence.* London: Routledge, pp. 110–29.

Holmberg, A. (2015) 'A demilitarization process under challenge? The example of Sweden' *Defence Studies* Vol. 15, No. 3, pp. 235–53.

Johnsson, M. (forthcoming 2016) *Strategic colonels: The professional discretion of Swedish force commanders in Afghanistan 2006–2014*. Ph.D. dissertation. Uppsala: Uppsala University.

Lindberg, M. (2015) *Aterinstitutionalisering av en policyfraga. Kvinnor, fred och sakerhetsagendan (WPS) i en skiftande sakerhetspolitisk kontext* [Reinstitutionalization of a policy issue. The agenda on women, peace and security in a shifting security policy context] M.A. thesis. Umeå: Umeå University.

Moskos, C.C. (2000) 'Toward a postmodern military: the United States as a paradigm' in Moskos, C.C., J.A. Williams & D.R. Segal (Eds) *The postmodern military: Armed Forces after the Cold War*. New York: Oxford University Press, pp. 14–31.

Osinga, F. & J.A Russell (2014) 'Conclusion: Military adaptation and the war in Afghanistan' in Farrell, T., F. Osinga & J.A. Russell (Eds) *Military adaptation in Afghanistan*. Stanford: Stanford University Press, pp. 288–326.

Pouliot, V. (2010) *International security in practice: The politics of NATO–Russia diplomacy*. Cambridge: Cambridge University Press.

Index

Abrahamsson, B. and Andersen, J.A. 123
Act on Training for Peace Support Operations (1994) 70
Afghan National Army *see* ANA
Afghan National Security Forces *see* ANSF
Afghanistan: assessment of mission 27; attitude of Swedish people 67; border with Pakistan 12; and changing Swedish image 2; civilian casualties 103; defence and security practices, 7, 8–11; international conflict parameters 64; involvement as transformative 4; politics and power 12; and potential war 60; poverty 11; security and development 21; social and cultural context 24; state-building 92; transfer to national forces 4, 5, 13
Agrell, W. 8, 9, 35
Al Qaeda 13
Alvinius, A. *et al.* (2014) 128, 129
ambiguity: and identity 183, 184; and internationalization 40; in military 39, 40–4; national and international 44, 45–8; and professionalization 40; and NATO 40, 41; strategic consequences of 49–50, 185
ANA (Afghan National Army) 78, 93–5; NTM–A evaluation of 94
Angstrom, J. 7
ANSF (Afghan National Security Forces): build-up of 92, 93; and gender mentoring 150
armed conflict, concept of 64
armoured vehicles 88, 104–5
Asnani, V. *et al.* (2003) 116

Battle Groups, EU 43, 46, 78
Bildt, Carl 160

Bosnia 163, 175
'boundary spanners' 123
Bourdieu, Pierre 26
Britain 82, 86, 107, 186
Brittain, J.R. 86

Canada: armoured vehicles 104; casualties 14, 103, 104; mission in Afghanistan 9, 10
casualties 14, 101, 103–4, 161, 162, 163, 171, 172–3
CFI (Connected Forces Initiative) 27
China, rise of 19
civil–military coordination 24, 47, 48; CIMIC teams 84, 86–7
civil–military relations approach 19, 20
climatological conditions 102, 107
coalition warfare 9, 10
COIN (counterinsurgency) doctrine 11, 26, 42, 47, 80, 108
Cold War: burden-sharing 22; Swedish neutrality 3; Swedish strategy 5, 31, 35, 45
Command, Control and Communication *see* C3
Common European Security and Defence Policy 5
Congo *see* DRC (Democratic Republic of Congo)
Connected Forces Initiative *see* CFI
conscription 33, 40, 101, 160, 169, 173, 174
constructivist turn 26
Copenhagen Process 65
counterinsurgency 141–2; and ANSF 93; as beyond mission 109; early 13; and gender 153; and tactical change 80; training 24, 42

counterinsurgency doctrine *see* COIN
C3 (Command, Control and Communication) 102
cultural sensitivity: and gender 91, 92, 150, 151, 153; importance of 141; and leadership 118fig, 120, 122, 128, 130t, 133, 134; training 88
Cyprus 169

Dalsjo, R. 46
data, accuracy of 160
DDR (Disarmament, Demobilization and Reintegration program), Afghanistan 109
Defence Bills: 2009 46, 161; 2015 6, 194
defence industry 31, 101
Democratic Republic of Congo *see* DRC
Denmark 10, 11, 65, 172
detentions 65–6
Disarmament, Demobilization and Reintegration program, Afghanistan *see* DDR
DRC (Democratic Republic of Congo) 72n2, 141, 142, 145, 160, 173
Durand line 12

Eastern Ukraine 154
Edstrom, H. and Gyllensporre, D. 46
e-Governance (e-Gov) 110, 111
Engdahl, O. 62, 63, 64–5
EU: Battle Groups 43; defence and security 6; framework on international operations 57; membership influence on defence policies 34; organizational change to Swedish Armed Forces 46; security and defence fields 22; Swedish officers and 43, 44fig; Swedish participation in operations 7, 8
European Armed Forces, transformation of 19
European integration, literature on 22

Farrell, Theo 23, 79, 80, 82, 83
Farrell, Theo *et al.* (2014) 22, 186
fast-track acquisition process 24
FETs (Female Engagement Teams) 85, 91, 147, 148
Finland 10
Finnemore, M. 37
force, legitimate use of 55–72; ambiguity and 37, 38; and identity 2; international norms 191; proactive 4; Swedish view of 56–9, 60, 67; and UNSC 68, 69

force transformation 81–3
foreign aid 160
Former Yugoslavia 56, 160, 173
Fors Brandebo, M. & Larsson, G. 117, 121, 127, 128
Forward Air Control 9

Garfield, A. 141, 142
Gates, Robert 108
Gaza Strip 160, 169
gender 90–2, 138–57; and Afghanistan mission 141–2; in 'comprehensive approach' 192; and female recruitment 155; Gender Field Advisors 142–54; institutionalisation of 145–50 *see also* UNSCR 1325
Gender Coach Program 141
Gender Focal Points 146, 147
Genderforce project 141
Geneva Conventions 64
Geo Cell 102
GEO intelligence and systems 102
Germany 11, 24, 105, 111
GNSS (Global Navigation Satellite Systems) 102
Gray, C.S. 32
Grissom, A. 82
ground forces, protection for 9

Haaland Matláry 10
Hazara people 12
Heier, T. 11
helicopters, procurement of 101, 105, 106
Hilpert, C. 11
humanitarian intervention, acceptance of 56, 57, 59

ICT (Information and Communication Technology) 101, 102
ICTY (International Criminal Tribunal for the Former Yugoslavia) 63, 64
identity: European states and 21; and ISAF 66, 67–70, 71; and relationships 189–91; slow change 22; Swedish 1, 3, 7, 183, 184; and transformation 20
IEDs (Improvised Explosive Devices) (road bombs) 101, 108; disposal teams 186
IFOR (Implementation Force), Balkans 163
IHL (international humanitarian law) 55, 56, 61, 62, 63–6, 68

India: 12, 107
Information and Communication Technology *see* ICT
infrared (IR) detection 104, 105
International Criminal Tribunal for the Former Yugoslavia *see* ICTY
'International Expeditionary Force' 168–9
international humanitarian law *see* IHL
international relations research *see* IR
International Security Assistance Force *see* ISAF
internationalization of conflict 13, 14, 187
interpreters, local 103, 149, 150
Inter-Services Intelligence Agency, Pakistan *see* ISI
IR (international relations) research 20
Iraq and international coalition against ISIL 59, 60, 67, 68–9; military training in 68, 69; Swedish presence in 183, 191
Iraq War 10, 11, 13, 80, 107
ISAF (International Security Assistance Force): and Afghanistan 8, 11, 12–14, 33; and ambiguity regarding Swedish intervention 36, 37; conclusion of mission 66; counterinsurgency 26, 27, 93; increased Swedish commitment 41–2; and international legal framework 55; NATO and 160; UNSC mandate 59, 61, 62
Isaksson, Charlotte 151, 152
ISI (Inter-Services Intelligence Agency, Pakistan) 13
ISIL (Islamic State in Iraq and the Levant) 59, 60
Islam 12
Israel 49, 50

Jalalabad 86
Jepperson, R.L. *et al.* (1996) 20
Johnsson, Magnus 48
Joint Operations field manual 41
Jowzjan province 85
jus ad bellum 55, 60, 61
jus in bello 55, 61

Kabul 12, 103
Karlsson, C. 174
Karzai, President Hamid 10, 108
Katzenstein, P.J. 20
Kemper, T.D. 130
Khojak Pass 107
Khyber Pass 107

King, A. 23, 189
Kissinger, Henry, *Diplomacy* 50
Korstrom, Per-Erik 173
Kosovo 57, 126, 127, 190

language 42, 121t, 134
Larsen, H.B.L. 10
Larsson, G. and Hyllengren, P. 117
Larsson, G. *et al.* (2000) 163
Lazarus, R.S. 124
leadership 116–34; acts of balance 126, 127, 128; behaviours 126; collaboration 128–30; 'developmental' 134; emotional contagion 130, 131; and environment 120–2; group characteristics 123, 124; individual characteristics 119–20, 121t; interactional person-by-situation paradigm 119; interpretation of task 124–5, 126; and irregular warfare 116, 120, 131, 133; and organization 122–3; and outcomes 132; and power 131, 132; and stressors 117; theoretical model of 117, 118–32; transformational model of 126; and trust 124, 125
Lebanon 160
Lebow, R.N. 20
Liberia 173
Libya 59, 64, 69
Lindstrom, Major General Anders 165
Lofvendahl, Peter 170, 174, 175
Lorber, A. 100

Mali 191
Masud, Ahmad Shah ('Lion of Panshir') 12
Mattelaer, Alexander 27, 177
Mazar-e-Sharif 41, 42, 48, 84, 86, 89, 103
McMichael, S.R. 105
medical evacuation 9, 106
mentoring 93, 94–5
METs (Mixed Engagement Teams) 91, 147, 148–9, 150
military capability building 80
military change 79–81
military observation teams *see* MOTs
military police readiness units 86, 87
Military Weapons Intelligence Teams *see* WITs
military-technological aspects, Swedish mission 100–12
Mixed Engagement Teams *see* METs

monitoring 78, 83, 87, 88
Moskos, C.C. 6, 187
Moskos, C.C. et al. (2000) 25, 133
MOTs (military observation teams) 78, 85–90; MOT J (MOT Juliette) 85, 90–2, 147, 148; MOT Y 148

Napoleon Bonaparte 131
National Strategy for Swedish participation in international peace-support and security-building operations (2008) 4, 57
NATO: and CFI 27; 'comprehensive approach' 47, 192; and defence and security strategy 6; exit strategy 93; framework on international operations 55, 57, 62; intervention without UNSC mandate 57; mission in Afghanistan 10, 13, 38, 39; peacekeeping missions 61; planning procedures 33; and relationship with Sweden 5, 7, 8, 33, 56, 67, 68, 69–70, 71, 72, 190–1; security and defence fields 22; standards adopted by Sweden 36, 40; Swedish officers 43, 44fig; takeover of ISAF mission 109
NATO Summit 2014 68
NBG (Nordic Battle Group) 173
NCGM (Nordic Centre for Gender in Military Operations) 138, 145, 146, 153, 156
Nesselrode, Count Karl von 107
Netherlands 10
Nilsson, S. et al. (2012) 117
Nilsson, S. et al. (in press) 131
9/11 attacks, US 10, 13, 183
no-blame procedure 112
non-international conflict, ICTY definition 64
Nordic Baltic Transition Support Unit 41
Nordic Battle Group *see* NBG
Nordic Centre for Gender in Military Operations *see* NCGM
Norrland Dragoon Regiment 87, 90
Northern Alliance 12
Norway 10, 11, 22, 65
not-for-profit veterans' associations 167
Nye, J.S. 131

Obama, President Barack 93
Odenberg, Mikael 170, 172, 173
OEF (Operation Enduring Freedom) 108, 109
offence–defence theory 50
Omar, Mullah 13
OMLTs (operational monitoring and liaison teams) 85, 92, 93–5; Afghanistan 78; and ANSF 93; and gender mentoring 150; Kandak 93–4
Operation Unified Protector, Libya 59
organizational culture 123, 145, 149, 151, 152, 153
Osama bin Laden 13
OSCE (Organization for Security and Cooperation in Europe) 57
Osinga, F. & Russell, J.A. 23, 24

Pakistan, relationship with Afghanistan 12
'Panshir, Lion of' *see* Masud, Ahmad Shah 12
Pashtun people 12
Peace Berets 165, 175
peace support operations 57–60, 64, 66, 162–4
Petersson, M. 6, 7
POs (provincial offices) Afghanistan 85, 88
postmodernism 6, 25, 187, 188, 189
Post-Traumatic Stress Disorder *see* PTSD
Pouliot, V. 26, 189
procurement procedures 33, 82, 101, 103–6, 109
professionalization of the military 26, 185, 193
provincial offices (Afghanistan) *see* POs
PRTs (Provincial Reconstruction Teams) 8, 78, 85–90; Swedish command of 41, 42, 45
psychological health problems 162, 163–5
PTSD (post-traumatic stress disorder) 134, 162, 163

Quebec Lima 89

Rashid, Ahmed, *Taliban* 12
Rasmussen, M.L. V. 11
realist approach 19
Resolute Support Mission, NATO *see* RSM
responsibility to protect 58–9
Rid, T. & Zapfe, M. 24
Ringmar, E. 3
RMA (revolutions in military affairs) 81
Roosberg, H. and Weibull, A. 9

RSM (Resolute Support Mission), NATO 13, 66
Rumsfeld, Donald 103
Russel, J.A. 14
Russia 107, 192
Rutgersson, L.-G. et al. (2011) 102
Rynning, S. 26, 27

SAF (Swedish Armed Forces): decline of 35; doctrine 48; institutionalization of 22, 23; and internationalization 61; NATO harmonization 41, 43; prioritization 9; professionalization 40; reorganization of 5, 6; training 47
Samangan province 85
Sandstrom, Colonel Bengt 90, 91, 92
SAR (synthetic aperture radar) 111
Sar-e Pul province 85
Sareen, J. et al. (2010) 162, 163
Särskilda Skyddsgruppen (SSG, now SOG) 109
Schylander, Lieutenant Colonel Olof 86, 87
'second-order adaptation' 23
security and defence fields 21–7, 191–3
security and defence policy transformation 184–5
Security Sector Reform 92
self-defence 4, 56, 58, 60–1, 69
Senior Gender Advisors 155
sexual violence 154
Sharia law 122
SIDA (Swedish International Development Agency 47, 110
social and political landscape, importance of 108
social constructivist approach 20
Social Democrats 3, 4
sociologically-oriented defence transformation literature 25
'soft' values 170
solidarity, Swedish declaration of 69, 70
SOM institute 39
Somalia 160
Sorenson, K. and Widén, J.J. 79
Soviet Union: and Cold War 31; demise of 19, 81; invasion of Afghanistan 11, 105, 107
Spatial Data Infrastructure 102
SSG see Särskilda Skyddsgruppen
Stach, A. 166, 169, 172, 176
strategy and technology 105–6, 107
strategic guidance, lack of 24, 48

strategic studies 20
stress, moral 125
Sudan 13
Suez Canal 107
Sweden 60–6; absence of strategy 185–7; Air Force 31; catch-all government narrative 33, 36, 37–9, 48, 183; changes in national policy 108, 109, 110; civilian and military elements to mission 9; coalition government 4; 'comprehensive approach' 192; cost of aid 8; criticism regarding PRTs 110; defence and security organization 5, 6, 7, 8–11, 21, 57; Defence Committee 2014 34; defence spending 31; doctrinal change to international mission 45, 46–7; domestic political consensus 36; EU membership 5, 184; identity 1, 3, 7; international coalition against ISIL 67, 68; international interventions 3, 33, 116; level of public support 38, 39; military non-alignment 5, 10, 31, 36, 41; and national defence 7, 10, 11, 45, 49, 67, 109, 183; Navy 31; neutrality 3, 5, 22, 31, 34, 184; peacekeeping 160; political opposition to European integration 22; post Cold War strategies 32, 33–6; professionalization of army 33; reduction in armed forces 33, 40; return to prior stance on foreign intervention 194; security policy 3, 4; self-sustainability 31; solidarity 36, 41; transformation of security forces 34
SWEDINT (Swedish International Unit) 88
Swedish Air Force, no-blame procedure 112
Swedish Armed Forces see SAF
Swedish International Development Agency see SIDA
Swedish National Audit Office 110
Swedish Official Inquiry 2011 63, 65, 66
Swedish Special Forces 103
synthetic aperture radar see SAR
Syria 67, 68

tactical adaptations 78, 79–83
Tadić, Duško 73n3
Taliban 12, 13, 60, 92
TDOODA 1 decision loop 112
'total defence' 47, 48
transformational leadership model 126

transparency, political 8
TSTs (Transition Support Teams) 8, 41

UAVs (Unmanned Aerial Vehicles) 9, 102, 105
UCAVs (Unmanned Combat Aerial Vehicles) 108
Ukraine 192
UN: international legal framework 55, 56, 57; in Gaza Strip 160; peacekeeping missions 69, 72n2; stabilization mission in Afghanistan 13; Sweden and 1, 7, 8
UN Summit 2005 58
UNAMA (United Nations Assistance Mission in Afghanistan) 109
United Nations Protection Forces *see* UNPROFOR
United States *see* US
Unmanned Aerial Vehicles *see* UAVs
Unmanned Combat Aerial Vehicles *see* UCAVs
UNPROFOR (United Nations Protection Forces) 163
UNSC (UN Security Council), mandate of 4, 55, 56, 58, 67
UNSCR 1325 9, 139–41, 151, 154, 187, 188
US (United States): Air Land Battle Doctrine 81; Canadian solidarity with 10; civilian agencies 14; international coalition against ISIL 68; mission in Afghanistan 9, 13, 14, 60; revolutions in military affairs 81; use of force 191
US Marine corps, *Expeditionary Force Development System* 82
USAID 47

veteran policy 160–77; and Afghanistan 9, 172–3, 176–7, 188; and awareness 170, 175, 176; holistic 162, 163, 165; modernization and 'internationalization' 160; not-for-profit organizations 175; peace support operations 161, 162, 163; reforms of 166–8, 172; and responsibility 165; and Swedish foreign policy 166; Swedish Official Inquiry 160, 164–6
Veterans Day celebration 167
Veterans Division (*Veteranavdelningen*), SAF 166
veto system, UN 56

Walldén, M. & Gyhagen, P. 95
Weisaeth, L. 162
Westerdahl, Major Frederick 86, 87, 88
Widman, Allan 61, 165, 169, 172
WITs (Military Weapons Intelligence Teams) 107
World Bank 8
Wranker, Bo 166, 173, 175

Yom Kippur war 49, 50
Yugoslavia 133

# Taylor & Francis eBooks

Helping you to choose the right eBooks for your Library

Add Routledge titles to your library's digital collection today. Taylor and Francis ebooks contains over 50,000 titles in the Humanities, Social Sciences, Behavioural Sciences, Built Environment and Law.

Choose from a range of subject packages or create your own!

Benefits for you
- Free MARC records
- COUNTER-compliant usage statistics
- Flexible purchase and pricing options
- All titles DRM-free.

Benefits for your user
- Off-site, anytime access via Athens or referring URL
- Print or copy pages or chapters
- Full content search
- Bookmark, highlight and annotate text
- Access to thousands of pages of quality research at the click of a button.

REQUEST YOUR FREE INSTITUTIONAL TRIAL TODAY

Free Trials Available
We offer free trials to qualifying academic, corporate and government customers.

eCollections – Choose from over 30 subject eCollections, including:

Archaeology	Language Learning
Architecture	Law
Asian Studies	Literature
Business & Management	Media & Communication
Classical Studies	Middle East Studies
Construction	Music
Creative & Media Arts	Philosophy
Criminology & Criminal Justice	Planning
Economics	Politics
Education	Psychology & Mental Health
Energy	Religion
Engineering	Security
English Language & Linguistics	Social Work
Environment & Sustainability	Sociology
Geography	Sport
Health Studies	Theatre & Performance
History	Tourism, Hospitality & Events

For more information, pricing enquiries or to order a free trial, please contact your local sales team:
www.tandfebooks.com/page/sales

 The home of Routledge books

www.tandfebooks.com